Impact Assessment and Evaluation in
Transportation Planning

Transportation Research, Economics and Policy

VOLUME 2

The titles published in this series are listed at the end of this volume.

Impact Assessment
and Evaluation
in Transportation Planning

by

PETER NIJKAMP

and

EDDY BLAAS

Free University of Amsterdam

KLUWER ACADEMIC PUBLISHERS
DORDRECHT / BOSTON / LONDON

Library of Congress Cataloging-in-Publication Data

Nijkamp, Peter.
    Impact assessment and evaluation in transportation planning / by
  Peter Nijkamp and Eddy Blaas.
        p.   cm. -- (Transportation, research, economics and policy ;
  2)
    Includes bibliographical references.
    ISBN 0-7923-2648-2 (alk. paper)
    1. Transportation--Planning.   I. Blaas, Eddy. II. Title.
  III. Series.
  HE147.5.N55 1994
  388'.068--dc20   93-42462

ISBN 0-7923-2648-2

Published by Kluwer Academic Publishers,
P.O. Box 17, 3300 AA Dordrecht, The Netherlands.

Kluwer Academic Publishers incorporates
the publishing programmes of
D. Reidel, Martinus Nijhoff, Dr W. Junk and MTP Press.

Sold and distributed in the U.S.A. and Canada
by Kluwer Academic Publishers,
101 Philip Drive, Norwell, MA 02061, U.S.A.

In all other countries, sold and distributed
by Kluwer Academic Publishers Group,
P.O. Box 322, 3300 AH Dordrecht, The Netherlands.

Printed on acid-free paper

Printed in the Netherlands

TABLE OF CONTENTS

PART A

TRANSPORTATION PLANNING: SHIFTING BOUNDARIES

PART B

IMPACT ASSESSMENT IN TRANSPORTATION PLANNING

PART D

METHODOLOGY OF EVALUATION IN TRANSPORTATION PLANNING

PART E

APPLICATIONS OF MULTICRITERIA ANALYSIS IN
TRANSPORTATION PLANNING

PREFACE

If one enjoys on a sunny day a nice cup of 'Hellenic coffee' on a terrace near the old Venetian port of Chania on Crete, one becomes impressed by the sophisticated way our ancestors have built up the necessary infrastructure around the port, ranging from roads to prisons and piers. The sudden disturbing noise of a throbbing motorbike embitters unfortunately too often our enjoyment and confronts us with the externalities of our modern transport systems. Transport is essentially a phenomenon which plays a central role in our economic and spatial systems. It is a necessary evil with all the good and bad things involved. This also makes transportation planning so difficult and at the same time so interesting.

The need for analyzing nowadays virtually all relevant aspects of a new transportation project in order to comply with environmental, economic and physical planning regulations and conditions has led to several analysis methods being developed. As a result, impact assessment and evaluation have become indispensable tools in modern transportation planning.

Planning means structured and analytical treatment of conflict and uncertainty. This also applies to transportation planning, a field which is rapidly gaining importance nowadays. Especially in case of goal conflicts in transportation planning, there is a need to rationalize complex decision problems, by providing both a tool for communication between all actors involved and rigorous analytical techniques for examining (implicitly or explicitly) the implications of policy choices. Flexibility in the design and use of such methods is necessary to ensure tailor-made research tools. The enormous variety in applications of such methods illustrates their great potential.

Clearly, in empirical applications in the transport sector difficult analytical problems will be faced, e.g., regarding the precision of measurement, the identification of priorities, the demarcation of the impacts, the negative externalities of transport, etc. Communication with all actors is then a sine qua non for an acceptance of results of such techniques.

Impact analyses and evaluation methods (e.g., multiple criteria analysis) offer the possibility to link appraisal methods much closer to political decision processes and hence have in principle the potential to enhance the quality of decision-making. The expositions and illustrations in the field of transportation planning offered in the present book serve to demonstrate that the use of such modern decision support methods may be of great importance for structured transportation planning, not only as an academic activity but also as a practical tool.

On the road towards completing this book, we have met many colleagues and friends with whom we shared many constructive reflections on operational transportation planning. We wish to thank them. The great hospitality of the Netherlands Institute for Advanced Study in the Humanities and Social Sciences (NIAS), Wassenaar, The Netherlands is gratefully acknowledged here. Special thanks go to Mrs. Anneke Vrins-Aarts and Mrs. Jody Kersten for their dedicated support in drawing this manuscript to a close.

Wassenaar / Chania / Amsterdam, July 1993

PART A

TRANSPORTATION PLANNING : SHIFTING BOUNDARIES

Chapter 1

TRANSPORTATION PLANNING : A THEATRE OF OPERATIONS

1.1. Planning as the Art of Communication

In the past years the context and substance of transportation planning in many countries have exhibited dramatic changes. Transportation planning is no longer a 'fixed route' planning, but is increasingly characterized by the need for flexible and visionary policy strategies and decision processes in an uncertain environment.

The external environment has a completely different 'face' compared to a decade ago. The drastic political changes in centrally planned countries, the return to market oriented societies and the new belief in competition and free entrepreneurship in many countries have destroyed the idea that public governments were the vehicles par excellence for ensuring 'the greatest welfare for the greatest number of people' (see also Button and Pitfield, 1991).

Furthermore, the substance of planning has changed. A fine tuning to a variety of democratic desires of citizens is more and more required, making planning a **theatre of democratic operations**. Thus external megatrends and internal system's movements force planning towards a client orientation. At the same time, more frictions between wish and reality become apparent, so that planning as a science tends to become the art of **conflict resolution**. This provokes a re-orientation in terms of scope and research methodology. This is clearly witnessed in transportation planning in many countries.

In the past decades transportation planning all over the world has been strongly dominated by engineering views on network use and its expansion. Only in recent years social science oriented views have begun to enter the discussion of transport behaviour and infrastructure, as transport policy nowadays is increasingly facing a dilemma between economic-technological potential and environmental-social constraints. Transport infrastructure is a critical success factor for competitive advantage and internationalisation of our economies, whereas at the same time a further network expansion of traditional infrastructure is generally incompatible with the need for a high quality of life. Thus transportation policy does not only require engineering solutions, but has to be implemented on the basis of broad actual and future concern for our societies. In consequence, there is a case for a strong social science orientation in transportation policy.

1.2.   The 'Climate' of Opinion and a 'Search Agenda'

Sky-rocketing mobility has become a widespread phenomena in all (developed and developing) countries, at all geographical scales ranging from local to international. This 'mobility drift' is clearly not only a technology - driven phenomenon ('technology push'), but also a result of far reaching changes in our ways of living, thinking and working ('market pull'). Our welfare societies are generating a complex array of contact patterns (material and immaterial) which require physical interaction at an unprecedented scale. Nevertheless and paradoxically, the daily travel time per person has hardly increased in the past decades; this 'law of conservation of travel time' means essentially that the average travel speed - and hence distance - has increased because of high efficiency increases in our transport systems (see als Bovy et al., 1993). Apparently there is an intrinsic resistance against an unlimited rise in travel time due to the high time preferences, so that the need for quality improvement of transportation networks (i.e., higher speed at relatively low costs) has come to the fore. It is also noteworthy that the travel frequency tends to rise in most countries.

Similar observations emerging from social science research can be made in the context of changes in labour force participation, life styles, demographic development etc. In all such cases social science research provides convincing empirical evidence that changes in our societies are major driving forces for the intensification of spatial interaction (persons, goods and information) in our Western world.

In addition, the awareness of the limits to growth in mobility has also dramatically increased (see Himanen et al., 1992). Environmental and safety considerations have become major factors in the social acceptance of our mobile society. Thus new transport solutions and technologies will have to be implemented within increasingly narrower limits imposed by our society. The range of such solutions is even further limited by the simultaneous behaviour of all actors in our modern transport systems generating congestion effects (including high accident rates).

Thus the transport sector has become a focal point of social concern and interest. The scene of the transportation sector can only be understood by means of rigorous social science research. Neglect of the findings from such research renders transport policy ineffective, as can be seen from the experience of 'transport solutions' in many European countries (e.g., parking policy, modal shifts etc.).

It should be recognized at this stage that the presence of various physical, geographical, political, economic or cultural barriers - causing altogether **the** transportation problem - has usually prevented most regions from becoming a self-organizing system with equally competitive conditions. This has led to various kinds of government interventions, in both market and non-market economies, in order to ameliorate spatial economic inequalities. Although the traditional dilemma between efficiency and equity is of paramount importance in economic policy and transportation policy, it is at the same time relevant to observe drastic changes in the orientation of regional policy in almost all countries. New policy initiatives and directions (notably deregulation, supply side orientation, decentralization and privatisation) have in the past decade led to a significant shift in the background and justification of regional-economic and transport policy.

In light of the previous observations, it is clear that there is a broad spectrum of questions which need to be addressed in policy formulation for the transport sector. The recognition of frictions and bottlenecks is the first stage in a policy life cycle. The policy agenda itself is of course much longer, as it includes also effective policy strategies and implementation (and maintenance) processes. In the past years where most countries have increasingly been faced with the negative externalities of the transport sector, social science research has been of critical importance for formulating issues that needed to be dealt with in comprehensive policy analysis (cf. Nijkamp et al., 1990). Some examples may clarify this proposition.

The 'undesirable' outcome of a highly mobile society (in terms of pollution, lack of safety and congestion) is - almost paradoxically - the result of rational and plausible actions of a great many individuals. Social science research has convincingly demonstrated that the neglect of social costs in individual decision-making must by necessity lead to a macro outcome that is far from optimal. This explains, for example, worsening quality of life conditions in major cities all over the world.

Another example concerns the inefficiency of transport systems in nationalistic planning traditions in separate countries that are causing extremely high costs. Europe offers a glaring example of inefficient trans-border transport. Such 'costs of non-Europe' are a result of nationalistic thinking in Europe, which hampers a standardisation in the hardware and software of European transport systems. The European airline sector and the European railway systems reflect much more a nation-centred interest than a search for European-centred benefits. Clear evidence of the need for a dramatic improvement of European transport systems can be found in a recent study on 'Missing Networks in Europe' (see the European Round Table of Industrialists, 1991; Masser et al., 1992).

Thus the transport problems are manifold and find their roots in socio-economic and cultural choices in our societies, rather than in 'missing technologies'. This observation is determining the agenda for transport policy evaluation.

1.3.   The 'Menu' of Operations and the Instruments Box

The set of policy actions that can be envisaged in the transport sector is vast. At the same time the number of actors and interest parties that are directly or indirectly affected by transport decisions and policies is large. A major challenge will be to formulate plans that convincingly incorporate non-zero-sum game strategies with gains for all parties involved. This may again be illustrated by means of some examples.

The 'user charge' principles in transport policy has in particular become a success in those countries where suppliers and users of transport infrastructure were all enjoying benefits (e.g., suppliers by receiving more revenues from road charges, users by increasing their travel speed etc.). The idea of intermodal substitution (e.g., from the car or lorry to the train) will critically depend on the willingness to implement such incentives in competitive transport systems which traditionally tend to be characterized by zero-sum games.

International competitiveness is nowadays regarded as a necessary condition for enhancing the level of economic performance in European countries. Segmented and nationalistic infrastructure policy may at best serve the short-run interests of infrastructure owners, but is in the long run to the detriment of all network owners and affects Europe's economic position. Thus transportation policy requires a balanced implementation of actions which ensure a consideration of both private and social costs, and a global orientation which exceeds country-based or segmented policy strategies. The current EC plans regarding the European high speed railway system are a clear case of a creative action-oriented policy strategy (despite a nationalistic bias in the present technology design).

Thus the 'menu' of operations in the transport sector needs a customized strategy toward a multiplicity of interest parties, which once more makes clear that transport (and infrastructure) policy analysis is essentially based on conflict resolution analysis. Thus policy implementation in the transport sector is not in the first place a clean 'technocratic' application of instruments, but requires a fine tuning between goals, measures, interest groups and social acceptance. Transport policy in most countries could be much more efficient, if the inertia embedded in our social and political system would be recognized prior to the formulation of technical strategies.

Such pro-active social science oriented strategies require creative policy and social science research, not only regarding technical solutions or financial means, but also regarding material resources, human responses etc. Those countries which have been able to develop and support such research tend to be relatively successful in their policies. A particularly important, but often neglected factor in this context is the organizational and managerial setting that is necessary for making a policy strategy successful. This can be well illustrated by the operation of new (privatized) bus lines in many European countries, where the necessary efficiency rise in mass transit systems (including bus lines) has been accompanied by decentralized responsibility of bus operators thus allowing a search for creative and cost-saving public transport solutions.

In this framework it is also noteworthy that in view of the great many negative externalities of transport (notably air and road), many social scientists in various countries have recently resorted to the so-called 'user pays' principle. This has had a significant impact on the direction of transport policy in various countries, witness the current plans in Hong Kong, the USA, Switzerland, Austria, Sweden, Norway or the Netherlands etc. to introduce tollroads, electronic road charging etc.

Another illustration of alternative transport strategy needs concerns the necessary improvement of transport systems in an efficient way by reducing the large number of protectionist regulations for specific actors. Research on deregulation principles in various countries (e.g., Great Britain, Germany, Greece) has had an important effect on political and societal thinking regarding the role of the government in transport policy.

In conclusion, transport policy is diversified and will not become uniform because of many indigenous cultural, physical and geographical factors. Much attention is needed for the identification of bottlenecks in transport systems operations, the socio-political barriers to geographical interaction, the reasons for missing links or networks etc. The recent past has shown a revival of a social science orientation in the transportation field, as is also witnessed in the policy/research agenda's of large international bodies such as the European Community, the Organisation for Economic Cooperation and Development (OECD) and the European Conference of Ministers in Transport (ECMT). It seems plausible to assume that this important position of social science research in the transport sector will become even much stronger in the near future, especially in light of the drastic socio-economic and political changes on the way towards a rapidly evolving network economy (see Camagni, 1993).

1.4.   The Position of Transport

Transportation - and spatial interaction in general - mirrors the socio-economic, spatial and political dynamics of our societies. In the **sixties,** a period with unprecedented economic growth in many Western countries, transportation policy was strongly oriented toward network and capacity expansion. From the **seventies** onward however, the limits to growth discussion marked a more modest role of infrastructure policy in which a more efficient use of existing networks received more attention than a straightforward physical expansion. In the **eighties** new views have come to the fore, reflected inter alia in the environmentalist movement (green parties, e.g.) with its strong concern about the negative impacts of transport on the general quality of life. From the **nineties** onward also a strong interest in the potential of modern technologies (telecommunication, e.g.) for network improvement emerged, notably in the context of the missing networks discussion and of the evolving new network economies.

Thus, to a large extent new socio-economic and political developments are projected on the field of transportation planning (see also Nijkamp and Reichman, 1987). This also implies that transportation planning cannot be undertaken in **isolation** from other fields of planning and policy-making (e.g., economic, environmental or technolo-gical policy), so that nowadays transportation planning is by definition a **multidimensi-**

onal activity focusing on multiple (public and private) interests with a strong emphasis on conflict resolution.

Furthermore, a wide variety of **new broader social developments** is taking place, which have direct or indirect implications for transportation planning. Examples are: uncertainty in income positions and labour market positions among various groups in society (leading to severe equity problems), an increase in female labour force participation in all industrialized countries (leading to complex journey-from-home-to-work travel patterns; see Fischer and Nijkamp, 1987), drastic cuts in governmental budgets for public works including infrastructure (leading to severe problems regarding the management and maintenance of infrastructure), new policies regarding urban revitalisation and gentrification (leading to structure changes in the direction and volume of commuting flows), a large scale introduction of informatics and robotics (leading to new types of logistic management and freight transport; see Giaoutzi and Nijkamp, 1988), an increase in car ownership and mobility (leading to severe environmental and safety problems), a reduction in the extent and scope of public policy (leading to various types of deregulation and privatisation principles in transportation planning), and a drastic socio-political re-orientation in Europe.

Such drastic changes are likely to exert a profound influence on the future spatial interaction pattern of our societies and will make it necessary for transportation planning to respond as efficiently as possible to new tendencies and new challenges. However, transportation planning is often marked by lack of resilience, so that flexible adjustments to new structural changes (e.g., deregulation, compact city design, new distributional policies) often take place insufficiently. This case of 'government failures' may then likely lead to **second best solutions** (including forced mobility, environmental decay, unequal distribution of costs and benefits, lack of safety, a high degree of functional separation etc.) (see also Barde and Button, 1991).

In the framework of our discussion on new roles of transportation it should be recognized that transportation is, generally speaking, **'derived demand'**. This assertion is no doubt valid, but it is only part of the truth. Seen from the viewpoint of transportation planning, it is more plausible to state that transportation has two different faces: **increased access to many facilities** (often resulting from an improved or advanced transportation technology and usually leading to a rise in general welfare) and an

increased deterioration of the quality of life (due to traffic congestion, pollution, noise annoyance and lack of safety). These contrasting roles of transportation planning, viz. **potentiality** and **externality,** have placed the mobility of man and society in the centre of scientific and political interest. These two poles also provoke the need for adjusted planning and evaluation methodologies for conflict resolution.

1.5.   Transportation Planning: A Field in Motion

In view of the above mentioned changing role of transportation, it is noteworthy that transportation planning is addressing nowadays complicated questions, partly of a methodological or theoretical nature, and partly of a practical policy nature (see also Van Gent and Nijkamp, 1987). Among policy-makers and researchers the awareness has grown that transportation research and planning should extend its scope by focusing also attention on those (sub)systems or domains that directly or indirectly interact with transport. For instance, in the case of passenger flows such subsystems include inter alia the population and household subsystem which - through its demographic and household formation processes, but also through changing lifestyles, work, consumption and leisure patterns - largely determine the demand for passenger transport (see Rima and van Wissen, 1988). In the same vein the freight transport sector is determined by the evolution of the economic subsystem, its changing location and relocation patterns, and the emergence of new production, storage and distribution technologies (e.g., logistic management and high speed connections). New information and communications technologies may also have profound effects on both passenger and freight transport, and there is undoubtedly a need to predict and evaluate these developments from a strategic perspective, including also the limitations set by the 'ecological paradigm'.

Another point worth mentioning here is the relationship between transport analysis on the one hand and policy implementation in a practical planning context on the other. There exists in many countries a gap between the increasing technical sophistication of transport planning studies or models and their practical usefulness in the planning process, and this gap is likely to increase in the future. Policy has not addressed itself so far to such fundamental questions as the legitimation of minimal levels of accessibility, the effect of the geographical concentration of public facilities and the districting of their service area on the supply of public transport, and the most important question of all, what the role of planning should be in society. One way out of this dilemma would be to increase the information-processing capacity of the planning system by installing computerized transport planning and management information systems. This would call for the need to design tailor-made **decision-support systems** in transportation planning. Complementary to this 'high-tech' approach, there is a 'low-tech' alternative of making the methods used more transparent and comprehensible to planners, politicians and the public at large. This may also require the design of user-friendly decision support systems and evaluation methods.

Another basic policy question in a changing planning situation concerns the relationship between transport infrastructure and land use patterns: is the spatial concentration into smaller numbers of public facilities (e.g., larger schools, hospitals, post offices, government offices, factories, warehouses, and so on) a response to a transport technology that has permitted these economies of scale to be realised, or have transport improvements merely helped to mitigate what would have occurred anyway and otherwise would have led to a general reduction in well-being? These are difficult questions, but central to our understanding of how society is changing, and hence of what could be done to modify (or accentuate) undesirable (or desirable) spatial mega-trends (cf. Armstrong and Taylor, 1985; Higgins and Savoie, 1988; Mclennon and Parr, 1979; Moore and Rhodes, 1976).

Mobility and transportation are thus essentially the spatial mapping of the dynamics of connectivity in our complex society. They are at the same time a multidimensional projection of various underlying forces, such as economic objectives, safety considerations, environmental standards, energy use, land use compatibility and maintenance of community lifestyle. Unfortunately, in industrial economies mobility and transport have often become a major driving force in their own right and have come to be regarded as an end in themselves, rather than as a means to an end ('derived demand'). This **isolationist** approach runs the risk of offering an incomplete and unbalanced view on the role of transport in society. Well focussed decision support and evaluation systems can help to restore the balance by providing a framework for looking at both positive and negative aspects of mobility, and for assessing its value in relation to social life and human well-being in changing industrial societies.

As a starting point for a more balanced view, it is noteworthy that mobility and transport have achieved a firm position in the hierarchy of needs and priorities of individuals, households and firms. The general rise in spatial mobility in the past decades is marked by various interesting features:

-   Mobility is an **integrated process** in which multiple actors with multiple motives (consumers, entrepreneurs and government agencies) play a joint role: residential mobility, job mobility, recreation, commuting, shopping, entrepreneurial relocation and geographical decentralisation reflect often the same tendency.

-   Mobility is - according to Say's Law - very often a **derivative of the supply** of a physical communications infrastructure (such as road and railway infrastructure): the 'hardware' determines the rise in 'locomotion' and 'automotion'.

-   Current mobility patterns reflect underlying deep **structural changes** in modern societies: increased interaction patterns, increased leisure time, simultaneous occurrence of geographical concentration and deconcentration, increased female labour force participation and differential economic dynamics (fast dynamics versus slow dynamics, or different adjustment speeds) between the components of an interwoven spatial system. It is noteworthy in this context that Kutter (1987) has questioned the trends in physical and transportation planning to design and select a spatial layout that supports the current status quo or its evolution: settlement and town planning fulfils the needs of an 'automotive' society, based on a segregation of functions (working, shopping, living, recreating, and so on) in which the transportation sector has become an important societal power as a driving force.

Clearly, predicting the spatial mobility and transportation effects of the great variety of structural changes in our dynamic economies is a complex matter, especially in the long run, and deserves much more attention in our research efforts. The societal value of mobility - from a long-term point of view - can only be assessed if adequate insight is obtained into the endogenous and exogenous dynamics of our complex spatial systems.

In this context, three remarks have to be made which indicate the relevance of the transportation sector from the end of the 1980s onwards. First, transportation is necessarily linked to the **production system**; it is an important input for many productive activities. Although the production system is at the moment going through a phase of structural transition, it has not become evident that future production systems will tend to be less transportation intensive (even though there is a trend toward high-value low-volume transport). On the contrary, future production systems may be expected to exhibit closely interwoven interactions, in which communications and transportation play a key role (see also Klaassen et al., 1982).

In the second place, the impact of **new technologies** has to be mentioned. Although from a technical viewpoint the modern telecommunications sector may be a substitute for many physical interactions, it is increasingly realised that this modern technology has become necessary in order to compensate for the rapid increase in physical and human interactions themselves (see Nijkamp and Salomon, 1987). In any case, we have incomplete evidence in this respect, especially because the developments in the field of transportation logistics and telecommunications are exhibiting a rapid growth (see Hewings et al., 1988). Substitution and complementarity seem to take place at the same time.

Finally, it is noteworthy that **modern settlement systems** (at both the urban and metropolitan level) may exhibit mutually contrasting impacts on the transportation sector. Transportation appears to be a major stimulus for the development of new urban centres, while at the same time transportation is endangering a balanced urban development. Positive and negative externalities appear to play an ambiguous role in the spatial and urban evolution of our modern societies.

1.6.   The Development Potential of Transportation Infrastructure

In recent years the potential of transportation (infrastructure) has increasingly received much attention, particularly in the context of a selective physical and transportation planning in which in addition to traffic aspects also economic, environmental, land use and safety aspects play a joint role. This also implies that transport impact analysis and evaluation is fraught with multiple problems, as the assessment of the spatial-economic consequences of (new) transport systems is a far from easy task. A major question, for instance, is whether modern infrastructure generates new benefits for the country as a whole or only - as redistributive impacts - for particular regions (especially those located on nodal points of a network). This important equity question - in combination with the efficiency question - deserves closer attention (cf.

Diamond and Spence, 1983; Giaoutzi et al., 1988; Meyer-Krahmer, 1985).

It is generally accepted that there is a mutual relationship between transportation infrastructure and regional development. On the one hand, regional development influences the growth of infrastructure, for instance, because an increase in regional welfare induces the demand for transport and hence for more infrastructure, while the public expenditures for financing this infrastructure are also generated by the same economic growth (a so-called Keynesian monetary effect). This is a so-called following (passive) infrastructure policy. On the other hand, the availability of appropriate infrastructure has a positive impact on the development of countries, regions and cities. In this case, the presence of transportation infrastructure allows for (potential) development of an area: infrastructure is a necessary - but by no means a sufficient - condition. Then one speaks of a **conditional** - or sometimes a steering - infrastructure policy. The latter type of policy will in particular be discussed here (see for a review Bruinsma et al., 1991, and Rietveld, 1990; see also Chapter 3).

It is interesting to observe that empirical evidence regarding the general role of transportation costs in industrial location decisions is inconclusive and leads to mutually contrasting results on the impact of transportation infrastructure. This paradox is co-determined by the following elements:

- The number and nature of location factors which have an influence upon the location decision of an entrepreneur are **heterogeneous** and differ from firm to firm and from place to place.

- Locational factors may shift in terms of impact and weight in the course of **time**.

- Entrepreneurs do **ex post** not always realize the major determining factors for a certain location, and in some cases posterior views are no more than an ex post rationalisation of earlier decisions.

- The impact of infrastructure on locational decisions of firms depends also on its **uniqueness**. An increase in an ubiquitous infrastructure category does not exert a major additional influence on a region. For instance, road expansion in an industrial area with a highly developed infrastructure network will have lower effects than that in an underdeveloped area (i.e., a case of decreasing marginal benefits).

Thus the conclusion can be drawn that infrastructure is **a conditio sine qua non**, but certainly **not a sufficient condition** for growth. Infrastructure policy requires a comprehensive and tailor-made supply of all relevant infrastructure categories (due to synergetic effects). Besides, infrastructure will only have a positive impact if the region at hand has already a favourable existing potential for new development. For instance, the implementation of new infrastructure in an economically weak region may even run the risk that the region at hand suffers from strong competition of enterprises in more distant regions. Next, infrastructure investments will only have a discriminating effect on regional development, if the competitive position of a region is improved. For instance, a simultaneous improvement of infrastructure in both central and peripheral regions is not necessarily beneficial - in a relative sense - for peripheral regions. And finally of course, the impacts of infrastructure are also co-determined by the general economic situation (see for more details also Chapter 3).

Altogether, network infrastructure is indispensable for long-run regional development, but the extent to which it will have a decisive influence on regional growth is not unambiguous. But in any case, it is evident that regions or countries with a poor infrastructure network ('missing links') run the risk of staying behind in the national and international economic restructuring process. The latter threat is an important driving force for assigning an **active** role to modern transportation planning.

1.7. Transportation as a Source of Conflict

The previous observations have shown that in our modern world transportation planning plays a central role in strategic policy-making and is hence also facing a wide variety of conflicts and tensions between a multiplicity of actors. Such problems originate amongst others from the following situations (cf. Cumberland, 1981):

- **ideological discrepancies** between economic planners;
- **political differences** regarding the desirable range of public policy measures;
- **lack of insight** into regional economic structures and growth processes;
- **rigidity** of instruments of economic policy.

In this context, Friedmann (1973) makes a distinction between **allocative** and **innovative** planning. Allocative planning is oriented towards the achievement of an optimal spatial allocation within the social and economic **status quo**, whereas innovative planning considers also the structure parameters of the socio-economic system and the institutional structure concerned as a variable. It is also noteworthy to refer here to Berry (1976), who distinguishes four **styles** of public policy:

- **ameliorative problem-solving**: this approach focuses the attention in particular on avoiding and tackling frictions and problems that are likely to take place on the basis of expected developments and trends;

- **allocative trend-modifying**: in this approach a future structure and reference pattern is required so as to have a frame of reference for current planning possibilities and directions;

- **exploitative opportunity-seeking**: in this setting, future spatial problems are identified in order to design future alternatives and to select the most favourable future alternative pattern;

- **normative and goal-oriented**: this approach aims at designing spatial alternatives on the basis of a priori specified aims, for instance, by means of systems-analytic methods.

In many cases, transportation - and especially infrastructure planning - is of the allocative trend-modifying type; it shapes the conditions for structural change in the space-economy (without however controlling directly or completely decisions taken by firms or households). Thus infrastructure policy is an **indirect** and **conditional** policy which focuses on **necessary conditions** for enhancing economic performance, without providing however sufficient or controlling conditions. This also means that the identification of a direct statistical or econometric link between (transport) infrastructure endowment and (regional or national) economic performance may sometimes be problematic, as the behaviour of relevant actors is characterized by much uncertainty, inertia and feedback mechanisms.

As mentioned before, transportation planning can be positioned at the crossroads of various economic, political and technological developments. Transportation and mobility have become key concepts in the modern Welfare State, so that it is almost regarded as a basic value in a modern society. Consequently, mobility rates are sometimes even taken as one of the performance indicators of an economic system.

In contrast to mobility as a positive welfare indicator, it is also worth mentioning that at the same time various negative spill-overs are caused by the increase in geographical movement. For instance, increased mobility causes intolerable consequences for the urban environment, it results in formidable fuel consumption, it leads to unacceptable changes in the physical environment, while especially car mobility conflicts strongly with other physical planning criteria (such as a pleasant residential quality of life).

It should be added that the increasing environmental concerns have not only led to a widening scope of transportation planning in most countries, but also to a wide spectrum of formal regulations and guidelines to be respected in any transportation project assessment. This means that in many countries environmental aspects are an obligatory part of transportation planning. This has of course led to far reaching implications for both the planning and implementation of transportation projects. For example, the joint impact of the enforcement of the 1990 Clean Air Act Amendment and the 1992 Intermodal Surface Transportation Efficiency Act in the USA on urban and regional planning in general, and on transportation planning in particular, is significant. The same holds true for the consequences of the Environmental Policy Act and the Structure Scheme for Transport and Traffic in the Netherlands. As a consequence, we observe a rapidly increasing need for the development and use of appropriate assessment and evaluation methods on the direct and cumulative impacts of new transportation plans. This new trend is not only instigated by national or federal concerns on the environment, but also by local and regional interests where the environmental awareness has become an important force field in urban and regional planning.

Clearly, it has to be realised that in an industrialised society (marked by labour division and specialisation) mobility is a necessary component, which also requires a satisfactory infrastructure system. The basic question is however, which type of mobility is desirable and compatible with the urban, environmental and residential system. It is evident that mobility based on private car use is by no means the only option. But as in our society (private) car mobility is a dominating trend, the question arises: what are the effects (in terms of costs and benefits) of increasing car mobility?

Debates on mobility and transportation planning often centre around two major issues: **internal** analysis focusing on mobility and transportation in a strict sense (for example, changing demands for travel, trends in settlement evolution, models of (dis)aggregate choice, transportation policy analysis) and **external** analysis focusing on the significance of mobility and transportation in a broad social context (for example, transportation as a means of achieving socio-economic goals rather than as an end in itself - the 'potentiality' view -, the basic needs approach to mobility, the negative externalities and social costs involved, the effects of a changing information and communications technology).

Generally speaking, **internal** transportation and mobility analysis appears to be relatively well developed in transportation planning, although there are important gaps in detail. For instance, in the case of actual trends there is considerable scope for further work in connection with the urbanisation/suburbanisation debate and its consequences for public transport usage. Similarly, in the field of methods there is an urgent need to expand existing accounting frameworks to make them more comprehensive in nature (including externalities), and to develop and strengthen operational methodologies relating to the use of 'soft' qualitative rather than hard data.

External research in the field of transport and mobility is in general much less well developed than that related to internal research. Nevertheless, in general, the position with respect to the analysis of trends is relatively good compared to the development of proper methods. Much more attention needs to be given, inter alia, to the analysis of non-cost factors and of indicators which incorporate social equity as well as cost-efficiency criteria. There is a particular need to introduce policy analysis and evaluation research thinking into the transport-planning field, for both the internal and external analysis. As mentioned before, there is also a clear scope for appropriate decision support methods in transportation planning.

In view of the conflicting nature of transportation planning, planners have to avoid two traps: to neglect meaningful and feasible alternatives (e.g., creative transportation plans) to be envisaged and to generate an overwhelming number of choice options which also renders planning useless and increases uncertainty. Thus, a combination of sound reasoning, 'plausibility', brainstorming, and Delphi-type and decision-theoretic methods seems to be necessary to ensure a balanced approach to transportation planning, based on a broad social science perspective. In all cases choice options have to be evaluated on the basis of relevant and up-to-date information (e.g., impact studies) and by means of appropriate evaluation techniques (e.g., multi-criteria analyses). The present book aims at providing such necessary decision support methods for transportation planning.

1.8. Organisation of the Book

Transportation planning takes place in a highly dynamic, conflictual and uncertain environment. Seen from the perspective sketched above, two tasks seem to be of paramount significance in a scientific reflection on transportation planning, viz. **the assessment of all relevant impacts of transport plans** (with a particular view on their social relevance) and **the evaluation of alternative choice possibilities** in transportation planning (with a particular view on conflict resolution).

Therefore, the present book has two main focal points, viz. **impact analysis** (Parts B and C) and **evaluation analysis** (Parts D and E). As an introduction to these main parts, Chapter 2 will first spell out the need for assessment, evaluation and decision support in modern transportation planning.

Part B of the book deals with impact analysis in a general sense. It describes models in transportation analysis and other statistical and ad hoc techniques for estimating the expected consequences of new transportation plans.

In Part C various illustrative applications of impact studies are described, with a particular view on their operational character.

Part D then introduces evaluation analysis as a major element of decision aid in transportation planning. Principles of evaluation, measurement issues and policy values are discussed, while a plea for the use of structured multicriteria methods is made.

Finally, in Part E various empirical illustrations of the significance of these evaluation methods for practical transportation planning are given.

All in all, this book aims to offer a broad set of modern methods and techniques for impact assessment, evaluation and decision support in the complex intriguing field of transport planning.

Chapter 2

NEED FOR DECISION SUPPORT IN TRANSPORTATION PLANNING

2.1.   Introduction

The actual impact of the research community on public decision making - both in general and in the transportation sector - is not always impressive. Institutional bottlenecks, administrative procedures, opportunistic behaviour or unanticipated events are often obstacles on the way toward clear and straightforward choice behaviour of policy makers (cf. Leman and Nelson, 1981). In a noteworthy article Verdier (1984) points to the need to bridge the gap between experts and policy-makers by suggesting inter alia the following guidelines:

- learn about the history of the issue;
- find out who will be making the decision;
- timing is critical;
- learn about everyone's interests and arguments.

These guidelines also suggest that planning presupposes a **communication** between experts and policy-makers, either as interactive decision procedures (based on a dialogue and information exchange about a given choice problem between all parties involved) or as cyclical decision procedures (based on an adaptation, feedback or restructuring of the planning problem at hand as a result of a consultation of parties involved; see Hickling, 1985).

The foregoing remarks indicate clearly that planning is closely connected with **information provision** to decision-makers (or in general to all actors in a decision-making process). This information has to be tailor-made for the decision-maker's wishes in all phases of decision-making, so that obviously a close cooperation between all actors involved in a decision is needed (cf. Batey and Breheny, 1978; Bracken, 1981; Masser, 1983).

21

According to Voogd (1984) various types of information provision may be distinguished, depending on the information need and decision style of actors. Examples of decision styles are:

-   a **monetary** decision approach, based e.g., on cost-benefit or cost-effectiveness principles;
-   a **utility** theory approach, based on a prior ranking of the decision-maker's preferences;
-   a **learning** approach, based on a sequential (interactive or cyclical) articulation of the decision-maker's views;
-   a **collective** decision approach, based on multi-person bargaining, negotiation or voting procedures.

It is noteworthy at this stage that each of the above mentioned four classes should all be based on sound principles regarding data collection, storage, retrieval, processing and inference (see also Nijkamp and Rietveld, 1984). In this context, it is evident that action-oriented planning approaches should generate comprehensible information which may facilitate the communication between various actors in a complex decision process; or in the words of the Greek philosopher Heraclitos: 'decision-making is communication'. Thus the decision support content of a planning or evaluation approach is of decisive importance for its actual influence. According to Janis and Mann (1977) the content of decision should not only be judged on the basis of their formal or substantive quality, but also on their procedural quality. This applies in particular to transportation planning, where in many cases the time horizon of a new project covers easily ten years, during which a variety of complicated administrative procedures - depending on the structure of the planning problem concerned - has to be followed.

2.2.   The Structure of Planning Problems

Planning concerns the analysis of conflicting choice options. In general the relative social ('public') value of effects of planning projects (e.g., a highway project) is co-determined by political priorities at different institutional levels. Sometimes these values are - directly or indirectly - a result of prices resulting from a market mechanism, but very often such values are more subjectively determined and, for example, based on desiderata of individuals and groups in society (for instance, the value of a natural park or the visual beauty of an old theatre). Consequently, many conflicting views may emerge in evaluating alternative plans (e.g., different highway investment projects). Especially modern approaches like multicriteria analysis may serve as a meaningful evaluation vehicle for taking explicitly account of such conflicts regarding the foreseeable impacts of a plan. For example, everybody may agree on the fact that the implementation of a road project will destroy x hectares of a forest, but not everybody will attach the same value to these x hectares of the forest. Multicriteria analysis may then be helpful in taking into account such conflicting issues by considering priority schemes or weights as an ingredient in an evaluation analysis for investment projects. Of course, this will not always lead to a unique final solution, but the structure and consequences of conflicts among decision-makers can be made more explicit, so that also the range of politically feasible alternatives can be analyzed in greater detail. Especially in Part D and E of the present book multicriteria methods as a tool for decision aid will be discussed in greater detail.

It should also be added that in many decision problems a multi-level policy structure is present, in particular in a decentralized policy framework. For example, a city council which wants to build a bridge across a river needs approval of its plans by a state government which may have different interests. This implies that conflicts may arise in two ways: **informally** between interested people whose well-being may be affected by the implementation of a certain investment project, and **formally** between official decision-makers (and other formal groups) whose institutional structure - reflecting a specific involvement - may give rise to sharp interest conflicts. As will be shown later on, both kinds of conflicts can be taken into consideration in multicriteria evaluation techniques.

The **general structure** of planning problems can be sketched as follows (see Figure 2.1 on page 24).

Clearly, the latter scheme can easily be extended with learning, interactive and feedback procedures for ill-structured decision problems, which form the backbone of decision support systems. In addition, it is noteworthy that before an evaluation starts, it is usually meaningful to eliminate less relevant choice options. In this respect, one may make the following classification of choice options which may be **rejected** for further implementation, based on **prior** considerations:

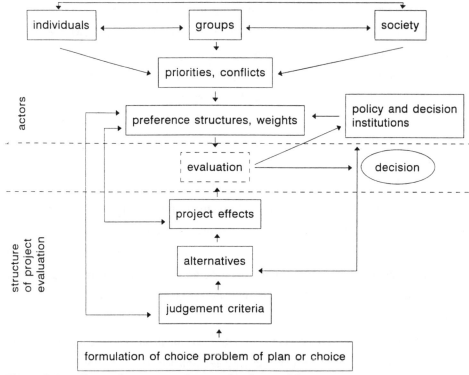

Figure 2.1.   General structure of an evaluation problem.

- options which are not feasible from a **technical** point of view. These projects can be eliminated **ex ante** due to technical constraints.

- options which are not feasible from a **financial** point of view. These projects can be eliminated after a careful financial budget analysis.

- options which are not feasible from a **political** point of view, in particular, due to conflicts with other policy constraints or desiderata (for example, environmental standards, safety requirements). These projects can be eliminated after a confrontation of project impacts with prevailing policy rules, standards or prohibitions. However, in some cases the political acceptability of a given choice option may depend on its relative position (e.g., ranking) vis-à-vis alternative choice options to be evaluated. In that case, a prior elimination is analytically not justifiable, as it violates the fairness principle that relevant alternatives should not be ruled out at the outset.

options which are not feasible after an **integrated** evaluation of all relevant aspects. It is clear that especially in the latter situation, decision support methods and multicriteria analyses may be an extremely useful tool, since in such cases a comparative judgement of all policy criteria is in order. This is also the reason for the current popularity of multicriteria evaluation techniques.

At this stage it should be emphasized that after a final decision to implement a certain investment project, the **ex ante** evaluation is completed. It must be added, however, that once the investment project concerned has been implemented, an **ex post** evaluation may be extremely important in order to monitor and judge the posterior social desirability of this project. In this respect, an **ex post** evaluation may be regarded as a necessary ingredient of an integrated evaluation procedure for alternative choice options, in particular because ex post evaluation provides also a learning mechanism to policy-makers and planners.

2.3. Decision Support Methods

After the illustrative sketch of some essential features of planning problems in Section 2.2., we will now focus our attention on decision support methods in planning. Decision support methods serve to enhance the quality of decision making by designing models, analytical techniques and related software which structure all dimensions of a complex decision problem, in particular by means of interactive (and usually computerized) information exchange procedures (cf. Bennett, 1983; Keen and Scott Morton; 1978; Lucas, 1980). Decision support methods deal usually with ill structured problems; they should in principle contain the following elements:

- a set of multiple (and usually conflicting) goal functions;
- an indication of uncertainty in model results;
- a discussion of the scope and transferability of (model) results;
- a presentation of (administrative, financial, technical, etc.) bottlenecks in the implementation of policies;
- a sensitivity analysis of the implications of alternative policy weights or new exogenous circumstances.

In all cases the interface analyst - decision-maker is of crucial importance, not only in terms of formal information exchange but also in terms of adjustments in decision processes. This is also necessary to ensure an integration of design, implementation and evaluation (cf. Keen and Scott Morton, 1978).

Decision support methods have gained a great deal of popularity in modern planning problems, in both the private and the public sector. The precise structure and mechanism of these methods is not fixed however, as such features depend both on the context in which planning and decision-making takes place and on the contents of the choice problem concerned (see for an interesting overview and various applications, Janssen, 1991).

Decision support methods in the field of transportation planning may adopt various forms ranging from interactive network planning to peak-load management of congested networks. Models to be used here may exhibit a large diversity and may be based among others on static distinct impact models or on dynamic multi-objective spatial interaction models. Such models may be used for network expansion or for modal split policy. In view of the multiplicity of actors involved and of policy objectives to be taken into consideration, straightforward conventional optimization procedures are often bound to fail. In this context, a flexible design and use of information systems and models as part of a decision support system makes much more sense, particularly because such a communicative vehicle is able to take into account heuristic decision styles and complex and rigid institutional environments which often prevail in the field of transportation planning (see also Fischer and Nijkamp, 1992).

Another advantage of the use of decision support techniques in transportation planning is that they do not take for granted the conventional rationality paradigm by assuming a comprehensive understanding of problems, objectives and constraints, full knowledge of all alternatives and a capability to make consistent judgements and decisions. Strategic behaviour in case of multiperson decision-making (e.g., the prisoner's dilemma case) can hardly be tackled by means of conventional optimization models, while decision support methods based on mutual communication between actors involved may provide a more appropriate framework here. Modern decision support methods may provide a useful complementary framework for complex and multi-person transportation planning. It should be emphasized that the expert - despite his ability to use or design complicated decision support techniques - can never take over the political responsibility of decision-makers. In this respect, impact and evaluation techniques are only aids for taking balanced decisions.

The systematic provision of information is extremely important, since many investment decisions have a process character. For example, a project to build a flood-control dam in a river will require a careful examination of all alternative locations and of all relevant judgement criteria (benefit-cost ratio, environmental impacts, risks, accessibility and so forth). After a first deliberation, alternative solutions and proposals may be put forward by policy-makers, experts or environmental action groups. Consequently, the evaluation of alternative plans has to be repeated. This process continues, until a final decision has been reached. During this process of evaluation, generating alternatives, judging the efficiency of the projects, comparing the intangible effects and so forth, the expert has to inform responsible policy-makers, interest groups, etc. about the trade-offs of alternative plans, so that people know precisely how much they gain or lose in a certain respect, when the first plan is substituted for the second, and so forth. So the expert or planner is essentially a communication agent. Thus the main task of the expert or planner is to rationalize decisions by offering a coherent, systematic and surveyable frame of reference during the entire evaluation process of plans or projects. Rather than employing evaluation or planning methods in a technocratic manner, the expert's responsibility is to confront decision-makers with the consequences of their priorities and choices, so that such methods serve as an aid to improve the quality of decisions. This is essentially the core of spatial impact analysis (see also Chapter 1 and Part B of the present book).

In this respect, decision support techniques have a learning character, based on an interplay between suppliers and users of information regarding a broad spectrum of consequences and scarce resources used. It has to be repeated here that the provision of information to policy-makers also requires the provision of insight into uncertainties, non-measurable effects, unforeseeable consequences etc., so that policy-makers may also take account of risks, uncertainties and stochastic information before taking a final decision on a plan or a project.

Provision of all relevant information and use of multi-dimensional and/or interactive decision or evaluation methods are two important characteristics of modern planning approaches, in particular of modern decision support methods. Such methods may also enhance the level of acceptance of such tools. Lack of acceptation or confidence in an evaluation tool may be caused by various factors; especially two factors have to be mentioned here:

- **time consuming** (or in general financially costly) **computational work**; this problem may lead to the following undesirable consequences:
  - neglect of a suitable evaluation methodology
  - use of an inappropriate evaluation method
  - neglect of complementary analyses (e.g., sensitivity tests)
  - use of a rigid evaluation method
  - imbalance between computational work and problem specification resolution
- **lack of comprehensibility of evaluation analysis**; this problem may have the following consequences:
  - lack of acceptability of (and hence less optimal use of) evaluation results
  - selective use of evaluation methods by experts only
  - unsatisfactory learning aspects of the method at hand
  - over-emphasis on technicalities instead of on substance.

Given the previous caveats, it is reasonable to design evaluation methods with at least the following characteristics (see also Nijkamp et al., 1990):

- user-friendliness;
- flexibility;
- reliability.

Under such conditions evaluation methods may play an important role in a decision support context. In general, the advantages of using decision support methods (including impact and evaluation studies) in transportation planning may be summarized as follows:

- They provide meaningful **information** which is necessary for a decision-maker in order to take a balanced decision (for example, the size of a forest to be cut when a new road would be constructed). In this context, also the use of geographic information systems (GIS) has to be mentioned (see Fischer and Nijkamp, 1993).

- They provide insight into all **trade-offs** (and sacrifices) of alternative choices (for example, the gain in traffic speed against the reduction in safety).

- They ensure the generation of **efficient** solutions, so that necessary optimality conditions are met; this means that interior (and hence less efficient) solutions can be avoided.

- They enhance the decision-maker's insight into the **structure** of the transportation problem at hand; of course, this requires that the method itself and its results should, in principle, be comprehensible for the decision-maker.

- The relationship between policy objectives, instruments and restrictions (of a technical or political nature) becomes much more clear in a **communicative** or an **interactive** process (for example, by exchanging information on some meaningful simulations or scenarios).

- The methods are also able to indicate the degree of **uncertainty** of forecasting statements (for example, the expected number of firms to be attracted by the construction of a new road should be assessed by providing also the uncertainty range of this expectation); see for further decisions on this issue also Douglas and Wildavsky (1982), Kahneman et al. (1982), and Pitz and McKillip (1984).

In conclusion, decision support methods are a communication tool in a multi-faceted planning environment based on adaptive planning procedures. In such cases, the relevance of decision support methods may be judged from four complementary angles:

- **indigenous** criteria, which are directly related to the **specific** nature of the choice problem or the relevant choice options. For example, if the choice problem at hand concerns a set of generally or loosely defined distinct policy programmes or plans (in contrast to a set of precisely defined distinct choice alternatives), the use of non-monetary or qualitative impact models is plausible.

- **functional** criteria, which are related to the following phases of an evaluation procedure:

  . structuring of choice problems (including information gathering, impact analysis, specification of constraints, design of heuristic rules, and generation of alternatives);

  . comparison of alternatives (including survey tables, graphical presentation etc).

.   ranking of alternatives (including e.g., multicriteria techniques);

.   judgement of evaluation results (including sensitivity tests on impacts, weights and methods);

.   presentation of final results (including user-friendly output).

-   **user** criteria, which are related to the expertise of potential users of the system at hand; the following elements may be mentioned here:

    .   easy use and accessibility;

    .   protection against abuse;

    .   early warning in case of wrong use of a procedure (or method);

    .   easy transfer of evaluation principles used.

-   **application** criteria, which are related to actual applications of the interactive system concerned:

    .   quick generation of new results;

    .   quick delivery of graphical results;

    .   broad applicability ranging from local to national level;

    .   emphasis on decision support (and **not** on replacement of decision-making).

It will be shown later on that multicriteria methods have their own indigenous values as multidimensional evaluation tools, but are also particularly appropriate vehicles in adaptive information systems or - in broader context - adaptive decision support systems. In this framework, multicriteria techniques may provide analytical support for a whole evaluation procedure (including evaluation of alternatives, generation of choice options, and structuring of choice procedures), with a particular emphasis on feedback (or interactive) processes in all phases of decision-making.

2.4.   Computerized Information Systems

The use of decision support methods has been induced particularly by the penetration of computers, notably micro-computers and personal computers (including the software); see also Fischer and Nijkamp (1992), Marin (1982), McNichols and Clark (1983), Rivers (1984) and Scholten and Stillwell (1991). In recent years also expert systems - sometimes based on artificial intelligence (cf. Laurini, 1988) - have come to the fore (see also Duda and Gaschnig, 1981; Stefik, 1982).

According to Kruijssen and Voogd (1988), an expert system can be described as "a computerized system which utilizes knowledge about a particular application area to help decision-makers solve ill-structured problems. This subset is characterized by the fact that it concerns knowledge-based systems" (p. 270). Generally, an expert system will include the following components:

- a knowledge system storing knowledge about the problem domain;
- a language system interacting with the users, and
- a problem processing system directing the problem-solving processes.

In the view of Kruijssen and Voogd (1988), usually six general classes of expert systems may be distinguished:

- consultation and advisory systems;
- evaluation systems;
- diagnostic systems;
- guidance and control systems;
- help systems;
- education systems.

The use of computer graphics may provide another stimulus for a wider application of decision support and expert systems (see Batty, 1987).

In many planning problems, however, computers are often used for more modest purposes, for instance, as a tool for storing and retrieving large data sets in the form of information systems (see e.g., Nijkamp and Rietveld, 1984). In physical and transportation planning especially the (relational) database management systems have gained much popularity, not only for administrative purposes but also for scientific analysis and evaluation.

In this framework also the significance of **geographic information systems** deserves closer attention (see also Burrough, 1986; Fischer and Nijkamp, 1992; Scholten and Stillwell, 1991). According to Scholten (1988), the main value of geographic information systems lies in the speed and accuracy with which maps can be produced by computers on the basis of a selection from a large amount of data, often of a differentiated type. Such geographic information systems may contain a wide variety of various objects. Examples are land use data, landscape and ecological data, data on built environment, etc. The presentation of data at different spatial levels is of major importance here. Such systems are particularly useful for monitoring long-term spatial developments. Various applications of the use of geographic information systems can be found in transportation planning, for instance, in the field of traffic safety policies, route choice policies etc. Information on traffic conditions is also increasingly available in a user-friendly way, e.g., via the Minitel-system (France).

It may thus be concluded that computerized decision support tools have shown a high penetration rate in physical and transportation planning, and it is foreseeable that this development will continue in the years to come. Such methods are not only important for ex ante planning problems, but also for ex post evaluation and monitoring (including a revision of implemented policies). Thus the necessary ingredients of decision support in planning - viz. information gathering, impact analysis and evaluation - are increasingly placed in a broader context of analytical and computerized research methods and models.

After this introductory Part A, which mainly dealt with the substance and context of (transportation) planning, we will in the next Part B focus attention on impact analysis in transportation, followed by various illustrative applications in Part C. The question of evaluation methodology will then be discussed in Part D, which will again be followed by various illustrative applications in Part E.

PART B

IMPACT ASSESSMENT IN TRANSPORTATION PLANNING

Chapter 3

PRINCIPLES OF IMPACT ASSESSMENT

3.1. Preamble

Rational and consistent policy analysis presupposes a reliable assessment and balanced evaluation of all foreseeable consequences and choice possibilities in relation to policy initiatives. The aim of generating and judging alternative frameworks of policy measures is a far from easy task for mainly two reasons. The process of **generating meaningful choice options** in the context of policy analysis is extremely complicated in an open, multi-actor social system with diverging interests, while also the **assessment of expected impacts** of policy measures - especially in a dynamic spatial system - is fraught with many difficulties inherent in the uncertainty context of decision-making.

The first problem refers essentially to the design stage of (transportation) planning (cf. Bracken, 1981). A major problem emerges from the task to seek for a fair balance between generating a comprehensible (but perhaps incomplete) set of choice options and generating a complete (but perhaps largely irrelevant or redundant) set of choice options. In the latter case, the so-called **combinatorial** approach (cf. Harris, 1978), a rather mechanistic and computational design method, is sometimes employed. However, it lacks focus and coherence in searching for a variety of feasible **policy-relevant** options. The first case however, runs the risk that certain relevant alternatives are neglected, a situation which has often emerged in case of environmental impact analysis. Therefore, the main challenge in (transportation) planning is to devise a set of representative choice options which serve as a first indicative frame of reference, so as to delineate a limited subset of relevant alternatives to be investigated more thoroughly in a next stage of the analysis (see Batty, 1974).

Various systematic design methodologies for physical and transportation planning have been developed in the past, for instance, the **strategic choice strategy** (see Friend and Jessop, 1976), the **potential surface analysis** (see Chadwick, 1976), or the **decision-**

theoretic approach (see Krueckeberg and Silvers, 1974). In this context, it is noteworthy that a major flaw in designing policy choice options is caused by the so-called **robustness principle**, which refers to the extent to which a set of policy measures designed for policy evaluation in a given period, leaves open as many choice options as possible for future decision-making (in particular, in order to account for adjustments in policy behaviour).

The second problem referred to above is known as **impact analysis.** In principle, one may distinguish four distinct levels at which **impact assessment of policy measures** may be applied (Cambridge Economic Consultants, 1990):

- an assessment (usually qualitative) of the contribution of policy measures towards the solution to a given policy problem.
- a consideration of the appropriateness of the package of policy instruments in the light of either changed economic circumstances or the contentions of economic theory.
- the measurement (as far as possible) of the range of benefits accruing from the package of relevant policy measures.
- the measurement of both the costs and benefits of the policy and the cost effectiveness of individual policy instruments.

These observations show that impact assessment is not a straightforward technical method, but has to be placed in a broad socio-economic and political context. In an **ex ante** analytical framework impact assessment aims in general at gauging the expected or foreseeable relevant consequences of a policy decision (project, programme or plan) in a given spatial socio-economic system. In particular, it serves to assess the extent to which a policy measure may cause a change in the desired direction of one or more relevant goal variables. Of course, impact assessment can also be undertaken as an **ex post** analysis. An ex post impact analysis includes information on the actual occurrence of (past) exogenous changes as well as the endogenous changes brought about by the policy intervention. Clearly, in this case factual information on policy-off situations is usually missing. It is increasingly recognized that impact analysis is the heart of policy analysis and deserves - in a broad perspective - much more attention than it has received in the past.

3.2. The Need for Impact Analysis

When analysing a certain policy (e.g., transportation policy, regional policy), one is interested in the assessment of the effects that **solely** accrue from that policy. Impact analysis thus aims at estimating all policy-relevant consequences (direct and indirect, intended and unintended) of (a set of) given policy measures. Usually, questions that emerge when dealing with impact analysis of a certain policy are the following:

- What would be the situation if there were no specific policy?
- What would be the influence of possible other relevant variables besides the specific policy instruments or measures used in this framework?
- Which are the interrelations between those different variables impacting on the system at hand?

The enormous financial implications of transportation (and regional) policy and its ambiguous results, have led to a growing interest in a systematic analysis of transportation (and regional) policy in both applied and theoretical research (see e.g., Armstrong and Taylor; 1985; Glickman, 1980; Pleeter, 1980). In particular, in recent years the need for a critical assessment of the success or failure of policy measures has increased, mainly for **two reasons**.

First, many countries or regions are now going through a process of **drastic socio-economic and technological restructuring**. This dynamic evolutionary pattern exhibits a clean break with the past which was - to a large extent - marked by stable dynamics. In the present circumstances, the assessment of the influence of policies is much more troublesome, as our current analytical models do usually not adequately reflect the present - much more turbulent - dynamics of our economies.

Secondly, the **slow (or sometimes declining) growth and drastic cuts in public budgets** in many regions and countries have called for a more careful analysis of the effectiveness and efficiency of public expenditures. Consequently, a systematic appraisal of (public) social and economic programmes is an important issue in transportation (and regional) policy analysis.

Policy evaluation requires thus a systematic and sound methodology, focussing on both the design and the implementation phase of policies (see also Diamond and Spence, 1983; Rossi et al., 1979). In particular, a **systematic assessment** and judgement of the various effects of a given policy programme is of great importance. Seen from this perspective, it is a sine qua non to develop systematic tools for assessing the meso and macro effects of transportation (and regional) policy.

3.3.   Elements of Impact Analysis

Impact analysis deals typically with **'policy-off'** versus **'policy-on'** situations. The 'policy-off' situation refers to the zero (initial) situation (assuming away the implementation of policies). The 'policy-on' situation refers to the evaluation of the system after the policy measures have been implemented. Clearly, different policies lead to different 'policy-on' situations, each of which has to be judged on the basis of multiple judgement criteria (see also Folmer, 1985). Sometimes also a desired alternative is (implicitly or explicitly) taken as a frame of reference. A simple presentation of the previous ideas is given in Figure 3.1.

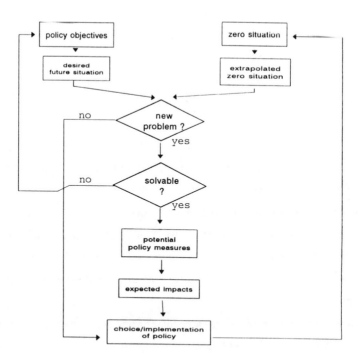

Figure 3.1.   A simplified representation of a decision-making process.

Impact analysis is only meaningful if it refers to a set of relevant alternatives. This means that usually from the set of choice options generated in the design stage a pre-selection has to be made, based on strategic considerations like (technical or financial) feasibility, flexibility, ease of implementation, risk level etc. The remaining subset then has to be evaluated in light of the successive effects emanating from the implementation of the policy concerned. The multiplicity of effects is one of the key issues in impact analysis and calls also for adjusted evaluation techniques in the decision-making stage (see Part D of the present study).

As mentioned already before, impact analysis is one of the central issues in policy evaluation. In the literature on impact analysis various types of impacts are usually distinguished (see, for instance, Van Kessel, 1983). We will use here the following **typology of impacts (or effects)**:

- **Intended** versus **unintended** impacts.

   Intended impacts are all consequences of policy measures which are deliberately strived for. Unintended (or side-) effects are not aimed at, but are usually inherent in the implementation of any policy. They may be either positive or negative, and should be an intrinsic consideration in any kind of impact analysis.

- **Direct** versus **indirect** impacts.

   Direct (or first-order) impacts emerge in a straightforward way from the implementation of a policy. Indirect (higher-order) effects occur after a 'detour' (or second-round effect) from the initial policy stimulus. The distinction between direct and indirect effects does **not** refer to the importance of these impacts, nor is it related to the distinction between intended and unintended effects. Indirect effects can be subdivided in second-, third- and higher-order effects.

- **Integral** versus **partial** impacts.

   Integral effects refer to all relevant effects (related to all relevant fields for a given decision), whereas partial effects concern only a limited class of effects (usually related to a single policy sector, e.g., transportation).

- **Single** versus **compound** impacts.

   Single impacts refer to the consequences of a single policy (policy measures or instruments), whereas compound impacts refer to policy packages (sets of policy instruments).

In principle, all relevant impacts have to be assessed in an impact analysis, but then an obvious question is: how relevant is relevant? The answer is that an impact is relevant for a policy decision, if its outcome is able to influence the ultimate choice of a policy option (or alternative) at a given level of detail. This has of course far reaching consequences for the **demarcation** of the impact system, as, in this view, this is not necessarily determined by institutional or administrative boundaries, but also by functional relationships or socio-economic repercussions in a broader setting. The same holds true for the desirable level of **aggregation** of effects; especially in case of equity problems (social, spatial) a detailed presentation of impacts is necessary. This had led to the notion of community impact analysis (Lichfield, 1991) in order to map out all distributive effects of a given policy.

3.4.   Caveats in Impact Analysis

There are many examples and applications in the field of impact assessment where serious methodological problems have emerged. For instance, is the type of impact to be assessed equal for all kinds of instruments, groups or regions? How to isolate the effect of a certain policy instrument from other kinds of variables, etc? The choice of an appropriate impact assessment method to be applied in a given situation is often sketchily dealt with in the literature. Thus there is a need for more systematics in impact assessment.

However, the solution to the above task is hampered by various bottlenecks. There are two difficult (and often neglected) aspects of impact analysis which deserve special attention here, viz. the **fuzzy nature** of many policies and the **role of uncertainty**.

The fuzzy nature of policy concerns both the policy objectives at hand and the effects of policy instruments used to attain these objectives (see Leung, 1989). It is widely recognized in policy analysis that effects upon a single decision criterion, as a result of different policy instruments, cannot always be measured in an unambiguous manner, since policy measures may be of a quite different and often multidimensional nature. Instruments can, for instance, be subdivided into quantifiable instruments, qualitatively defined plans and broad legislative measures (e.g., in environmental policy). Similarly, policy objectives may vary from quantifiable targets (for instance, a four percent increase in employment) to qualitative policy desires (for instance, a rise in social well-being).

Next, the measurement of values of objectives and of instruments incorporates much uncertainty, as it may be based on different scales, ranging from metric information (cardinal scales) to nominal or qualitative information (see also Nijkamp et al., 1985). In the case of a nonmetric measurement of objectives and instruments, the concept of both the effectiveness of a policy (i.e., the extent to which a policy measure contributes to the fulfilment of a policy target) and the cost efficiency of a policy is fraught with difficulties. This may, for instance, take place in case of qualitative scenario analysis for regional policy (Folmer, 1985).

In general, there is quite some scope for **qualitative impact models** (see also Chapter 5). Recently developed qualitative calculus models (based on the mathematics of signs or directions of impacts) can be considered as special cases of qualitative impact models (see Brouwer 1986, 1989; Brouwer et al., 1989; Fontaine et al., 1991; Garbely and Gilli, 1990). The same applies to graph-theoretic models and Boolean representations of complex policy systems (see Berndsen, 1992). In this context also causality analysis and specification theory have to be mentioned (see e.g., Blommestein and Nijkamp, 1983).

3.5. Criteria for an Appropriate Impact Assessment

In order to arrive at an appropriate impact assessment method it is desirable to formulate some general **methodological** criteria for impact assessment methods. Besides such methodological aspects, we may also discern some **practical considerations** in order to ensure that impact methods are operational. By **methodological** criteria we mean all (theoretically and conceptually) relevant research aspects inherent in each particular kind of impact assessment. Methodologically weak points arise, when a given method fails to consider all aspects that are necessary for a (theoretically) valid impact assessment. The **practical** considerations refer to those aspects which make a certain method feasible or unfeasible when it is put in operation, even though certain methodological aspects may be adequately fulfilled.

In general, most **methodological** criteria in socio-economic (including transportation) impact analysis concern the relationship between a certain policy measure (or a package of measures) as an explanatory variable and economic development as the goal variable (or target objective). In investigating the latter relationship we may distinguish **three circumstances** which make it often difficult to meet methodological criteria.

The first problem stems from the fact that in the relationship mentioned above, economic development (as a goal or target variable) is not only affected by a given policy measure, but also by many other (endogenous or external) conditions. Thus one has to bear in mind that normally there will be **more than one explanatory variable** (no mono-causality), so that simple stimulus-response models are often not very adequate.

The second problem is the fact that the explanatory variable (e.g., a policy measure) does not only affect the goal variable. There are **indirect (second-order) effects** influencing the goal variable and emanating indirectly via a causal chain from the explanatory variable. Thus indirect effects of a policy measure might also cause a change in economic development.

The final problems follow from the two causes mentioned above. Because of subsequent and indirect effects and because of the existence of more than one explanatory variable for the dependent goal variable, conclusions concerning the effects of a policy measure are **often ambiguous**, so that also the order of magnitude of the relevant effects is sometimes difficult to assess and to explain. Figure 3.2. represents the relations between these influences.

Besides an underestimation or a neglect of the relationships outlined in Figure 3.2., most methods for impact analysis do not explicitly consider the fact that such methods should be capable to include also adjustments in terms of specific policy instruments, the regions concerned, the relevant sectors or the time horizon in the study. One should not only look into demand responses, but also into supply (dynamic generative) impacts, if one really wants to achieve a reliable, realistic and complete representation of the impact of a policy measure on economic development.

It is obvious that impact methods incorporating in a satisfactory way also other (non-policy) explanatory variables and higher-order effects have strong methodological advantages. This allows also a consideration of various important effects for different policy measures, regions, sectors and time horizons (including time-lag effects).

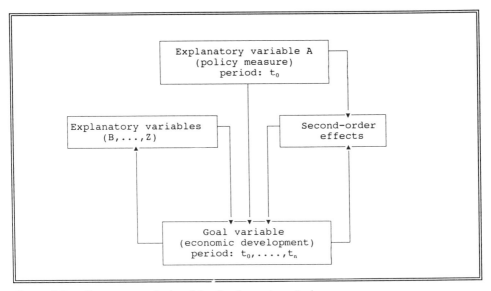

Figure 3.2.   Important relationships for impact analysis.

Besides these methodological criteria, we need to distinguish also **practical criteria**. In practice, the weak points of most impact methods consist mainly of problems concerning **collecting relevant data** or **valuable information**. The difficulty of collecting all relevant data increases with the complexity of the method used. The difficulty of collecting reliable data increases also with the extent to which the data are collected in a micro based way (e.g., from panel surveys).

There may also be difficulties connected with impact assessment methods emerging from a tension between what is considered to be essential from a **theoretical viewpoint** and what is (im)possible to achieve in **practice**. We can distinguish here two kinds of problem.

The first kind of problem concerns the **frame of reference** used for making and interpreting an impact assessment. Significant differences in such frameworks (e.g., other regions or time periods) may drastically limit the usefulness of impact studies. The problem is thus to find a region that is in all respects identical to the region under study, or to use a time period that is in all respects equal to the time period of study (except for the existence of a certain policy measure).

The second problem arises when some effects with a high importance in **theory**, are difficult to assess in **actual practice**. For example, a certain method may wish to assess the systems-wide (programme) effects of an infrastructure investment, but when applying this method it may be difficult to assess or even identify such programme effects in an adequate way (or to assess their degree of adequacy). To isolate a specific effect or to measure an effect that leads to a meaningful interpretation is not always very easy in assessment practice.

Given the previous observations, it may be useful to distinguish the following desiderata that ideally would have to be fulfilled for a meaningful impact analysis in a spatial context (see Nijkamp, 1987):

1.   **Relevance**: impact and indicators are to be associated with the objectives and instruments of urban, regional or transportation policies.

2.   **Completeness**: all relevant (direct and indirect, intended and unintended, integral or partial) impacts are to be included.

3.   **Consistency**: the statistical and relational information base should provide a coherent and non-contradictory impact system.

4.   **Pluriformity**: impacts should reflect the variety and multidimensionality of an urban, regional or transportation system.

5.   **Comparability**: impacts should preferably be comparable to analogous impacts measured at different places or in different points in time.

6.   **Flexibility**: the information about impacts should be comprehensible for decision-makers and should be adaptable to new circumstances.

7.   **Data availability**: impacts should be measured on the basis of available data, so that long-lasting research procedures are not necessary; in this context, ordinal and soft information may play an important role in impact assessment.

8.   **Comprehensiveness**: the successive steps in an impact study should provide an integrated picture of all spatial interactions and effects - including distributional effects.

9.   **Effectiveness**: estimated impacts should preferably allow for a confrontation with a priori set policy goals (or costs).

10.   **Feasibility**: impact analysis should fit in the prevailing pattern of urban, regional or transportation planning systems.

Having now made a long check list of guidelines for impact analysis in general, we will in the next section pay more specific attention to various problems inherent in transportation (infrastructure) impact analyses.

3.6.   Impact Analysis in Transportation Infrastructure Planning

When we regard investments in infrastructure as a policy instrument for general economic or regional development, we are essentially referring to an **active strategy**: a strategy where infrastructure is inducing private investments (Rietveld, 1989). A survey of the relevant literature teaches us that the relationship between infrastructure and (economic or regional) development can be based on various theories. De Wit and van Gent (1986) distinguish three kinds of theories, viz., **general development theories**, **regional development theories** and **development theories based on transport systems**.

Despite some variation, a central and common aspect in all these three kinds of theories is the significant influence of infrastructure investments on the development of a certain region. The development and implementation of transportation infrastructure is often used as a strategic policy instrument to fulfil the efficiency and equity goals of (regional) economic policy. Consequently, in the past various specific impact assessment methods have been developed to estimate all relevant consequences of such kinds of policy measures (e.g., input-output methods, Keynesian multiplier methods, etc.). In Chapters 4 and 5 we will give a more complete overview of methods and models for impact assessment. The aspects related to impacts analysis in general and discussed in the previous sections should of course also be taken in consideration when dealing with impact analysis focused on transportation infrastructure policies.

In assessing the consequences of transportation infrastucture upon (regional-) economic development, one may distinguish the following two classes of impacts (cf. Bartels et al., 1982; Pleeter, 1980):

(1)   **Temporary (direct and indirect) effects**. These are effects which occur during the building/construction phase of infrastructure. These effects will arise in both the economic sectors directly concerned with this activity and the remaining sectors that are indirectly related to the first type via intermediate deliveries. Via multiplier/accelerator mechanisms these infrastructure investments will exert a demand stimulating effect (in the Keynesian sense). In general these effects can

reasonably well be estimated via input-output analyses or economic base methods. Similar assessments can be made for maintainance activities of infrastructure.

(2)   **Long lasting (structural) effects.** These are effects which emanate as a consequence of infrastructural investments in the field of production, employment, locational shifts and migration movements. Infrastructure projects may - via a reduction in travel time and in transportation costs - have an influence on (regional) economic development, because it leads to an expansion of the market for products and labour. Firms will benefit from this increased accessibility, so that they will be induced to move to the areas concerned.

One word of warning is in order here, as the latter phenomenon brings us into the field of location theory for entrepreneurial behaviour. In conventional location theories (Weber, Von Thünen etc.), transportation costs do play a central role. However, the development of modern transportation technology has led to a reduction of the share of transportation costs in total production costs, so that transportation costs are only one of the many factors in locational decisions. It should however be added that the importance of infrastructure as a location factor is not only limited to its impact on transportation costs, but also to attributes like speed, reliability, flexibility and capacity.

Besides, when analysing the impacts of the development and implementation of infrastructure on the economic development of a region or a country, one has to take in account the following series of specific characteristics of infrastructure. Some of these characteristics have already been shortly mentioned in the first chapter (Section 1.6). Here we will give a more detailed description of the specific characteristics in light of operational impact assessment methods for transportation (infrastructure) policy.

First of all, infrastructure is often subjected to **decreasing returns to scale**, depending upon the intensity of utilization (Rietveld, 1989). The marginal effects of an infrastructure investment are dependent on the infrastructure already available in a region. For example, when a region is already provided with an extensive railway network, the addition of an extra connection will not have such a great effect on the economic activities of a region per unit of investment expenditure, as it would have had in a situation when there were hardly a railway network at all. On the other hand, when an infrastructure investment leads to the elimination of a missing link in an already developed infrastructure network, this might result in high marginal effects. The contribution of infrastructure investments to regional developments depends thus on its uniqueness for a specific region.

In the second place, the implementation of a certain kind of infrastructure in a region will **not necessarily** lead to a positive economic development for that region. If a region with a weak economy is provided with new or improved infrastructure, surrounding regions might benefit relatively more. The region at hand might suffer from strong competition of enterprises located in more distant regions but which see now a new perspective for entrepreneurial activities in a more accessible region (Bruinsma et al., 1990). Thus for infrastructure investments to be really beneficial to a target region, this region must already have a favourable existing potential for economic development.

In the third place, an acceleration of economic development in a region will not only be dependent on improvements in the local infrastructure. Infrastructure is a **necessary condition** for economic growth (a minimum threshold level is a prerequisite), since infrastructure influences directly or indirectly all other regional potentialities and mobile production factors (Nijkamp, 1986). But infrastructure is not the only condition that ensures economic development. However, it is very difficult to isolate the effects of infrastructure on regional development from other factors. For example, the general economic situation of a region influences in general significantly the actual effects of infrastructure improvements.

In the fourth place, if infrastructure investments in a region are relatively equal to the investments in surrounding regions and if this leads to the same relative (qualitative or quantitative) improvement in all regions, there may be **relatively no extra benefit** for that region compared to the others (there may even be less dynamic effects), although overall living standards in absolute sense may rise in the target region.

In the fifth place, **synergetic effects** are essential in improving the ultimate results of infrastructure investments. Linking (different kinds of) infrastructure to further private and public investments has a greater effect than an isolated infrastructure improvement. For example, investments in harbours have a limited effect, if the infrastructure for transport from the harbour to the hinterland is poor. Supporting a complementary infrastructure is thus equally well needed.

In the sixth place, it is clear that if the level of investment is higher and results in the elimination of more bottlenecks, the effect of this investment on economic development will also be higher. But we also know that in general eliminating one bottleneck leads soon to the emergence of another **new bottleneck**, if the total capacity of a network is not sufficient.

In the seventh place, one has to consider that infrastructure is subject to **technological improvements.** Like for every economic good, infrastructure categories have life cycles (Rietveld, 1989), although one has to keep in mind that a technological improvement of an existing type of infrastructure may result in an extended life cycle (for example, the development of high speed trains). It is desirable to discourage investments in infrastructure that will be rendered outdated in a few years. When a region anticipates in the future new technological developments in a given form of infrastructure, this will possibly already at present lead to a comparative advantage vis-à-vis other regions (e.g., due to a relocation of firms). This technological dimension is difficult to assess because investments in infrastructure take a long time and have a long life span.

In the eighth place, a recurrent issue in studies on infrastructure and (regional-economic) development is the problem of **causality.** Is investment in infrastructure a stimulus to economic development? Or does economic performance give rise to the need for infrastructure investments (which can also easier be financed because of the better economic prospects of that region)? In actual practice both aspects will influence one another and might lead to a mutual cumulative reinforcement.

In the ninth place, the effects of infrastructure investments on (regional) development is mainly of a **long term** nature. Such long effects are associated with structural and/or programme effects. Long term interrelationships between infrastructure and other potentiality factors (often only observable after several years) should ideally also be considered, in order to take into account structural changes in a (regional) economy (Nijkamp, 1986). In the long run infrastructure investments could lead to a productivity improvement in other input factors that affect the output sectors (Rietveld, 1989).

In the tenth place, nowadays the financing of new infrastructure projects often involves a **mixture of public and private investments**, in which many different parties are involved. Consequently, it is not always clear how far the effects of the infrastructure investment on the (regional) economy can be ascribed to the contribution of public regional policy institutions alone.

Finally, one has to recognize that infrastructure leads to both **generative** effects and **distributive** effects. The **generative effects** may promote overall growth in the national economy, while at the same time **distributive effects** may result in unequal growth rates for the different regions in a country.

Given these aspects inherent in the nature of infrastructure, an impact assessment method for transportation (infrastructure) policy should - besides the methodological desiderata from Section 3.5 - ideally fulfil the following substantive conditions:

- isolate the effects of infrastructure (investments) on the economic development of a region;
- consider the possible negative consequences of infrastructure for a region;
- consider the contribution of infrastructure in the context of transportation networks (taking into account synergetic effects, missing links, total capacity of networks etc.);
- consider the change in comparative advantage relative to other regions when investing in infrastructure which anticipates new technological developments;
- consider the interaction between infrastructure investments and (regional) economic develoment;
- consider both generative and distributive effects;
- consider possible decreasing returns to scale;
- consider the long-term consequences;
- assess which part of total effects on regional development is due to the public contribution to investments in infrastructure;
- assess the environmental and safety impacts of new infrastructure.

It goes without saying that in practice these criteria are not always met.

3.7. Concluding Remarks

Impact analysis is undoubtedly a useful tool in the evaluation of public policies. However, using impact analysis leads also to the necessity to be aware of the great many problems inherent in its implementation. In the context of impact assessment methods for the evaluation of transportation infrastructure planning, one has to take into account the specific characteristics of network infrastructure marked by a complex connectivity structure. Finally, it is clear that the **scope of impact analysis** may be very broad, covering a multiplicity of policy sectors, spatial entities, time horizons etc. To the same extent there is a wide variety of different impact assessment methods, as will be outlined in the next chapter.

Chapter 4

A REVIEW OF IMPACT ANALYSIS METHODS

4.1. Introduction

In the past, various methods and models have been designed in order to analyze the allocative efficiency of (urban, regional or transportation) policies, their equity consequences and their impacts on a broader set of socio-economic and environmental development objectives (e.g., energy use, environmental quality). Some good illustrations of spatial impact analyses can be found in Moore and Rhodes (1973, 1976). Clearly, the impacts of policies can be measured by means of a multiplicity of indicators, such as employment, income, investments, amenities, and so forth. In general, policy objectives (and hence the achievement of these objectives) have to be represented by a multidimensional profile, so that in principle the appraisal of policies has to be based on multiple indicators (see Nijkamp, 1979).

The different kinds of impact studies discussed in the literature can be typified in various ways. For instance, they may be classified according to the kinds of policy instruments used or the kinds of regions under consideration, the (national or supranational) level of policy implementation and so forth. For our purposes, it seems meaningful to distinguish various impact studies according to the **kind of method used**. Of course, this does not imply that the aspects mentioned above are not of any importance, but our main goal is to present here a methodological overview.

Also in this context there are different ways of classifying the various methods. Although we find in the literature various classifications (see e.g., Bartels and van Duijn, 1981; Folmer and Nijkamp, 1986; Cambridge Economic Consultants, 1990), it is noteworthy that most of them appear to make a general subdivision into **micro approaches** and **macro approaches**. Before we will present this typology, we will first discuss a subdivision of impact assessment methods into **ad hoc and structured approaches**.

Ad hoc impact analyses refer to a measurement problem in a situation where no possibility exists to develop standardized operational models, due to time constraints, non-repetitive situations, or lack of data (for example, the impact of an entirely new, large-scale high tech plant on a depressed rural region). Such approaches may preferably be used in a first exploratory stage of analysis in order to support the application of structured approaches later on. We can distinguish two kinds of analyses here.

The first approach is called the "**expert view**" approach. This method calls for a critical analysis of the results of a specific impact study by experts in the field concerned. Such experts may be able to analyse the results of a specific study more precisely and to interpret and explain them in more detail, although there may always be a danger of subjectivity when an expert is consulted. An example of an expert view method is the Delphi-technique. Different (groups of) experts try to judge a particular policy. The results of the expert views (of each group of experts) are circulated among all experts. After having reviewed all other opinions, the experts are asked to reconsider their own opinions and views. This procedure is repeated several times; usually the different opinions tend to converge showing a clustering around a mean opinion. The strength of the Delphi-technique is dependent upon on the quality of the experts involved and the manner in which the process is undertaken.

Secondly, we may mention an other approach, called **comparative analysis**. This approach is based on cross-regional, cross-sectoral or cross-national experiences concerning situations with more or less similar problems and policy solutions (for instance, the regional effects of the creation of new science centres or technopolises in different countries).

Despite the low costs and easy use of ad hoc impact analyses, they usually do not offer the same rate of precision, controllability and transferability as **structured impact analyses**. A structured impact analysis refers to a testable statistical or econometric method or model, based on quantified data describing the phenomenon under consideration (see for more details and expositions also Chapter 5). In theory, by means of structured impact analyses the effect of (a set of) policy measures on (a set of) relevant policy variables can be traced more reliably. A first path finding influential contribution to structured economic impact analysis can be found in Tinbergen (1956), where the first models for quantitative policy impact assessment were offered. When we talk about structured impact analyses based on formal (usually quantitative econometric or statistical) techniques and models, we can also make the already above mentioned distinction between **micro and macro approaches.** In the next subsections we will discuss the various methods according to this classification in greater detail. The methods described will be illustrated with some examples of studies focusing on the assessment of impacts of transportation infrastructure.

4.2.   Micro Studies

4.2.1. Introduction

At the micro level one deals with **individual observations** on actors who are (supposed to be) exposed to and hence affected by policy measures. Micro studies are normally related to survey methods (e.g., questionnaires, interviews, self-administration). The information is obtained from surveys explicitly referring to policy issues. Examples are surveys among companies receiving aid in the context of (regional) government programmes (e.g., incentives) or among companies located in a region in which an improvement of the locational profile as a result of new infrastructure has taken place. A central question is thus whether such companies have decided to start up, expand or relocate their operational activities - entirely or partially - because of the various policy instruments implemented in the area. With these micro based methods, it is possible to collect very **detailed and precise data** at a disaggregate level.

It should be noted however, that acquiring this kind of information is **costly and time consuming.** There is also a chance on biased information due to the survey techniques used. For example, there may be measurement errors caused by the interviewer or - in case of interviews - errors on account of communication barriers and perception disturbances of the respondent (Folmer and Nijkamp, 1986). Besides, for information on attitudes of firms one has to rely on the perception of the executives in a company who respond to the survey. They may be tempted to use a survey to manipulate future policy decisions in order to reach a desirable direction of policy measures ('strategic reply'). Also researchers may interpret the results of surveys in a subjective way in order to come to a proper ex post rationalization of the survey results. Furthermore, in some types of surveys also an instrument bias may arise, in particularly when a policy measure is not adequately specified in all its facets.

A central question in micro studies that aim to analyse the importance of infrastructure for (national or regional) economic development is the extent to which the quality and quantity of infrastructure (in particular economic infrastructure) is an important location factor (and hence a cost factor) for a company. Empirical research in this field yields contradictory results. Different studies end up with different conclusions concerning the importance of infrastructure as a strategic location factor for companies. In most of these studies, firms involved in a survey appear to have difficulties in isolating the various effects of infrastructure on their activities and in assessing its indirect effects. Besides, it is hardly possible for them to give an impression of possible effects in case of a "policy off" situation (see also Bruinsma et al., 1991). Furthermore, distributive and generative effects are generally not distinguished. All such problems are mainly due to the characteristics of infrastructure investments which are indirect, diffused and varied.

Micro studies can be further classified into **controlled experimentation, quasi-experimentation** and **non-experimentation**. This will be discussed below.

4.2.2. Controlled experimentation

With controlled experimentation one wants to collect detailed information on two classes of actors: one class of actors who have not been exposed to a policy experiment and one contrasting class who have indeed been exposed. In both classes, detailed information is used to determine the difference between the policy-off and policy-on situation. A major problem is the near impossibility of finding two identical classes of actors with the same characteristics, in such a way that the differences found can only be ascribed to a specific policy measure. Therefore, in practice this method has hardly been used to analyse the impacts of (regional, urban or transportation) policies.

However, noteworthy and interesting examples can be found in studies undertaken by Hitchens and O'Farrell (1988, 1989). They compare small firm performance between assisted and non-assisted regions. The non-assisted regions act as control areas to assess the need and/or influence of specific government assistance. The selection of firms to compare those two categories of regions is based on matched pairs of firms, i.e., the sample design controls for variables such as size, age and product of the specific firm (which otherwise would have a negative influence on the comparison of the different regions). By investigating several dimensions of performance (e.g., regarding markets, transport costs, price and quality, design etc.), the key strategic issues are judged in terms of their importance for a good small firm performance. Based on these results it is possible to assess the appropriateness of the policy at hand and the changes brought about by this policy in order to improve the performance of small firms in these assisted regions.

4.2.3. Quasi-experimentation

Quasi-experimentation as a general research method has amongst others been discussed by Campbell and Stanley (1966). They suggest to use quasi-experimentation when it is not quite clear when the exposure of a certain stimulus will arise and to whom or what the exposure will be extended. Therefore, quasi-experimentation in the field of regional, urban or transportation policy analysis is based on surveys among those actors who **most likely** have been affected by the policy measures at hand. This is a common approach in industrial questionnaires. Clearly, the impact of policy may be either direct or indirect or both (dependent on the kind of instrument and the way this is presented), so that it is not easy to disentangle the amalgamated impacts of various instruments. There also is the difficulty of considering subsequent effects for the actors who are surveyed. They probably can only assess the direct effects of a certain policy measure. For instance, when they are asked to estimate the increase of investments due to a certain incentive, it will be difficult for them to estimate the employment effects resulting from the increased investments. An additional problem for the respondents is to provide reliable quantitative estimates of the various effects.

Quasi-experimentation has often been used for examining the impacts of infrastructure policies on regional development. For example, Diamond and Spence (1988) surveyed the importance of infrastructure for the economic activities of companies. The main question was how and why the quality of infrastructure influences the cost structure of the industry and whether it has an impact on securing employment. The survey was done by a questionnaire among 190 manufacturing and service establishments in four regions in England. The questions were asked in the form of a self-completion questionnaire. It appeared that it was hardly possible to make any reliable estimates of the employment effects of new infrastructure or infrastructure improvements.

Another micro-based quasi-experimental study worth mentioning here and also related to infrastructure, has been undertaken by the Cambridge Economic Consultants (1990). From an overall survey of a sample of companies within the European Community, it appeared that infrastructure provision was not extremely important in the location decision of companies, at least compared to other location factors. Many companies attached a higher importance to regional development incentives in their location decision than to the infrastructure provision. Nonetheless when asked whether the level of infrastructure provision (and its quality) was a factor in the company decision to locate in a less favoured region, it still appeared to be an important factor.

Of course it has to be observed that with these kinds of studies - mainly concerned with locational choices - a relevant distinction has to be made between infrastructure-rich countries - where most types of infrastructure are amply available - and infrastructure-poor countries facing many bottlenecks (see also the observations made in Chapter 3).

4.2.4. Non-experimentation

A third kind of micro studies is called non-experimentation. In this case no attempt is made to control for the effects of non-policy variables. This approach can only be used if effects of non-policy variables are supposed to be absent or uniform, or if these effects can be taken into account as external factors. Such approaches have hardly been used in regional, urban and transportation research.

4.3.   Macro Studies

4.3.1. Introduction

The class of macro approaches is not entirely separated from micro analysis, as macro studies are often based on **aggregated results** of micro-based surveys held by bureaus of statistics. These surveys however, do usually not explicitly refer to policy issues (and related impacts) and hence involve less risk of biased information like in the case of the micro studies mentioned above. Moreover, macro studies are sometimes less costly and time consuming than micro approaches (see also Chapter 5).

Macro studies in the field of impact analysis of regional, urban or transportation policies are often related to statistical and econometric analyses, although one may also find methods not using an explicitly specified model. Therefore, we will classify macro studies according to methods **without and with an explicit model**. The methods using an explicit model may be subdivided into **single-equation** and **multi-equation models**.

4.3.2.   Macro studies without an explicit model

Macro studies without an explicit model can be distinguished into **qualitative system approaches, numerical statistical analyses without an explicit model, and quasi-experimental control group analysis**.

The **qualitative system approaches** are normally used in cases of a weak information and data base. Then a qualitative approach is to be preferred instead of mathematical models, which would lack statistical validity. Another motive for using qualitative system approaches is that policy impacts are not exclusively limited to economic impacts that can unambiguously be translated into measurable (monetary or physical) units. Then a (qualitative) impact analysis aims to assess all relevant quantitative and qualitative (economic and social) consequences of external changes in a system within a given time period, so that in principle all system's variables may have a relevance (Nijkamp and Van Pelt, 1991). For a qualitative system approach one can use qualitative information such as ordinal, nominal and binary statements. Relationships between the successive variables can then amongst others be represented by means of graphs and/or arrows. Inclusion of direct/indirect and intended/unintended effects is also possible, although usually only the first-order effects can be quantified. The inability to come up with numerical estimates is one of the weakest features of this approach. In most cases only indicative results can be given. An example of a qualitative system approach is given in Nijkamp and Van Pelt (1991) for a case study on strategic development policy for the city of Bhubaneswar in India.

Numerical statistical analyses without an explicit model can inter alia be found in studies based on **differential growth indicators** (for instance, for regions or sectors with and without a strong public policy). Possible explanatory (non-policy) variables are not explicitly included in this kind of simple methods. The performance variable which has to be explained is standardized without a subdivision into policy influences and endogenous influences. Therefore, results may be biased in favour of a certain policy instrument.

Another kind of numerical analysis is a performance assessment based on so-called **frequency tables**. This method was in particular developed for regional impact analysis (see Blaas and Nijkamp, 1991). The frequency tables are based on a **cross-sectional comparison** of a number of regions in a country concerning two or more strategic policy variables in a given year. The frequency analysis can be described in the following way. Consider a relevant **policy (control) variable** B_r and a relevant **impact (dependent) variable** A_r, observed on a set of regions r (r = 1, ..., R). All values of the variables can be standardized and related to population figures of the specific regions to ensure a properly weighted comparison of all regions. The average values of the variables are denoted by B^* and A^*, respectively. Then a dichotomous classification of these regions according to the question whether or not these variables are above the regional average can easily be made. This is indicated by means of the following cross-classified table:

	$B_r > B^*$	$B_r < B^*$
$A_r > A^*$	I	II
$A_r < A^*$	III	IV

Table 4.1.   A cross-classified impact table

The frequency table involves four quadrants, where each of the four entries in this matrix indicates the number of regions performing according to the features represented in the margin. These tables can now be used to explore the hypothesis that there exists a **positive correlation** between the variables A^* en B^*. Clearly, the direction of causality cannot directly be derived from these tables. The variable that is supposed to be the dependent variable is represented in the vertical column (i.e. variable A). Clearly, in general the main interest is in the figures in the quadrants I and IV. By adding up the figures in these two quadrants, one may plausibly assume that a frequency above fifty per cent of the total number of regions implies a positive correlation between the two variables. This conclusion is of course more strongly valid if the number of regions in quadrant I and IV far exceeds the frequency figures from quadrant II and III. It should be added that statistically more valid influences might be drawn when the number of regions considered would increase (e.g., by chi-square test statistics or contingency table tests based on log-linear models; see also Chapter 5). There is one important advantage in this method: it is also possible to use **time series** in order to examine the stability of correlations over time, **time lags** (if the influence of the explanatory variables on the dependent variable takes some time) and **moving averages** (a method to be used if possible outliers in the data set of a specific variable are to be eliminated). This frequency table analysis is mainly meant to be an exploratory tool in the sense of offering evidence on the average effect of a policy instrument on a target variable and of offering support for a subsequent evaluation of expenditures related to a specific policy measure. In Chapter 8 we will discuss in more detail the results of a case study that applies this method in order to examine the impact of financial amounts committed by the European Regional Development Fund (ERDF) to Italy and The Netherlands.

Finally, another class of numerical statistical impact methods without an explicit model is base on **shift-and-share analysis** (see also Dunn, 1982; Moore and Rhodes, 1976; Tervo and Okko, 1983). Shift-and-share analysis is a technique that subdivides a regional change (e.g., a change in employment) into two components. The first component is called the shift component and the second the share component. The first part can be separated into a proportional and a differential component. The shift-and share method can then be represented as follows:

$$G = \underbrace{S_p + S_d}_{\text{"shift"}} + \underbrace{R}_{\text{"regional share"}} \qquad (4.1)$$

In this equation, G stands for absolute growth (e.g., employment) in a given region. The regional share (R) is the increase in employment if the regional employment growth rate would equal the national employment growth rate. Sp represents the growth (or decline) in employment for the region in relation to the region's industrial structure. Sd is the differential shift (or regional component) that represents the growth or decline in employment that cannot be explained from R or Sp and may be due to a specific regional policy (Bartels and van Duijn, 1981).

This method has some weak points which are worth mentioning. Firstly, there is an inadequate representation of non-policy variables. Only growth due to the national development and due to a region's industrial structure is considered, but in general many more variables will influence the growth rate of employment in the region considered. Secondly, the national growth rate is possibly also influenced by regional policy. Thirdly, the assumption that both the shift component and the share component will remain constant over time is doubtful; this is not necessary because - due to a positively developing comparative advantage of a region - in the long run the shift component may decline. Finally, an evident limitation of these methods is that effects of different policy instruments on regional objectives cannot be disentangled.

In many cases the shift-share analysis is used for its simplicity and the low costs involved. Also the amount of data required is limited. But in light of the weak points mentioned above, this kind of method should preferably be used experimentally in an exploratory stage of analysis.

More rigorous statistical tools are also offered by multivariate methods, such as **contingency table analysis** applied to the realized values of policy instruments and objectives, while the high-order effects can then be tested by means of **log-linear models** (see e.g., Brouwer, 1989). This approach will be further described in the modelling Chapter 5.

The third class of methods not using an explicit model is formed by **quasi-experimental control group analysis**. The difference with respect to quasi-experimentation - mentioned in relation to the micro studies above - is that these methods are based on aggregate information from bureaus of statistics. The influence of non-policy variables on the results of a certain policy measure is controlled by the random assignment of regions to relevant groups and contrast groups. This method requires less understanding of the underlying processes of change in the output indicator selected and analyzed. Compared to statistical analysis, it also requires less data. Forkenbrock et al. (1990) describes the results of several studies concerning the impact of infrastructure on regional development all using quasi-experimental control group analysis and macro-economic indicators (viz., population, employment, income per capita etc.). The results of these different studies appear to be different. Some authors appeared to find a positive relationship between infrastructure and regional development, but others did not. This may be due to some weak aspects of the control group analysis. As already mentioned in relation to controlled experimentation in micro studies, the selection of valid control groups is difficult. Besides, by focussing on group differences no understanding is obtained of the question why the order of magnitude of the treatment effect varies across individual cases and which factors determine this varying order of magnitude.

For this reason, Isserman (1990) discusses different methods for control group analysis. He proposes a variant focussing on **individual treatment cases.** The individual treated place is compared to a control group of untreated places. The control group is selected on the basis of pre-treatment similarity to the treated place. This approach controls for external factors affecting both the individual treated place and the control group, but controls weakly for place-specific occurrences during the post-treatment period.

This kind of approach can be combined with **statistical methods** for analyzing the results of the studies of the individual treatment cases. The statistical method focuses on explaining variation in the treatment and can incorporate factors that were missed by selection control. The control group analysis focuses on documenting and measuring the existence of treatment effects. Although not all objections against control group analysis can be eliminated and although there is still a limited understanding of the determinants of the size of the relevant effects, this is a more useful approach than the conventional quasi-experimental control group analyses. The combination with statistical methods leads of course at the same time to a devaluation of the strong point mentioned earlier, viz., the lower data requirements when using quasi-experimental control group analysis. In the next subsection we will now turn to explicit impact models.

4.3.3. Macro studies with an explicit model

4.3.3.1. Single-equation models

Single-equation approaches - most of the time used as partial models - are able to describe the impact of a relevant policy variable. The analysis is based on a comparison of the actual policy-on situation with the extrapolated policy-off situation. It is also possible to compare different time-periods and/or regions with fluctuating policy strength and to make use of different kinds of time series, variants of shift-and-share analysis and/or cross-section data.

Models based on a single-equation approach have various advantages. Firstly, these kinds of models are very easy to use. Secondly, the amount of data required is relatively limited compared to, for example, multi-equation models. Of course, there exist also some weak aspects of this kind of methods. It is only possible to assess the direct effects of a regional policy measure if one uses only one equation (unless this equation is a reduced form of a more complicated multi-equation model). Furthermore, there is often a neglect of the interrelation between national and regional effects, of the distinction between short-term and long-term effects and of the interdependence among the independent variables. Those weak points lead to uncertainties in relevant conclusions concerning such policy effects.

The models based on single equations can be subdivided into **single-equations with non-policy variables only** and **single-equations including instruments of policy**.

Models without policy variables aim at comparing the actual policy-on situation with the extrapolated policy-off situation. Instruments of policy are not explicitly incorporated as explanatory variables.

The **single-equation models incorporating policy instruments** are able to assess the direct impacts of policy measures - explicitly incorporated - on policy objectives. This is done, for example, by estimating the effect of financial assistance policies on employment or the effects of individual regional policy instruments on the movement of industry (Armstrong and Taylor, 1985) by using time series data or cross-section data.

The single-equation models which are useful for impact analysis of infrastructure can also be subdivided into single-equation models **with non-policy variables only** and single-equation models **with instruments of policy included**. Besides this subdivision, single-equation models used for infrastructure impact analysis can be based on different approaches viz., **the production function approach** and **the location factor approach**. Both approaches will briefly be discussed here.

In the **production function approach** one assumes a production function in which infrastructure - as an input - plays a role next to traditional production factors. A lack of supply of infrastructure means that the productivity of the private production factors (i.e., labour and capital) decreases. A general formulation of such a so-called quasi-production function for region r is:

$$Q_r \quad = f_r \, (L_r, \, K_r; \, I_r), \tag{4.2}$$

where

Q_r = value added in region r

L_r = employment in region r

K_r = private capital in region r

I_r = infrastructure in region r.

This standard function may be extended with various sectors in a region and various types of infrastructure. This is important because the impact of infrastructure is not the same for all kind of sectors and infrastructure. This function is - if used in his simplest form as formulated above - usually supply-oriented (i.e., production output is only determined by the supply of production factors) and of a bottom-up structure (i.e., regional variables are determined prior to national variables).

There are two weak points worth mentioning in using the production function approach in the transport sector. Firstly, when considering transport infrastructure it is difficult to take into account the network properties. Such a consideration is necessary because a certain infrastructure investment has to be seen in the context of the synergetic effects of infrastructure networks. The best approach seems then to consider the impacts of a given type of infrastructure on a relevant intraregional, interregional, national or even supranational level. The level to be considered is dependent on the characteristics of the infrastructure investment. In practice, one might then look at the improvement of the service provided by the newly added infrastructure, e.g., the time saving in the transport sector.

Another problem related to the above production function aproach to infrastructure is that its impact may supersede the boundaries of regions. Not every region has its own university or airport, but it may nevertheless benefit from a nearby university or airport. A solution to this problem may be to introduce an accessibility measure for a certain type of infrastructure in the production function (Rietveld, 1989).

Next, in the **location factor approach,** infrastructure plays a role - besides other factors - as a strategic location factor. Among these other factors are the sectoral structure, the labour market, the existence of public policies and so forth. In this kind of approach the effects of infrastructure as a locational factor for employment and capital are measured. This approach can be based on various key variables, notably **assessibility, marginal transportation costs** or **private investments.**

When the location factor approach is based on **accessibility,** one presupposes that an improvement of infrastructure leads to a better network linkage through a reduction of travel time. This may in turn lead to a relocation of labour and capital to the benefit of the region that has become more accessible. Clearly, as mentioned before, it may happen that a higher accessibility of a certain region may also lead to negative effects, while also a gain in overall productivity to the advantage of all regions is possible. Examples of the location factor approach based on accessibility can be found in Evers et al. (1987) and Rietveld (1989).

The location factor approach based on **marginal transportation costs** argues that the attractivity of a location will increase if the transport costs to that location will be minimized. An obvious meaningful way to reduce these costs is to improve the infrastructure in that region. This approach uses normally linear programming models; it is a method that is most appropriate for sectors producing homogeneous goods.

The last variant of the location factor approach is based on **private investments.** This variant focuses on the relationship between government (infrastructure) investments and private investments. Besides multiplier effects of public sector investments (i.e., increasing investments in the private sector in the short run caused by increasing demand), it distinguishes spin-off effects (i.e., increasing investments in the private sector in the long run because of the improvements in infrastructure). The following causal single-equation model can be used as a starting point for assessing the impacts of government (infrastructure) investments on the private investments in a certain region r:

$$I_{pr} = \alpha_o + \alpha_1 . I_{gr} + \alpha_2. \Delta GVA_r \tag{4.3}$$

with:

ΔGVA_r = change in gross value added in region r

I_{gr} = government investments

I_{pr} = private investments

α_0 = intercept

α_i = reaction coefficient (i = 1, 2)

This basic equation (4.3) can be represented in terms of three complementary types of investment equations. If the hypothesis of **rational expectations** is used (which means that realized or foreseen increases in value added will also lead to a rise in private investments), then this approach may be based respectively on an **active response** model, a **conventional** model and a **passive response** model. For the active response model we may then have the following specification:

$$I_{pr} = \alpha_0 + \alpha_1.I_{gr} + \alpha_2. \Delta GVA_r^{(+\sigma)}, \tag{4.4}$$

where it is taken for granted that private investments depend among others on the economic situation entrepreneurs expect to take place in the future. This forward looking behaviour is represented by the change in the gross value added with an expected positive (forward) time lag σ.

For the second case, the conventional investment behaviour, we assume:

$$I_{pr} = \beta_0 + \beta_1.I_{gr}^{(-\sigma)} \tag{4.5}$$

where the investments in the private sector only depend on the (past) investments made by the public sector.

The third equation:

$$I_{pr} = \delta_0 + \delta_1.I_{gr} + \delta_2.\Delta GVA_r^{(-\sigma)} \qquad (4.6)$$

is based on a passive response model, i.e., the private investments undertaken by the entrepreneurs depend among others on the economic situation in the past years. This is represented by the change in gross value added with a negative time lag σ.

In Chapter 11 we will present an application of the single-equation model by assessing the impact of the European Regional Development Fund (ERDF) expenditures in regions in the European Community.

4.3.3.2.   Multi-equation models

Multi-equation models aim at providing a coherent picture of direct and indirect impacts of policy measures on policy objectives. These kinds of models make it possible to consider the various effects of policy measures on various regional profile elements. Multi-equation models are able to catch the causal relations between infrastructure and regional development. The problem is again the direction of causality. Is a positive regional economic development a result of increased infrastructure investments? Or are those investments increasing because of positive economic development in the area? Both directions may occur in actual practice and should ideally be included in a (dynamic) multi-equation model. The main weak point of all multi-equation models is that in most cases a large amount of information is needed on many variables.

Multi-equation models can be subdivided into **input-output models** and **general simultaneous equation models**.

Input-output models focus on inter-industry transactions and related employment and income flows. These models calculate the effects of policy inputs originating from income or production variables. From all tools available to regional policy-makers, regional and interregional input-output models remain the most widely used. Regional input-output models may be employed for an impact analysis of direct policy influences (e.g., fiscal incentives, infrastructure subsidies), besides the standard input-output impact analysis approach.

Input-output models have the advantage that it is possible to calculate effects for different sectors and for different regions, provided an interregional sectoral input-output model is available. It provides also insight into the various linkages between sectors and/or regions.

Admittedly, it has often been demonstrated - regardless of the many virtues of interregional models - that if the analyst is only interested in the impacts on a single study region, little is lost by neglecting interregional feedbacks (see Miller and Blair, 1985).

Like any other method discussed so far, input-output models have weak points too. First of all, the structure of input-output models is very rigid. Adjustments to changing circumstances are difficult to make and these models require an extremely high amount of data. Furthermore, there are some stringent assumptions inherent in input-output models. The first one is that doubling output requires a doubling of inputs (linearity of production processes). But in practice it is possible that the larger the output the lesser the inputs needed (economies of scale). The second assumption concerns the ignorance of the existence of supply constraints, as the input-output models focus only on the demand side. Conversions to a supply-constrained model might then be useful to analyse regions characterized by resource constraints.

General simultaneous equation models comprise a large variety of models which are not restricted to a recording of transactions between industrial sectors. At the regional level, there are general integrated regional economic models. These models can be described as a system of equations. Each causal variable belongs to the explanatory variables impacting on others (Folmer and Nijkamp, 1986), representing a comprehensive picture of the economic mechanism of a regional economy. Both direct and indirect effects are considered. Nijkamp et al. (1987) describes in a general context a model useful for measuring the effectiveness of policy instruments that could function as a basis for various types of general simultaneous equation models. In Figure 4.1 this basic model is represented as a general stimulus-response model for policy analysis.

When this basic model is used in a dynamic spatial context, the model should be extended with several feedback relationships, spatial spillover effects and spatial interaction linkages. When this kind of model is used for an impact analysis of regional

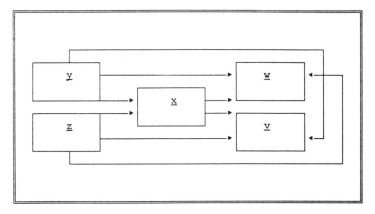

Figure 4.1.   A stimulus-response model for policy analysis.
                   Source: Nijkamp et al. (1987).

The types of variables considered are the following:

$\underline{w} = (w_1, ..., w_i)'$:   objectives (or goal variables to be optimized)

$\underline{x} = (x_1, ..., x_j)'$:   intermediate variables (endogenous economic variables, but not objectives)

$\underline{y} = (y_1, ..., y_k)'$:   instruments of policy

$\underline{z} = (z_1, ..., z_l)'$:   autonomous variables (data)

$\underline{v} = (v_1, ..., v_m)'$:   non-economic side-effects (e.g., pollution)

policy, it aims in most cases to measure the effects of government expenditures (as well as induced private investments) and investments in infrastructure on the basis of general macro-economic indicators such as income, employment and GDP. Several weak points inherent in general simultaneous equation models have already been mentioned for the single-equation models. They mainly concern the neglect of the interrelation between national and regional effects and the distinction between long-term and short-term effects. In most cases, regional models are very similar to those at the national level and reflect more or less the same theoretical framework. But the assumptions and considerations laid down in national econometric models are not necessary valid at a regional level. Spatial computable general equilibrium models are then needed.

Given the need for completeness, coherence and multi-dimensional representation in integrated policy assessment models, it is clear that - despite some weak points - such models are to be preferred in empirical policy analysis. However, it has to be added that data problems often preclude an empirical estimation of such models, especially in case of ad hoc impact analysis of distinct public projects. On a more structural basis of systematic impact analysis, the latter shortcoming can - to some extent - be removed by using spatio-temporal data or using data "created" from national variables.

In the context of integrated regional policy models it is useful to employ a multi-modular design, in which classes of related policy objectives are regarded as relevant modules. The same holds true for classes of mutually linked policy instruments and of external variables. In this way it is also better possible to disentangle effects from non-relevant stimuli as well as effects of policy packages. An example of such a model that can be used in a multiregional context is the integrated multiregional model developed by Isard and Anselin (1982).

In conclusion, an appropriate integrated regional policy model should measure the impacts comprehensively (also concerning high-order effects), incorporate non-economic impacts and be able to consider alternative policy mixtures. The multiregional aspects concern the interrelationships between regions and/or the interrelationships between regions and the national economy. Issaev et al., (1982), describe and discuss in a broad overview a wide variety of such multiregional economic models.

When using **general simultaneous equation models** for an impact assessment of infrastructure, it is also possible - like the single-equation models (4.3.3.1) - to distinguish again between two kinds of approaches, viz., the production function approach and the location factor approach. A related approach, the **interregional trade approach**, treats the impact of changes in transportation infrastructure on trade flows in regional development. This class of models contains various kinds of linkages as presented in Figure 4.2. The development of a region is supposed to be influenced by transport infrastructure via transportation costs and trade flows. This interregional trade approach is a promising tool for detailed impact studies of changes in transportation networks regarding regional development. Until now, most operational models in this field have given a rather crude treatment of networks (see also Rietveld, 1989). In most studies the dynamic generative impacts are not adequately considered. The possibility that the impacts of the infrastructure investment will continue to emerge several years after the initial investment is often ignored in modelling efforts.

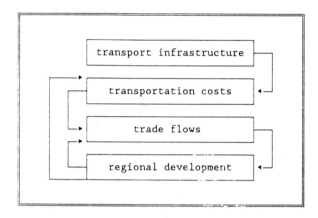

Figure 4.2.   Important linkages in the interregional trade approach.

Impact assessment methods are useful tools to measure the various effects of policy instruments put in operation in order to achieve the goals of a certain economic, regional or transport policy. There appears to exist a wide range of impact assessment methods that may be useful in the evaluation of a policy in general and of transportation (infrastructure) planning in particular. However, the above review has shown that each of the different classes of impact analyses has its own weak points. Until now there is no overall optimal impact assessment method. The choice of the method to be used in the evaluation of a regional policy or transportation infrastructure plan will depend on different factors, such as the specific policy to be evaluated, the kind of policy instrument that is used, time and budget constraints, the type of region examined etc. Chapter 5 will provide now a further exposition on the use and potential of various impact models in transportation planning.

Chapter 5

BEHAVIOURAL IMPACT MODELS IN TRANSPORTATION PLANNING

5.1. Models as Replica's

In the previous chapter it has been asserted that models are one possible structured method - and certainly not the only one - for assessing the impacts of a certain policy measure. Clearly, impact assessment requires a careful estimation of all expected consequences of a stimulus (e.g., a rise in gasoline tax, a new underground system) on the behaviour of individuals, groups or society as a whole. In order to generate testable results, very often researchers have to resort to statistical and econometric techniques.

Models serve to replicate - under certain conditions and within certain ranges - part of a complex real-world system. This replication may be of an **ex post** nature (e.g., in case of descriptive models) or an **ex ante** nature (e.g., in case of predictive models). Clearly, models are usually much more rigid than the real-world patterns to be analyzed. Nevertheless, in the post-war period an avalanche of attempts has been made to design models for social systems which were 'as close as possible' to real-world phenomena. However, a consistent mapping of such real-world phenomena into a stylized model framework is fraught with many difficulties, as is also witnessed in Hempel's 'bridge principle'. And consequently, the majority of models in the social sciences is suffering from 'semantic insufficiency' caused by specification problems (see for convincing arguments Blommestein, 1987).

Models in the social sciences - in particular spatial models - are largely based on the following assumptions:

- all relevant (endogenous and exogenous) variables can appropriately be measured;

- all relationships between variables are known and quantified by means of an operational - often causal - model;

- technical, institutional, social and economic impacts are known and can be specified in a testable form;

71

- uncertainty in (the state of) the system can be taken into consideration by means of the a priori probability distribution of stochastic elements;
- in case of a dynamic system, the time trajectory of all variables can be reproduced accurately;
- in case of spacial interaction effects, a spatial distribution function (transfer or filter) is able to generate precisely all geographical impacts.

Clearly, these modelling assumptions take for granted a high level of **precision** of measurement of variables (usually a cardinal metric). It is noteworthy however, that in recent years also much progress has been made in the area of imprecisely measured variables, witness the popularity of categorical data analysis, path analysis and fuzzy set analysis (see for instance Nijkamp, 1985). Despite many statistical problems in the area of 'soft econometrics', such models may be extremely useful in social science research where precise measurement is an exception rather than a rule (see also Sections 5.3 - 5.4).

A more serious problem however, which is directly related to specification issues is the **causality** structure in a model. Social science models are sometimes extremely weak in this respect. Causality presupposes a stimulus-response (or cause-effect) relationship from one variable toward another one. Theoretically, this would require also the incorporation of a time dimension for analyzing, understanding and interpreting causal orderings, so that in this strict sense mutual causality is even excluded (see among other Simon, 1957; Wold, 1954; Harvey, 1969; Bennett and Chorley, 1979). Static models are thus essentially at odds with causality analysis, unless one assumes that adjustment (or response) time is very short or that only equilibrium situations are to be considered (comparative statics).

Clearly, not all components of models in the social sciences are necessarily reflecting causal patterns. For instance, identities (e.g., in an input-output model), technical relations (e.g., in a production function), or institutional relations (e.g., income tax rates in the determination of net disposable income) do not have any clear causal component from a social science perspective (see also Blommestein and Nijkamp, 1983; Gilli, 1980; Nijkamp and Rietveld, 1982). However, a major class of components (structural relationships) in social science models is governed by behavioural key forces, and such behavioural relationships should be considered from the viewpoint of causal explanation. Behavioural models aim at describing or predicting responses of individuals or groups in a social system as a result of (endogenous or exogenous) stimuli (including policy measures). Seen from this perspective, mechanistic location-allocation models used in spatial modelling, do not seem to be particularly meaningful - at least not without a behavioural interpretation - in a social science context.

5.2. Models as Replica's of the Space-Economy

Chapter 4 was devoted to a general typology of impact models. Here we will focus on models for spatial systems.

In the past decades a wide variety of spatial models has been developed (see among others Bertuglia and Rabino, 1990; Mills, 1988; Nijkamp, 1987). The complicated and interwoven pattern of human activities in space and time is evidently not easy to model and many flaws in this area do still exist (see for a critical review also Issaev et al., 1982). Three major shortcomings still seem to be predominant in modern spatial modelling approaches:

- A proper treatment of **space**. Space is a projection of human activities and acts at the same time as a potential (or sometimes a barrier) to further socio-economic development. Spatial interactions are hard to model however, despite the progress made in spatial autocorrelation analysis, spatial interaction models and multiregional input-output models (see also Fotheringham and O'Kelly, 1989, and Nijkamp and Reggiani, 1992).

- A proper treatment of **behaviour**. Human behaviour - and the resulting spatial processes - can be studied from two angles, viz., a micro viewpoint (focussing attention on individual perceptions, motives and decisions) and a macro viewpoint (focussing attention on aggregate entities such as groups, regions, a country as a whole, etc.). A major problem here is a consistent linking of these two levels of analysis, especially because complicated feedback mechanisms often hamper a methodologically sound approach.

- A proper treatment of **time**. Spatial decisions and processes take necessarily time, but the number of models where time plays an indigenous role is still very limited (see for instance Beckmann and Puu, 1985). In recent years the awareness has grown that the behaviour of a dynamic system (individuals, groups) does often not follow a continuous and smooth time path, but may exhibit sudden fluctuations (e.g., catastrophes, singularities, bifurcations). In the past years several studies have been devoted to the relevance of catastrophe theory for spatial analysis (see for instance Wilson, 1981, and Nijkamp and Reggiani, 1988). In this context, very recently the theory of **chaos** has come into being and gained a great deal of popularity, not only in the physical sciences but also in the spatial sciences and transportation science (see for an overview Nijkamp and Reggiani, 1992). Such models may be used at both a micro and a macro level of analysis and may provide more insight into (seemingly) irregular behavioural patterns of individuals and groups.

In any case, a spatial economic model (e.g., a transport systems model) needs an appropriate **causal** (i.e., stimulus-response) specification in order to be suitable for impact assessment. However, the need for causal explanations in spatial modelling does not yet provide clear guidelines regarding the **level of analysis** for spatial decisions and processes. Decisions can be analyzed at the level of individual actors (i.e., disaggregate choice modelling) or at the level of collective agencies (e.g., a political party, the government, a labour union, etc.). The same holds true for processes in space and time.

Aggregate analyses deal thus with phenomena at a meso or macro scale (e.g., regions, groups, sectors, etc.), whereas disaggregate analyses focus attention on individual or micro phenomena (e.g., personal income, individual mobility, personal car ownership etc.).

Although it is often more usual to analyze processes at a more aggregate level, there is an increasing trend toward a more micro level of analysis (e.g., in longitudinal data analysis, see Golob et al., 1989; or in company life history analysis, see Van Geenhuizen et al., 1989).

It is evident that - although the micro level of analysis is critical for understanding the choices made by individual actors - micro and macro levels cannot be examined in isolation from each other. For instance, spatial processes (e.g., mobility behaviour) may be aggregate consequences of macro decisions (e.g., infrastructure measures), but are nevertheless a result of numerous individual decisions (e.g., on mode and route choice).

However, a consistent linking of these two levels of analysis is far from easy and needs in general some form of a market clearing system (based on e.g., price incentives, rationing, institutional regulations and the like). A promising example of a causal spatial choice analysis - where micro utility maximization (based on discrete choice models) is consistently connected with the behaviour of the (housing) market as a whole (based on distributional assumptions on actors and 'states of the world') - can be found in Rouwendal (1989). Previous attempts in this area were also made by Anas and Cho (1986).

In the past decade, the problems of micro and macro levels of analysis have also extensively been discussed in areas outside the social sciences, notably in physics and chemistry. And to a large extent, in these disciplines similar questions arose as to the stability of a dynamic system in which the behaviour of individual elements is governed by a high degree of stochasticity, whilst also synergetic effects make the system at an aggregate level sometimes hardly predictable (witness also recent developments in the area of the theory of fractals and of turbulence). It is interesting to observe that such non-linear modes of explanatory analysis can also be combined with modern behavioural modelling of space-time processes (see also Barentsen and Nijkamp, 1989, and Haag and Weidlich, 1986).

An important stream in current modern spatial modelling approaches and in transportation analysis is connected with **discrete choice theory**, dealing with individual choices for distinct alternatives. Two reasons can be mentioned for the popularity of these models: (1) they are compatible with economic principles based on (random) utility maximization, and (2) they provide an operational tool for empirical analysis where micro data are used for meso and macro inferences (see Golledge and Timmermans, 1988). And besides, recently also time-dependent choice determinants related to (both true and spurious) state dependence have been incorporated in such models (see also Fischer and Nijkamp, 1987, and Heckman, 1981).

Despite the progress in recent modelling attempts in the spatial sciences, the question still remains whether such research efforts are sufficiently appropriate for encapsulating the complex changes in spatial patterns of human activities. It is plausible however, to claim that a proper (transportation or spatial) impact assessment needs to reduce uncertainty in prediction.

The necessity to map dynamic spatial processes has caused the current popularity of quantitative analysis of complex geographical patterns and processes (e.g., urban growth, demographic developments, mobility processes, and residential location patterns). This development is also reflected in modern transportation planning, where uncertainties in individual and group responses are increasingly addressed as an urgent issue.

In the past decade much attention has been given to the specific - often socially undesirable - consequences (e.g., externalities and conflicts) of the spatial distribution and interaction of activities for the research methodology in the spatial sciences. Examples are found **inter alia** in spatially hierarchical models, spatial interaction models and spatial choice models. Illustrations and surveys of statistical and economic modelling techniques in the area of regional economics, geography and transportation science can be found in among others Bahrenberg et al. (1984), de la Barra (1990), Fischer et al. (1990), Hutchinson et al. (1985), Issaev et al. (1982) and Nijkamp et al. (1985).

In the methodology of spatial analysis, usually a distinction is made between **exploratory** and **explanatory** analysis. Exploratory analysis refers to attempts at identifying structures in complex phenomena without the explicit aim of testing behavioural hypotheses. Often, such exploratory analyses take the form of statistical data analysis (for instance, contingency table analysis, chi-square tests, cross-classifications). On the other hand, explanatory models aim at analysing behavioural cause-effect relationships, for instance, in the context of micro- or macro-spatial choice behaviour. Models for causal inference are usually based on a stimulus-response structure so that behavioural hypotheses can be tested by means of appropriate statistical and econometric techniques. In reality, the distinction between exploratory and explanatory models is less sharp, as any exploration has to assume by definition a certain behavioural structure in the underlying data set, while explanatory models have to take for granted some exploratory plausible results.

Another distinction which is often made concerns the **level of measurement** of the variables under consideration. Although many traditional models (e.g., regression models, spatial interaction models, programming models) are based on cardinal variables (measured on a metric - i.e., ratio or interval - scale), in reality many variables have a less precise level of measurement.

In contrast to natural sciences, the measurement levels of many variables in the spatial sciences (and hence also in transportation science) are **discrete, non-metric or categorical** rather than **metric**. This is a consequence of the fact that measurement procedures such as interviews, panel surveys or questionnaires have only a rather limited degree of precision. The term 'discrete' (non-metric or categorical) is used to refer to dichotomous and polytomous nominal variables as well as to dichotomous and polytomous ordinal variables. In contrast to metric variables discrete variables take values only in a limited set of categories.

Models and methods for dealing with categorical data are important in planning sciences, just as in other social and economic sciences. Therefore, it is no surprise that in recent years there has been an increasing interest in handling such categorical data in the framework of multiple criteria models and disaggregate choice models. It is interesting to observe that many methods and models widely used in the spatial sciences have been originally developed in quantitatively more advanced social and economic science disciplines such as psychometrics, sociometrics and econometrics. The presence of such categorical (or qualitative) variables has led to the emergence of a wide variety of adjusted methods, in the field of both **categorical spatial data analysis** (with emphasis of exploration) and **categorical spatial choice analysis** (with emphasis on explanation).

Finally, it is also noteworthy that often a distinction is made according to **static** or **dynamic** models (see also Nijkamp and Reggiani, 1992).

Thus, models in the spatial sciences (and hence in transportation analysis) can be classified as follows:
- aggregate versus disaggregate
- metric versus non-metric
- exploratory versus explanatory
- static versus dynamic

In the next section some important classes of models which are often used in transportation impact assessment will briefly be described.

5.3.   Aggregate and Disaggregate Models

Aggregate models centre around the behaviour of groups, regions, sectors at a meso or macro level of analysis, where both spatial elements (e.g., regions) and activities (e.g.,trips) are classified according to major discrete categories (cf. Liew and Liew, 1985).

A major class of models at an aggregate level of analysis is formed by conventional (linear or non-linear) **programming models.** Examples are trip assignment models, location-allocation models and the like. These models serve to identify an optimal spatial configuration of activities or flows, given assumptions on the size of origins and destinations as well as on distance friction costs. Special cases are formed by dynamic programming models and optimal control models.

A related class of models is based on a **utility framework,** where the socio-economic 'performance' of a spatial system - in terms of its spatial allocation of activities or flows - is optimized, given side-constraints on marginal totals related to origins and destinations. Such models play also an important role in the context of spatial **equilibrium models.**

Another class of aggregate models can be found in **spatial interaction models.** Such models, originally based on gravity theory, but later on also on entropy theory or information theory, may be seen as a general class of spatial models including also the previous models as special cases (see Nijkamp and Reggiani, 1992).

It is noteworthy at this stage that the class of spatial interaction models (at an aggregate level) is formally compatible with the class of **discrete spatial choice models** (at a disaggregate level), based on **random utility** theory. Such models use normally micro-based **categorical information,** and are often based on panel surveys, interviews, questionnaires etc.

Such categorical choice analyses aim to study the behaviour of populations of individuals in a given choice context. Clearly, in general, spatial choice theory and interaction analysis have already a long history. This issue was essentially the heart of economic geography and regional economics, in so far as these disciplines focussed attention on the location of firms or the settlement patterns of families or groups in a country.

The first formal contribution to spatio-temporal aspects of choice behaviour can be found in traditional **space-time geography** (Hägerstrand, 1970). In a modelling framework, **location-allocation models** based on programming theory have played an important role in aggregate spatial choice and interaction analysis. In the 1970s, categorical spatial choice models focussing on distinct alternative choices have come to the fore. Categorical spatial choice models aim at describing, explaining and forecasting disaggregate choice behaviour in a spatial context, for instance, in housing market, transportation and labour market analysis.

Later on, **panel studies** and **longitudinal data analysis** also have drawn a great deal of attention in spatial choice research, while simultaneously the spatial **activity-based approach** came into existence. More recently, **event-history analysis** has demonstrated its potential in discrete spatial choice analysis.

Spatial choice models may be classified on the basis of criteria such as (van Lierop and Nijkamp, 1991):
- the level of **aggregation**;
- the nature of the **choice process**; and
- the element of **time**.

On the basis of these criteria, the following main classes of spatial choice models may be distinguished:
- micro simulation models;
- deterministic utility-based models;
- conventional random utility models;
- generalized random utility models;
- psychometric behavioural models;
- activity-based choice models;
- search models.

The past decade has exhibited an avalanche of studies in the area of categorical (or discrete) choice models based on random utility theory. Well-known model approaches in this framework are multinomial logit and probit analyses. Especially in transportation studies such models have gained much popularity and they belong nowadays to the standard toolbox of a transportation analyst.

Finally, in recent years there has been a surge of interest in developing more reliable discrete panel models for spatial choice behaviour, sometimes on a longitudinal basis. Conventional panel data models are essentially of a cross-sectional nature leaving aside dynamic aspects of choices, but more recently dynamic models also have been designed in order to take into account the intertemporal aspects of spatial choices and decisions (see Fischer et al., 1990).

This concise list of models shows that categorical data and choice analysis has become a major vehicle in spatial research. And particularly in the field of transportation analysis, in many countries attempts have been made at designing and estimating models describing the complex web of interactions in space and time.

Altogether, there seems to be a fairly extensive set of analytical instruments which may serve as technical tools for transportation impact assessment. Having discussed now spatial models mainly from an aggregate/disaggregate viewpoint - but also with an indirect focus on metric (cardinal) or non-metric (categorical) features -, we will in the next section pay some attention to exploratory non-metric methods.

5.4.   Categorical Spatial Data Analysis

Categorical spatial data analysis aims to analyse statistical relations between independent variables (**stimuli**) and one or more dependent variables (**responses**), where at least one variable is discrete (or categorical) (see also Fischer and Nijkamp, 1985). A standard approach in social science research is **contingency table analysis,** where simple chi-square tests can be used to detect statistical patterns in a large multi-category data set (see for instance Brouwer, 1989). Such approaches are extremely helpful in exploratory stages of research.

Recently, much effort has been made in integrating different models for categorical data analysis into a **generalized linear models** approach provided by Nelder and Wedderburn (1972) and implemented in the GLIM (Generalized Linear Interactive Modelling) computer package. The class of generalized linear models (GLMs) is obtained by extending classical regression models to allow a distribution from an exponential family and a link function which relates mean and linear predictor. The unifying methodology enables all members of the class of GLMs to be fitted by means of a common unified estimation procedure, the iterative weighted least squares procedure. GLMs for categorical data include linear logit models, probit models and log-linear models as special cases.

Since logit and probit models were already discussed in the previous section, we will pay some attention here to **log-linear models**. Log-linear models closely resemble the regression and analysis of variance models for metric data. They are linear in the logarithms of the expected cell frequencies of a multi-dimensional contingency table. When all variables in a dependence relation are discrete, the sample data can be displayed in the form of an asymmetric contingency table where one dimension is treated as the dependent variable. By imposing restrictions on the parameters to be estimated, a wide range of unsaturated and hybrid log-linear models describing the relationship between the dependent and independent variables can be specified. If the number of dimensions of a contingency table increases, the number of possible log-linear models will also increase. The question as to which model may be considered to be reasonable and adequate should be solved on the basis of the principle of parsimony and its goodness-of-fit to the data at hand. For this crucial task there are different approaches which are based inter alia on F-statistics, partitions of the likelihood-ratio chi-square, standardized values of the parameter estimates and residual analysis.

The parameters and the expected cell frequences can be estimated by means of (non-)iterative weighted least square procedures, or alternatively by means of the iterative proportional fitting approach combined with linear contrasts of the design matrix method. Further discussions on the use and scope of log-linear models in a spatial context can be found in Wrigley (1986). Such models are in particular useful in case of panel data on individual spatial behaviour, and the statistical results found may be used to generate causal (behavioural) hypotheses to be tested in an explanatory framework (e.g., by means of discrete choice models).

Clearly, there is a wide variety of other categorical data methods, e.g., event history analysis, sign solvability analysis, rank order statistics etc. (see for an overview Nijkamp et al., 1985). The previous sample of methods has shown however, that there is a variety of technical tools available for adequate research in transportation planning. The main bottleneck however, is in many cases the lack of available or accessible information. This explains also the popularity of (micro-)simulation models and of scenario experiments. These issues will be further examined in the next section.

5.5.   Scenario Analysis for Uncertainty Analysis

Uncertainty is an indigenous feature of transportation planning. The main aim of the methods described above is to improve the quality of transportation planning by using the most appropriate tools, given the available data. Thus a kind of 'plausible reasoning' (see Polya, 1954) is in order here to derive justifiable inferences about 'states of the world' (cf. Fishburn, 1970).

The previous methods and techniques can also be extended with complementary analytical tools, such as **scenario analysis**. Scenario analysis is one of the methods and techniques of prospective policy research that have become very popular since the late sixties. Especially in the case of unstructured decision problems with uncertain outcomes, scenario analysis may be an appropriate instrument. The main difference between scenario analysis and conventional methods of policy analysis is that scenarios do not only contain a description of one or more future situations, but also a description of a consistent series of events that may connect the present situation with the described future situation(s).

Instead of giving a formal definition of scenario analysis, it may be more helpful to explain this approach by means of an illustrative figure (see Figure 5.1).

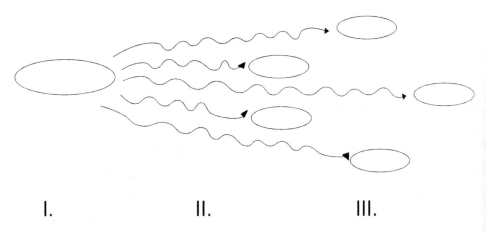

I.   II.   III.

I.   Description of the present situation
II.   Description of a number of future situations
III.   Description of a series of events that may connect the present situation with future situations

Figure 5.1.   Series of events between present and future situations.

Figure 5.1. shows that a scenario analysis contains three components:
- present situation.
- future situation.
- paths from the present to future situations.

Each of these components must be a part of the scenario analysis, otherwise the scenario will not provide useful information for a better structuring of a choice problem. For instance, if there is no description of the present situation, then it is very likely that the construction of the future situations and the paths that may lead to it, are based upon incorrect assumptions about the present situation. Also, the description of the future situations may not be absent, because scenarios try to provide a description of the future in the medium and long term. If only the characteristics and developments of the present situation are extrapolated to get a picture of the future, then this picture will be full of many uncertainties, so that an essential part of a scenario analysis - the provision of (clear) pictures of some plausible and desirable future situations - will fail. Also, the construction of a path leading from the present situation to the described future situations is an essential part of a scenario analysis; without these paths, the links between the present situation and the future situations under study will be missing, which might lead to inconsistencies.

Depending on the specific circumstances under which a scenario is constructed, some of these three components may not require as much attention as the other one. If, for instance, a scenario is constructed for a problem that has already been examined in greater detail, then it is probably quite easy to find the information that is required for the description of the present situation. Then evidently most emphasis can be placed upon the two other components of the scenario analysis. On the other hand, if the paths from the present to the future are well known, then only a brief description will be sufficient to perform a meaningful scenario analysis.

Finally, sometimes the future may be surrounded with so many uncertainties, that it is hardly possible to describe a plausible future situation. In such cases, especially the feasible paths to the future may be a topic of discussion.

Scenarios can be identified by four characteristics (cf. Van Doorn and Van Vught, 1981):

-       A scenario is either **descriptive** or **normative**. The prospective paths and pictures
        of a descriptive scenario are based on the know-how developed in the past and
        present. The question whether these paths and pictures are desirable or not, is not
        raised. The first scenarios designed by Kahn and Wiener (1967), are in agreement
        with this description. The construction of normative scenarios is based upon the
        ideas of the scenario-writers or scenario-users. The future paths and pictures are
        selected by these writers and users. The so-called Ozbekhan-scenarios (see
        Ozbekhan, 1969), as a response to Kahn and Wiener, may be regarded as
        member of this category (cf. Van Doorn and Van Vught, 1981).

-       Another distinction that can be made is the difference in direction of the scenario
        analysis. If future pictures are based upon the present situation and future paths
        leading to it, then the scenario is said to be **projective**. On the other hand, if at
        first the future situations are determined and next the paths leading to this
        situation, then in fact these paths lead from the future backwards to the present.
        As they are composed afterwards, the scenario belongs to the class of **prospective**
        scenarios. Prospective scenarios are always normative, while projective scenarios
        are either descriptive or normative.

-       A scenario can be characterized as a **trend** scenario or as an **extreme** (or contrast)
        scenario. Trend scenarios are in fact an extrapolation of the present situation.
        Extreme scenarios on the other hand, try to construct future paths and future
        situations that are considered to be in principle feasible, though very unlikely.
        They are both always projective scenarios.

-       The last distinction to be made is whether a normative scenario is based upon the
        preferences of the **majority** of people, or whether it is based on the preferences
        of a **small minority**. The first group may be characterized as "common opinion"
        scenarios, and the second as "happy few" scenarios.

The relation between these characteristics are shown in the following figure.

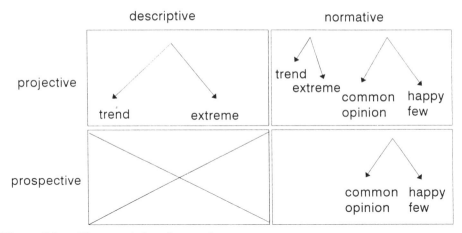

Figure 5.2.   Characteristics of scenarios.
Source: Van Doorn en Van Vught (1981)

On the basis of Figure 5.2, various compound scenarios can be constructed, each made up by features of the successive individual scenarios. This is illustrated in Figure 5.3 where the entries S I,1 ... indicate a blend of characteristics of various scenarios.

It is assumed in Figure 5.3 that state 1 at the top of the table is a trend, while the remaining states 2, ...,N are alternative, feasible (maybe sometimes extreme) states of the system concerned. The (linear or non-linear) combination of these states makes up the external boundaries of all possibilities of the system. The policy priorities are reflected in the common opinion view I, the normative (maybe sometimes extreme) priority schemes II, ... (the happy few, e.g.), and the endogenized priority responses upon the external conditions (1, ...,N) indicated by X_1, ... The latter category is by its very nature essentially a set of descriptive scenarios.

It is evident that the use of such scenarios is of great importance - as a complementary tool - for multidimensional planning problems.

In view of the uncertainty incorporated in many planning analyses also information systems should be given due attention in transportation and physical planning. This does not only hold true for monitoring systems, but also for decision support systems and expert systems. Clearly, such systems form also an extremely

alternative external conditions various societal values	States of exogenous conditions			
	1	2	3	N
I II ⋮	$S_{I,1}$ $S_{II,1}$	$S_{I,2}$		
X_I X_{II}				

Figure 5.3.   Various compound scenarios.

useful contribution to a rationalization of complex planning problems.

Thus, both scenario experiments and information systems may provide useful decision support methods for transportation planning under uncertainty.

5.6   Concluding Remarks

Having presented now in part B some basic elements of transportation impact analysis, we will in the next part (part C) offer a set of empirical studies on the assessment of effects of transportation and infrastructure investments.

Four types of approach will basically be presented: a micro-based investigation among entrepreneurs on the regional impacts of new infrastructure (Chapter 6), a multivariate statistical analysis and economic single-equation model for assessing the regional growth effects of infrastructure endowment (Chapter 7), a statistical analysis based on the mentioned frequency analysis (Section 4.3.2.) for identifying the regional performance of new infrastructure investments (Chapter 8), and an explanatory impact model for gauging the regional impacts of infrastructure subsidies from the European Community (Chapter 9).

PART C

CASE STUDIES IN TRANSPORTATION IMPACT ANALYSIS

Chapter 6

A MICRO-ORIENTED INQUIRY AMONG ENTREPRENEURS
ON REGIONAL IMPACTS OF INFRASTRUCTURE

6.1. Introduction

In this chapter we will discuss the results of a case study which was undertaken for assessing the impact of infrastructure endowments on three different regions in the Netherlands. This case study was part of a study on infrastructure and employment effects with the aim to provide a more solid empirical basis for the question whether (public) infrastructure investments are significantly contributing to an improvement of the employment situation in the Netherlands (see Bruinsma, 1990). For the case study a micro-oriented approach - related to the method of quasi-experimentation (see Section 4.2) - was used to assess the programme effects of infrastructure endowments. Programme effects refer to the supply of infrastructure promoting long-term structural employment effects based on maintenance and management and spin-off effects caused by changes in the relative locational attractiveness of places or regions for new enterprises. In the study both the direct effects (related to the design, construction and building aspects of infrastructure provisions) and indirect employment effects of infrastructure investments (related to derived (second-order) consequences of the creation of infrastructure) were assessed also for the Netherlands as a whole. Our main interest however, is in the regional programme effects.

6.2. Methodological Aspects

As outlined in Chapter 4, micro studies for impact assessment of policy measures deal, in general, with individual observations on actors who have been influenced by a specific policy measure. The information needed for an impact assessment is provided by a survey method. The case study discussed here focuses on the programme effects of infrastructure (in terms of employment). **Because** of synergetic effects resulting from various infrastructure components, it is plausible to focus on the programme effects of an infrastructure complex rather than on those of separate infrastructure categories. Therefore, in the case study programme effects of various coherent and compound infrastructure classes are analyzed in an ex post way. It is taken for granted that the programme effects result - exclusively or mainly - from infrastructure investments, based on a stimulus-response model.

First we will discuss a few difficulties that arose in using such a regional survey. In the first place, it is hard - if not impossible - to make a distinction between **distributive** and **generative** effects. Are the observed effects the result of the growing internal strength brought about by infrastructural investments? Or are these effects the consequence of a shift in employment from the surrounding areas as a result of a better competitiveness? Most employers appear to be unaware of such aspects.

Secondly, it is for most employers difficult to **distinguish** the influence of a change in the infrastructure from the general upgrading of the total regional economic production structure and environment.

Thirdly, in addition to jobs created as a consequence of infrastructure investments, one would also have to account for jobs that would have been lost if the infrastructure investments concerned would not have been carried out (the **'policy-off'** situation). The order of magnitude of the latter category is largely unknown.

In the fourth place, no attention could be paid to **household** effects (e.g., better access to markets or information). For instance, when new recreation or shopping trips are generated which provoke growth of employment in those sectors, it is not possible to include such information.

Finally, entrepreneurs may adopt a **'strategic behaviour'** by overrating the potential benefits of infrastructure projects in the hope that the research results will convince policy makers that such public project investments should be continued. To cope with this problem, we have only covered effects of infrastructure that was already implemented during the period of the survey.

The above observations mean that the results presented here have to be interpreted and used with great caution in the context of a specific region under investigation.

6.3. The Regions under Study

In three Dutch regions which have been exposed to a clear infrastructure impulse in the last decade, a postal questionnaire - focusing on the influence of new infrastructure on the number of employees - was sent out to relevant firms with at least 50 employees. In Figure 6.1 the three regions used in the case study are shown. These regions in the Netherlands were: Leiden and the Bollenstreek in the Randstad (the economic heartland of the country), Southeast North-Brabant (Zuidoost Noord-Brabant) in the intermediate zone, and Twente in the peripheral zone.

Figure 6.1.   Three selected Dutch regions

In selecting the three regions for the case study, the following criteria played an important role:
-    the functional economic position of the region;
-    the investments in the ground-, water- and highway construction sector;
-    the geographical position of the region at hand in the Netherlands.

The regional level of analysis has to correspond to the geographical coverage and spatial functioning of the infrastructure complex studied (hence so-called 'functional' regions had to be selected). In this case study the regions selected corresponded to a standard statistical level in the Netherlands (so-called COROP-regions). In most cases this spatial level is in agreement with the sphere of influence of an infrastructure complex. Besides, for this level sufficient statistical data are available from the Central Bureau of Statistics (CBS) in the Netherlands.

Concerning the second criterion, it is necessary to select regions which have invested substantially in infrastructure in the past 10 to 20 years. The higher the level of infrastructure investments, the higher and better measurable the programme effects.

Finally, the geographical position of the regions selected has to ensure a reasonable representative coverage of existing economic areas in the Netherlands. In regional studies in the Netherlands usually three different economic areas/zones are distinguished, viz., the economic heartland, an intermediate zone and a peripheral zone. A representative study is thus guaranteed by selecting three regions each representing one type of the three functional economic area classes in the Netherlands. Of course, it has to be recognized that not each of these three different regions will react in the same way to infrastructure investments: besides infrastructure investments other intermediate variables have an influence on the growth of employment in a certain region (e.g., production environment and sectoral structure).

In Figure 6.1 the three regions selected for the case study have been sketched. Below we will discuss shortly some aspects of these regions which are important in light of the subject of our study, viz., growth of employment and infrastructure investments in the past years.

6.3.1. Leiden and de Bollenstreek (heartland)

In this region employment growth has been higher compared to the average trend in the Netherlands. Also the unemployment figures have been lower. Employment is overrepresented in the industrial sector and agriculture (see Table 6.1).

	EMPLOYMENT				UNEMPLOYMENT		
year	Leiden absolute	Leiden index	Netherlands index	year	Leiden absolute	Leiden percent	Netherlands percent
1971	74,470	100	100	1972	2,577	2.4	2.2
1976	81,100	109	104	1977	3,489	3.0	3.7
1980	88,000	118	111	1980	4,229	3.3	4.3
1984	98,500	132	116	1984	13,837	9.3	13.6
1986	102,700	138	123	1987	10,500	6.8	11.1

Table 6.1.   Employment and unemployment figures for Leiden and Bollenstreek
Source: CBS

The most important new infrastructure components in this region are the following:

-       in the period 1980-1988 98.6 hectare of business parks has been distributed;

-       the highway A4 has been extended to 2 x 4 lanes (costs not precisely known);

-       removal of several bottlenecks in provincial highways (costs about 96 million Dutch guilders);

-       construction of a strategic new railway connection (the Schiphol railway; costs about 500 million guilders);

-       improvement (optical fibre) of the telecommunication network (costs unknown).

6.3.2. Southeast North-Brabant (intermediate zone)

Employment growth in Southeast North-Brabant has been poor compared to the average trend in the Netherlands, although in the past years there has been a slight improvement. The unemployment figure of 1986 is even better compared to the unemployment figure for the Netherlands as a whole. Employment in the industrial sector has been more and more replaced by employment in the service sector (see Table 6.2).

	EMPLOYMENT				UNEMPLOYMENT		
year	Brabant absolute	Brabant index	Netherlands index	year	Brabant absolute	Brabant percent	Netherlands percent
1971	181,200	100	100	1972	4,490	2.2	2.2
1976	178,710	99	104	1977	11,312	5.2	3.7
1980	190,200	105	111	1980	14,326	5.9	4.3
1984	198,600	110	116	1984	40,010	15.2	13.6
1986	216,100	119	123	1987	27,500	10.0	11.1

Table 6.2.   Employment and unemployment figures for Southeast North-Brabant
        Source: CBS

The most important new infrastructure components in Southeast North-Brabant are the following:

-   in the period 1980-1986 131.9 hectare of land for new business firms has been allocated;
-   extension of highway A58; improvement of highway A2 and of some provincial highways (total costs about 180 million Dutch guilders);
-   opening of a new railway station in Eindhoven;
-   extension of civil air traffic on Eindhoven airport;
-   improvement of the telecommunication network on various places.

6.3.3.   Twente (peripheral zone)

In Twente employment growth has been much worse compared to the average development in the Netherlands (see Table 6.3). This is mainly due to the loss of employment in the textiles and clothing industry. The unemployment is also higher than in the Netherlands as a whole (although in very recent years a significant improvement has taken place).

	EMPLOYMENT				UNEMPLOYMENT		
year	Twente absolute	Twente index	Netherlands index	year	Twente absolute	Twente percent	Netherlands percent
1971	143,290	100	100	1972	5,737	2.2	2.2
1976	143,760	100	104	1977	7,749	5.2	3.7
1980	151,300	106	111	1980	14,326	5.9	4.3
1984	151,100	105	116	1984	40,010	15.2	13.6
1986	161,100	112	123	1987	27,500	10.0	11.1

Table 6.3. Employment and unemployment figures for Twente
Source: CBS

Also in Twente some major infrastructure investments have been implemented in the past years. The most important are the following:

- in the period 1983-1988 154 hectare of business parks was distributed;
- construction of the highways A1 and A35 (total costs 490 million guilders);
- strong improvement of the telecommunciation network.

6.4. The Questionnaire

To assess the programme effects of infrastructure, a postal questionnaire was sent to 781 firms in the three regions. In Table 6.4 the distribution of firms over the three regions and all relevant sectors is given. Most responding firms are large companies (over 100 employees); such firms are probably more capable to assess the effects of infrastructure investments on employment. In Table 6.4 also the response rate is given. Generally speaking, this response shows a reasonable distribution over all sectors and size classes of firms.

Sector	Leiden		Brabant		Twente		Total	
	response		response		response		response	
	absolute	percent	absolute	percent	absolute	percent	absolute	percent
agriculture	3	17	2	67	1	-	6	27
minerals	0	-	0	-	0	-	0	-
industry	18	23	43	29	51	39	112	32
construction	5	8	18	43	17	36	40	26
trade	23	37	6	29	8	27	37	32
services	10	34	2	13	5	83	17	33
transport	8	32	6	26	10	26	24	28
unknown	0	-	0	-	1	-	1	-
total	67	25	77	30	93	37	237	30

Table 6.4.   Regional distribution of number of firms according to sectoral responses

The response is fairly satisfactory for the aim of this case study, i.e., to obtain an adequate assessment of regional employment effects of infrastructure investments on various sectors in the Netherlands. To assess these effects the questionnaire contained the following items:

-    location and type of firm;

-    year of foundation and spatial locational behaviour of firm; and effects of infrastructure (and intermediate variables) on this behaviour;

-    growth in the number of employees; effects of infrastructure (and intermediate variables) on this number;

-    effects of specific infrastructure projects on the number of employees in a firm;

-    effects if those infrastructure projects would not be realized ('policy-off' situation);

-    specific benefits for the firm resulting from several other infrastructure components.

The response to these questions would have to lead to more empirical insight into the programme effects of infrastructure. It is also important that the entire context of regional development and the role infrastructural improvements play in this context, are clearly indicated, before the employers are asked to answer questions specifically dealing with such infrastructural improvements. So in the introductory part of the questionnaire the regional infrastructure was positioned and described in the broad regional context.

6.5. Results of the Study

The result of our analysis appeared to be in agreement with most outcomes suggested in the literature. The two factors which appear to be of decisive influence on the fluctuations in the number of employees are market perspectives and internal company considerations, like for instance automation. A second group of major influencing factors is: labour market, availability of industrial sites, new infrastructure and investment subsidies. Thus infrastructural factors are well represented in this second group. The influence of other factors - like the already existing infrastructure, contacts with the government and the image of the region - appear to be marginal.

A slightly different pattern appears to exist when the reasons for a relocation of the firm are brought to attention. Dominant factors are then the availability of industrial sites and market perspectives. Factors with a significant influence are the internal company structure, new infrastructure and investment subsidies. Rather striking is the fact that the main reason to relocate is for nearly 50 per cent of the relocated enterprises the inappropriateness of the former location; only 5 per cent of the enterprises had moved to a new location (mainly) because of the suitability of the new location. Another rather striking result is the close connection with the former location. Over 60 per cent of the enterprises appeared to relocate inside the same city boundary.

Although these figures are interesting from the general viewpoint of location theory of firms, in this case study the central focus concerns the spin-off effects ('programme effects') of specific infrastructural investments. In general, it is plausible to assume that infrastructural improvements should originate from a significant improvement of the regional infrastructure complex (the synergy of all individual infrastructure components), before we may observe a spin-off effect that is sufficiently significant to be measured. The survey therefore focused on such important infrastructure projects like, for instance, motorways, railways, regional airports and the replacement of old copper telecommunication networks by new optical fibre ones.

The employment spin-off effects of the railway investments and regional airports appeared to be marginal due to the fact that those infrastructure elements are not in common use by any of the economic sectors. The employment effects of highways appear to be fairly substantial (see Figure 6.2).

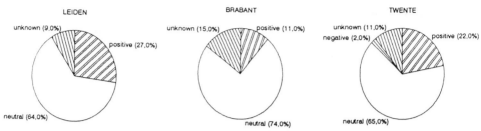

Figure 6.2.   Employment effects of new road infrastructure

In Leiden, for instance, 27 per cent of the entrepreneurs indicated a positive employment effect as a consequence of the improvement of the highways in the area. In Brabant 11 per cent and Twente 22 per cent of the enterprises signalled an employment growth for the same reason.

The effect of the optical fibre networks seem to be smaller (see Figure 6.3); however, in 1988 only 1 per cent of the Dutch telecommunication network was based on optical fibre.

To check whether the figures provided by the firms were correct, a control question was built in. The employers were also asked their opinion about how the firm would have acted if the new infrastructure would not have been realized. In between other questions about firm size, the firm's investments and its relocation behaviour, the question was raised what the consequences would have been for the numbers of employees.

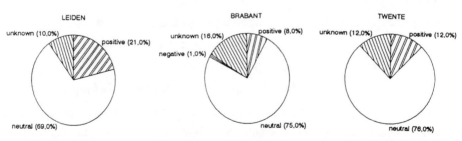

Figure 6.3   Employment effects of new optical fibre telecommunication networks

The results of this question (see Figure 6.4) are quite consistent with the figures shown before. In this respect Leiden appears to score with 17 per cent a little lower than would have been expected, and Twente somewhat higher with 26 per cent.

In both Leiden and Twente a relatively high percentage of firms indicated that their firm size would have been smaller without the new infrastructure. The effect on the investment level of firms appears to be substantial. Nearly 40 per cent of the firms in Leiden, 30 per cent of the firms in Twente and 20 per cent of the firms in Brabant expected lower company investments, if the infrastructure would not have been realized. About 15 per cent of the relocated firms would not have looked for a new location.

The overall view from these results is that the impact of new infrastructure in these regions on company behaviour is rather significant, especially in the cases of Leiden and Twente.

Keeping the difficulties inherent in a questionnaire in mind, it is nevertheless possible to measure at least threshold or minimum effects, considering that a positive employment effect as reported by a firm means at least one new created job.

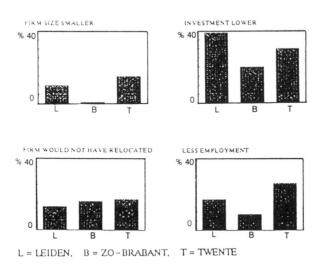

L = LEIDEN, B = ZO-BRABANT, T = TWENTE

Figure 6.4.   Effects if the infrastructure were not realized

For example, in Twente the construction of the highways A35 (Almelo-Hengelo) and A1 (Amsterdam-Osnabrück) had a minimum effect of 383 new jobs in the basic sector. Assuming a multiplier of 1.4 for the second-order effect in the nonbasic sector, the total minimum employment effect is then 536 jobs. The total investments in highway construction in Twente amounted to 346 million Dutch guilders. This means that an investment of 650.000 Dutch guilders generated at least one new job as an absolute minimum estimate (note the difference between the temporary effect of 'one man-year of labour' and the more structural notion of 'job'). As indicated in Bruinsma (1990), the actual employment spin-off effects of the construction of these highways may be considerably higher, since these are only minimum estimates. Altogether the programme effects of infrastructure investments tend to be significant.

6.6. Conclusions

The following factors were found to have a positive influence on the size of the employment effects. First, the region should possess a clear economic potential. The labour market should not only have a reserve capacity of labour, but it is also necessary that it contains a good quality of labour. There has to be also a good entrepreneurial spirit, while the political climate has to be in favour of economic development.

Secondly, the new realised infrastructure has to serve the needs of all economic sectors. As a consequence, important spin-off effects can be expected from an expansion of the following infrastructure elements: road infrastructure, telecommunication networks, energy and water supply infrastructures. Energy and water supply infrastructures are basic infrastructure elements and normally already available, without any capacity constraint. It is not reasonable to assume that increasing investments in those networks will lead to substantial spin-off effects, unless these networks were absent ('missing networks').

The construction of highways or the replacement of the copper telecommunciation cables by optical fibre networks on the other hand may result in substantial structural employment effects. Through those expansions, the whole infrastructure complex of the region may be upgraded.

Substantial employment effects were found in two situations. Employment effects appeared to be particularly significant, when an essential but missing link in the infrastructure network was constructed or when the new investments led to a capacity increase in a clearly congested network. Although it has to be admitted, for the reasons mentioned in Section 4.2, that it is very difficult to measure the exact employment spin-off effects of the different infrastructure elements within regions, the above analysis suggests substantial economic benefits from the synergy of infrastructure investments, with particular emphasis on advanced road, rail and telecommunication infrastructure.

Chapter 7

INFRASTRUCTURE ENDOWMENT AND
REGIONAL GROWTH POTENTIAL:
AN EMPIRICAL ANALYSIS

7.1. Introduction

Infrastructure policy is one of the popular components of regional development policy. Infrastructure has in general a long range impact on the structure of regions or nations. Since socio-economic disparities are usually not the result of short-term economic fluctuations but of structural differences in space, it is conceivable that regional policy often assigns a critical role to infrastructural provisions. Moreover, in most cases, transport infrastructure appears to have the highest financial share among all public infrastructure endowment expenditures.

Infrastructure as part of a regional development strategy aims to redress imbalances among regions by providing the necessary conditions for making less favoured regions more competitive (e.g., in terms of accessibility, attractiveness or locational profile). Analytically, it is therefore an important question whether more and better infrastructure endowments lead also to a higher growth potential. This question will be dealt with in the present chapter and illustrated by means of an empirical application to Dutch regions.

The main idea here is thus that regional disparities are the result of **long-run developments** and not of short-term cyclical fluctuations. Consequently, much emphasis is put on the supply - and hence capacity - side. In this context, the problem of regional disparities is essentially a global allocation problem, viz., which share of total (e.g., world or national) demand will be attracted by the more favoured regions in an open competitive spatial system? This allocation problem is also connected with the extent to which regions succeed in efficiently utilizing their production capacity, so that then the question of which factor composition has an optimal influence on the regional development potential becomes crucial (cf. Biehl, 1980).

The regional development potential depends in general on:

-   **regional potentiality factors** (such as availability of natural resourses, locational conditions, sectoral composition, international linkages and existing capital stock)
-   **mobile production factors** (such as various kinds of labour and new investments).

The optimal composition of all these elements is of decisive importance for the competitive advantage of a region (cf. Porter, 1990). In our empirical study we will mainly focus on Dutch regions.

7.2.   Analytical Framework for the Contribution of Infrastructure to Regional Development

As mentioned before, infrastructure can be seen as one of the regional potentiality factors, which determine the long-term development perspectives of regions. It is clear that all these different potentiality factors may contribute in different ways to the regional development potential. Therefore, it is important to assess the relative contribution of various infrastructure categories to the regional development potential.

For a systematic treatment of this problem, it is meaningful to distinguish the following steps in our impact assessment:

(1)   specification of discriminating criteria in order to distinguish infrastructure from other potentiality factors, followed by an analysis of various kinds of infrastructure categories by means of their characteristics or attributes;

(2)   regional dimensions of infrastructure attributes and characteristics;

(3)   classification of regions and infrastructure categories;

(4)   evaluation and ranking of various infrastructure categories on the basis of their contribution to regional development.

These steps will now be described in a concise manner.

7.2.1.   Identification of infrastructure categories

In general, infrastructure capital can be separated from other types of public capital by means of the following discriminating criteria: mobility, indivisibility, non-substitutability, polyvalence and non-exclusiveness (see Biehl, 1980). Thus those types of public capital which imply relatively high values of these criteria will be selected as critical elements of a regional infrastructure strategy. This means that infrastructure is regarded here as a broad potentiality factor.

Given the available Dutch data, the following items are included in an infrastructure list (see also Table 7.2):

(a)   Transport infrastructure

(b)   Communication infrastructure

(c)   Energy supply infrastructure

(d)   Water infrastructure (including pollution abatement technology)

(e)   Environment infrastructure

(f)   Educational infrastructure

(g)   Health infrastructure

(h)   Special urban (local) infrastructure

(i)   Sports and tourist infrastructure

(j)   Social infrastructure

(k)   Cultural facilities

(l)   Natural infrastructure

Clearly, the abovementioned main infrastructure categories can be subdivided into various subcomponents and attributes. For instance, transport infrastructure can be subdivided into a road network system, a railway network system, a waterway network system etc., while each of these components can be further subdivided into characteristic attributes such as roads, highways, tunnels, parking places etc. Consequently, a long list of infrastructure attributes can be obtained (see Biehl et al., 1986).

7.2.2. **Regional infrastructure endowment**

For all regions of the spatial system concerned, the values of the infrastructure attributes and characteristics can in principle be assessed. This leads to a coherent matrix of regional infrastructure endowments (see Table 7.1.).

regions

infrastructure
attributes

```
┌─────────────────────────────────────────────────┐
│                                                 │
│                                                 │
│              regional attributes                │
│                                                 │
│                                                 │
│                                                 │
│                                                 │
└─────────────────────────────────────────────────┘
```

Table 7.1.   Matrix of attributes of regional infrastructure

In accordance with the regional development potential theory, the elements of
Table 7.1. should be expressed as much as possible in **maximum capacities,** so that by
applying next user indicators significant regional **bottlenecks** can easily be identified.

7.2.3. Classification of regions and infrastructure categories

The grouping of infrastructure categories will enable us to structure the
relationships with regional development more easily, while a clustering of regions
according to infrastructure endowments will help us eventually in formulating policy
recommendations about the spatial distribution of policy instruments in future regional
development programming and the potential contribution of infrastructure investments
to regional development.

The classification of regions can be based on various principles. The following
multivariate techniques will successively be employed here:
-       hierarchical cluster analysis;
-       multidimensional scaling analysis (MDS);
-       principal component analysis.

7.2.4. Assessment of infrastructure impacts on regional development

In this chapter, we will deal with the following three questions:

- **which** groups of infrastructure categories are most likely playing a dominant role in the regional development process?
- **when** may infrastructure (probably) become a successful instrument in regional development programming?
- **where** could infrastructure investments be a useful instrument in future regional planning?

To provide meaningful answers to these questions, **multiple regression methods** and **shift and share analysis** are suitable statistical techniques which will be used in our empirical application (see also Chapters 4 and 5).

Having described now briefly the structure and the methods to be used in the present impact study for the Netherlands, we will in more detail describe the results for each of these four elements in Sections 7.3 - 7.6.

7.3.　Assessment of Infrastructure Indicators

The data on infrastructure for Dutch regions stem from different sources and were collected at a detailed level for many infrastructure indicators for all eleven Dutch provinces (the administrative regions in the Netherlands). These eleven provinces are:

1.　Friesland
2.　Groningen
3.　Drenthe
4.　Overijssel
5.　Gelderland
6.　Utrecht
7.　Noord-Holland
8.　Zuid-Holland
9.　Zeeland
10.　Noord-Brabant
11.　Limburg

The location and size of these provinces can be seen from the map in Figure 7.1.

Figure 7.1.   Provincial subdivision of the Netherlands for the relevant period.

In some cases regional data are difficult to obtain (e.g., communication, energy, water and education). We have used the periods 1970 - 1975 and 1976 - 1980, as these were the periods with rather severe regional disparity problems and hence intensified regional policy efforts (see also Table 7.2., and for further details De Graaff and Nijkamp, 1986). In general, a detailed investigation of the data for the Netherlands leads to the conclusion that the majority of regions is relatively equally endowed with most infrastructure categories. Only the transport network shows a noteworthy exception, since the peripheral areas in the North (and to a lesser extent in the South) are lacking sufficient motorway and railway infrastructure. In addition, it is noteworthy that the less central regions outside the industrialized heartland of the Netherlands have a much higher endowment of environmental capital, which may be an important asset for potential growth in the future. Finally, the changes in regional disparities have been modest in the seventies, which forms a contrast to the eighties where regional economic development shows a more clear trend towards convergence (except for a few structurally stagnating areas in the northern part of the country).

Infrastructure categories		monthly	yearly	3-5 years	irregularly	availability at provincial level: + good ± fair - poor
(a)	. roads			x		+
	. railways		x			±
	. waterways/ports		x			-
	. airports		x			+
(b)	. telephone		x			-
	. telex		x			-
	. radio/tv		x			-
(c)	. electricity network		x			±
	. gas network		x			+
	. petroleum	x				+
	. district heating		?			-
(d)	. water network				x	-
(e)	. water sewage			x		+
	. waste disposal			x		+
	. pollution control			x		+
(f)	. number of schools		x			±
	. number of classrooms		x			-
	. number of teachers		x			-
	. number of pupils/students		x			+
(g)	. number of hospitals			x		+
	. number of hospital beds			x		+
	. number of physicians			x		+
	. number of dentists			x		+
(h)	. fire protection		x			+
	. number of urban parks				x	±
	. industrial estates				x	-
(i)	. sports facilities				x	+
	. camping grounds				x	+
	. youth hostels		x			-
(j)	. old age homes		x			+
	. child centres				x	+
	. youth centres				x	-
(k)	. museums			x		+
	. theaters		x			+
	. operas, concerts, ballets		x			+
	. libraries		x			+
(l)	. natural parks			x		+

Table 7.2.   Availability of data on various infrastructure indicators.

7.4.   Regional Infrastructure Endowment

The first step in analyzing the relationship between infrastructure and regional development in more detail is to classify regions according to their infrastructure endowment. For the sake of statistical ease, our analysis will concentrate on the twelve **main infrastructure categories** distinguished in Subsection 7.2.1. Subcategories within these main classes will not be dealt here. This choice is also justified by a correlation analysis, which showed in general a high correlation between items **within** each of the twelve main infrastructure categories (see De Graaff and Nijkamp, 1986).

In order to reduce the effects size of population and areas on the statistical results, each infrastructure item is standardized as follows:

-       items related to network and space-opening infrastructure by means of a joint spatial potential (i.e., the surface of a region)

-       items related to point infrastructure by means of their demand potential (i.e., population size).

In order to ensure comparable statistical scales for all infrastructure data (which were measured in different units), a simple normalization method was used by dividing the regional value of each of the twelve main indicators by its maximum value across all regions. In other words, if a_{ir} is the level of quantitative endowment (or capacity) of infrastructure category i (i = 1, ..., I) in region r (r = 1, ..., R), then the normalized value of a_{ir}, denoted as a^{*}_{ir} is written as:

$$a^{*}_{ir} = a_{ir} / a_{i,max} \cdot 100 \tag{7.1}$$

An expression for the total regional infrastructure endowment, denoted by a_r, can also be found by taking the unweighted arithmetic mean of the normalized indicators for each regional infrastructure category:

$$a_r = a^{*}_{ir} / I \tag{7.2}$$

In Figures 7.2. - 7.4., the aggregate pattern of regional infrastructure endowments and their infrastructure endowment growth over all 11 provinces is given.

provinces infrastructure endowment	provinces infrastructure endowmend	provinces growth in infrastructure endowment

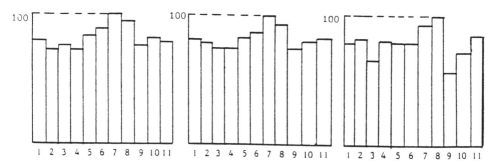

Figure 7.2. Average infrastructure index for 1970-1975.

Figure 7.3. Average infrastructure index 1976-1980.

Figure 7.4. Average infrastructure growth index.

The results lead to the following conclusions:

- the discrepancies among provinces are fairly low, although the central regions (Utrecht (6), Noord-Holland (7), Zuid-Holland (8)) clearly demonstrate a higher infrastructure endowment.

- the spatio-temporal dynamics of the average infrastructure endowment in the seventies is fairly low; apart from minor changes (viz., the province of Limburg), the relative position of provinces has been fairly stable.

- the average infrastructure index suggests, a reasonably equal spatial distribution of infrastructure.

7.5. Classification of Regions and Infrastructure

On the basis of the average infrastructure index derived above, we are now able to construct a simple hierarchical classification system, based on the distances between the eleven infrastructure indices (see Nijkamp and Paelinck, 1976). The results of the clustering are presented in Figures 7.5. and 7.6.

provinces

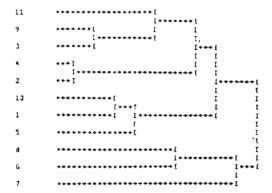

Figure 7.5.   Hierarchical classification of Dutch provinces, 1970-1975.

provinces

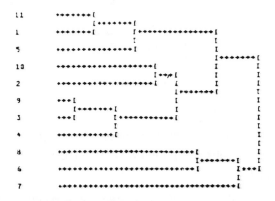

Figure 7.6.   Hierarchical classification of Dutch provinces, 1976-1980.

These results appear to be very stable over the time period considered. Now we may also carry out a clustering of regions. If this clustering would be based on only one overall infrastructure characteristic, we may expect neither a high degree of diversity **between** clusters, nor a high degree of homogeneity **within** each cluster. However, we may also apply the clustering method to all 12 infrastructure indicators. Then we may use the hierarchical classification system presented above. The results of this clustering are presented in Figures 7.7 and 7.8.

provinces

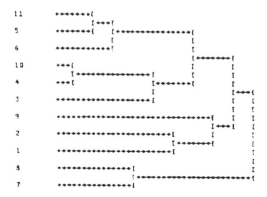

Figure 7.7. Hierarchical clustering of Dutch provinces, 1970-1975.

provinces

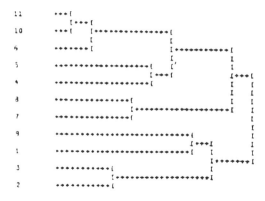

Figure 7.8. Hierarchical clustering of Dutch provinces, 1976-1980.

These results give rise to the following observations:

-   As one would expect, the results shown above are rather different from the ones presented in Figures 7.2. - 7.4. The only similarity between both results seems to be the hierarchical position of the cluster which includes the provinces Noord-Holland and Zuid-Holland.

-   Spatio-temporal dynamics is here more visible. The changes in the positions of Noord-Brabant, Drenthe and Zeeland are examples of intercluster dynamics of provinces, while the changes in the hierarchical positions of the Noord-Holland and

Zuid-Holland cluster illustrate alterations in the spatial distribution of infrastructure.

The general impression from the hierarchical clustering therefore, seems to be that the construction of infrastructure during the seventies has caused **decreasing** discrepancies between most of the provinces. Especially the convergence between the provinces Utrecht, Overijssel, Gelderland, Noord-Brabant and Limburg has increased, while the relative disparity between these provinces and two western provinces has become smaller. The insufficient growth of certain infrastructure categories in the provinces of Groningen and Friesland, Drenthe and Zeeland has caused an increasing discrepancy between these provinces and the rest of the Netherlands.

Next, it may also be interesting to identify which infrastructure categories have caused the shifts in the relative position of provinces and clusters. Here the use of multidimensional scaling (MDS) techniques may be an extremely useful tool (see Nijkamp, 1979). MDS analysis is a multivariate technique which aims at reducing an original data set to a smaller subset. The original rationale behind the use of MDS techniques was to transform ordinal data into cardinal units. Suppose that the matrices in Table 7.1. were measured in ordinal units. Then a transformation to a metric (cardinal) system can be made by assuming that each region r ($r = 1, ..., R$) can be represented as a point in an I-dimensional Euclidean space. Since there are R such points, a whole pattern of regions emerges such that the Euclidean distances among each pair of these R points may be regarded as a measure for the discrepancy between each pair of regions. The co-ordinates of these R points can be gauged by means of a similarity rule stating that the R points have to be located in the Euclidean space in such a way that their positions correspond to a maximum extent to the ordinal information in the original data matrix.

In a similar way, the values of the twelve infrastructure categories can be depicted in a Euclidean space, while also a joint representation of both regions and infrastructure categories may be given in the same space. The latter picture which will be used in our case allows one to identify correspondences between regions and their endowment with specific infrastructure categories.

The two-dimensional results of the MDS analysis for both time periods are included in Figure 7.9. and 7.10., respectively.

dimension 2

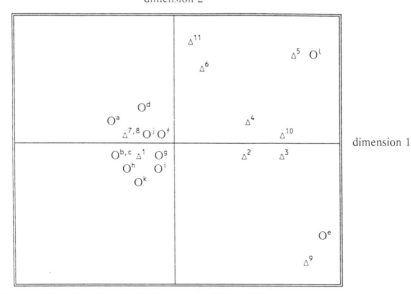

Figure 7.9. Results of MDS analysis (1970-1975)
  Δ = Provinces
  O = Infrastructure categories

dimension 2

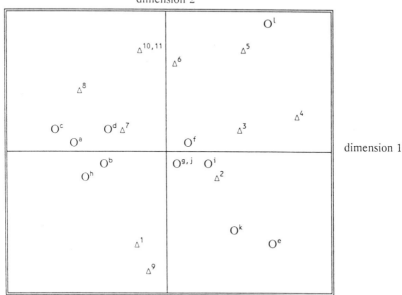

Figure 7.10. Results of MDS analysis (1976-1980)
  Δ = Provinces
  O = Infrastructure categories

In both figures, we can observe approximately the same clusters of provinces as presented in the linkage trees of Figure 7.7. and 7.8., except for the position of Groningen. Figure 7.9. shows an overall dominance of the provinces Noord-Holland and Zuid-Holland. Almost all main infrastructure categories are closely related to these two provinces, indicating a high correlation with their degree of urbanization and regional development. Since nearly all infrastructure categories are clustered in one group, Figure 7.9. cannot provide us with a meaningful description of the various clusters of provinces. Figure 7.10. provides a better basis in this respect, as we can distinguish here three more or less independent groups of main infrastructure clusters, viz., a network or regional infrastructure cluster (all infrastructure categories included here serve the entire region), a local social-welfare infrastructure cluster, and a separate infrastructure class composed of natural endowment.

Due to the decreased discrepancies caused by a more equal distribution of social-welfare infrastructure, the differences between the various clusters of provinces are mainly determined by a different performance on network and natural infrastructure. The clusters can therefore be characterized as follows. In the provinces of Noord-Holland and Zuid-Holland, network infrastructure is dominating, at the expense of natural endowment. Centrally positioned between network, socio-cultural and natural infrastructure endowment, the provinces Utrecht, Gelderland, Noord-Brabant and Limburg seem to have a more balanced infrastructure endowment. A serious lack of natural infrastructure characterizes the otherwise satisfactory profile of Groningen and Zeeland. The provinces Drenthe and Overijssel show relatively a lack of sufficient network infrastructure.

The clusters of infrastructure identified in our MDS analysis, are not only useful to characterize different groups of provinces, but they will also be extremely valuable in identifying and assessing relationships between infrastructure categories and regional development.

To arrive at a weighted aggregation of infrastructure categories in each cluster, the application of principal component analysis might be a useful tool, since the hereby produced **factor score coefficients** can be interpreted as weights to express the relative importance of each component within the relevant cluster or factor concerned. The results of a principal component analysis are given in Table 7.3.

Component	Eigenvalue		Pct. of variation	
	Period 1970-1975	Period 1976-1980	Period 1970-1975	Period 1976-1980
1	4.50	4.95	52.4	51.8
2	2.27	2.51	26.5	26.3
3	1.81	2.09	22.1	21.9

Table 7.3. Results of principal component analysis.

Component 1 includes - in descending order of importance - the following infrastructure categories: transport, communication, energy and water. Hence, this component can be regarded as a **network** indicator.

Component 2 includes sports and tourism, cultural facilities, social infrastructure, education and health, so that this component may be interpreted as the **social welfare** indicator.

Finally, component 3 is composed of **urban** and **environmental** infrastructure. As we have already observed from the MDS analysis, the natural endowment indicator has an entirely different character compared to the above mentioned indicators.

After this exploratory analysis of regional infrastructure data, we will use this information in the next section to study the relationship between infrastructure and regional development from an explanatory perspective.

7.6. Impact Assessment of Infrastructure and Regional Development

In this section, we aim to investigate whether (the dynamics of) the spatial distribution of infrastructure (as observed in the previous sections) has had an influence on the level of regional welfare. The first step is to test statistically, by means of a static **quasi-production function** (see Section 4.3.3.), the nature of the relationship between infrastructure clusters and the level of regional development (i.e., regional product). The quasi-production function takes for granted that regional product is determined by traditional (substitutable) production factors (such as capital and labour) as well as by specific regional determinants (such as agglomeration, sectoral structure and infrastructure). Due to the lack of quantitative information regarding regional productive capital and sectoral structure, and due to the fact that agglomeration factors are already partly incorporated in employment opportunities and infrastructure components, only the two last mentioned potentiality factors will be included as production factors. Hence, the following quasi-production function, based on a Cobb-Douglas specification, will be used:

$$Y = \alpha L^{\beta} \cdot I_1^{\gamma_1} \cdot I_2^{\gamma_2} \cdot I_3^{\gamma_3}$$

with Y = average regional product

L = employment opportunities ($\dfrac{\text{total population in age class 15-65}}{\text{total number of jobs}}$)

(7.3)

I_1 = network infrastructure

I_2 = social welfare infrastructure

I_3 = urban infrastructure

The results of a multiple regression analysis, based on aggregate infrastructure components in combination with data on regional product and employment opportunities for both periods together, are:

$$
\begin{aligned}
\ell n \quad \alpha &= .17 \ (.36) \\
\beta &= .58 \ (.33) \\
\gamma_1 &= .15 \ (.07) \\
\gamma_2 &= .03 \ (.15) \\
\gamma_3 &= .19 \ (.07) \ ,
\end{aligned}
$$

(7.4)

$$R^2 = .671$$

where figures in brackets represent the standard deviation. It turns out that as far as infrastructure is concerned, both network and urban infrastructure give a (statistically) significant explanation for regional development. The social welfare infrastructure indicator gives a slightly less significant explanation which may be due to the fact that it may depend more on **population size** than on the level of economic activity.

It should be noted however, that from these results the conclusion cannot be drawn that new infrastructure investments in the relevant categories will lead automatically to an improvement in regional development. We have stressed the fact that infrastructure is a **condition** for regional development; the above mentioned results prove mainly that bottlenecks in **network** and/or **urban** infrastructure are likely to have serious repercussions for the regional development process. Removing such bottlenecks is then a prerequisite for further development. This leads us to the question whether and when investments in infrastructure have positive effects on regional development.

In this respect, it may be useful to separate out, by means of a **shift and share analysis** (see Section 4.3.2.), the national contribution to regional growth performance from the specific intra-regional impacts, of which infrastructure forms a part. The **structural component** in the regional shift can then be interpreted as a measure of the quality of the regional economic structure, while the **regional component** indicates whether the combination of the other potentiality factors succeeds in obtaining relative locational advantages which may explain the tendency for industries in some regions to grow faster than in others.

The results of a shift and share analysis based on **employment growth** can be used to classify and explain regional growth in the following way (see Table 7.4).

		Regional component	
Structural		+	-
	+	I	II
component	-	III	IV

Table 7.4. Classification of regions

The characteristics of the groups of regions are (cf. Paraskevopoulos, 1974):

group I   :   regions with a satisfactory industrial structure and locational conditions that favour the realisation of agglomoration economies.

group II :   regions with favourable conditions for attracting growth industries but where other industries tend to stagnate due to bottlenecks in either potentiality factors (available floor space, accessibility, wage level, etc.) or governmental restrictions (see also Pellenbarg, 1977 and Andrioli et al.,

1979).

group III : regions where growth industries are relatively underrepresented but where locational conditions are sufficiently favourable to benefit from the spread effects occurring in industries in group II. These are the so-called 'intermediate' regions, located at the fringe of the national core areas.

group IV : the regions in this category are losing on both grounds, i.e., industrial mix and regional share, respectively, because the locational conditions are so unfavourable that neither growth industries nor spread effects are likely to be attracted to these areas. In short, the development prospects in these regions are not very promising.

Since infrastructure is one of the elements making up the regional component, one may assume that the contribution of infrastructure as a policy instrument in regional planning will be most successful in those cases where the regional component shows a negative sign, i.e., in **group II** and **group IV**. As the structural component in group IV is also negative, a combination of both **sectoral** and **locational** policy instruments seems then advisable.

7.7. Retrospect

After the above analysis of the relationship between infrastructure and regional development, the following final remarks and suggestions may be made:

- The degree to which infrastructure contributes to regional development depends strongly on the spatial level of analysis. A more refined spatial subdivision may reveal more (perhaps different) interesting relationships.

- The time periods for studying the impacts of infrastructure policy were essentially very short. Long term interrelationships between infrastructure and other potentiality factors should therefore receive more attention.

- The conclusions drawn from the analysis are co-determined by the definition of the variables, the aggregation procedures, and the normalization and the standardization methods.

- The statistical results demonstrate a high degree of correlation between detailed infrastructure indicators within one category. This justifies the aggregate level of analysis.

- Regional infrastructure endowments appear to be represented in some interesting clusters such as a network cluster, a social-welfare cluster and a quality-of-life cluster.

- Densely populated industrialized areas tend to have a higher network infrastructure endowment than peripheral, agricultural and less populated areas.

- Interprovincial discrepancies among infrastructure categories have decreased during the seventies.

- Locational conditions have become increasingly important in explaining regional employment and growth differences. New infrastructure-oriented factors such as accessibility and space availability tend to become important pull factors in the relocation process of firms.

- Due to the variety of instruments used in regional planning, an exact evaluation of the contribution of infrastructure investments to regional development is hard to give. Only indicative conclusions can be drawn which support the idea of infrastructure as a **conditional** growth stimulus.

Chapter 8

IMPACTS OF INFRASTRUCTURE ON REGIONAL DEVELOPMENT: RESULTS FROM A FREQUENCY ANALYSIS

8.1. Introduction

The improvement of infrastructure is one of the major policy instruments of the European Regional Development Fund (ERDF), created in 1975 in order to support and develop backward regions in the European Community. Infrastructure is regarded here as (material and immaterial) public capital which forms the foundation of - and is a critical success factor for - all other productive or socio-economic activities in a country or region. Especially since 1978 - when it was decided that a wide variety of public goods could be considered as infrastructure to which the Regional Fund (and other financial policies of the Community) might financially contribute - subsidies for infrastructure projects gradually rose to a significant part of the Regional Fund's annual budget.

The European regional development policy is essentially based on two different principles:

-       maximum contribution to national and regional (socio-) economic objectives, and
-       decline in undesirable (socio-)economic disparities among regions.

Especially the latter (convergence) objective is of major importance in the regional policy of the EC. In this respect, the Regional Development Fund plays a dominant role in reducing spatial disparities.

The necessary policy measures in the EC are in general related to both **institutional and financial aspects**. As far as financial aspects of infrastructure are concerned, especially the European Regional Development Fund plays a critical role in financing infrastructure investments. It is clear that a balanced regional policy needs sufficient insight into the impacts and effectiveness of infrastructure policy on regional development. Given the large amounts of money involved, there is a permanent need to monitor and evaluate the achievements of the Fund. In the present chapter we will offer some empirical results of a frequency analysis (see Section 4.3.2.), which has been used to assess the regional implications of EC infrastructure subsidies or expenditures.

In Section 4.3.2 the methodological aspects of **frequency tables** as an impact assessment method have already been discussed. Here we will discuss the results of a case study in which a frequency table analysis is used to assess the effects of amounts committed by the Regional Fund, with particular emphasis on Italian and Dutch regions. These case studies are used to test the validity and applicability of the above methodological framework developed for a systematic assessment of the regional economic effects of the ERDF. The frequency analysis is an exploratory analysis in which we use dichotomous frequency tables which show the number of regions which experienced an economic development - caused amongst others by the ERDF commitments - that is higher than the regional average in a country. A major advantage of the frequency table analysis is its **user-friendliness**. Besides, the method can be used for most **available data** in the statistical data bases in the countries of the European Community and does not require painstaking statistical field work.

8.2.   Illustration of a Frequency Analysis

The frequency table analysis outlined in Section 4.3.2. can be illustrated by means of a simple example sketched below. Let us assume a country with 25 regions, where we want to identify the impact of public expenditures on employment in the 25 regions. We define first:

E_r =   employment in region r relative to regional population

G_r =   public expenditures in region r relative to regional population

We now assume that the statistical data can be included in the following 2 x 2 table (with G^* the average of all G_r's and E^* the average of all E_r's).

	$G_r > G^*$	$G_r < G^*$
$E_r > E^*$	9	2
$E_r < E^*$	3	11

Table 8.1.   An illustrative frequency table.

In our example illustrative figures are given concerning employment and public expenditures (standardized for population size). This frequency table - and in consequence the calculation of the regional averages - is based on all relevant 25 regions of the nation. If we add up the number of regions in quadrant I and IV, we find a total of 20. This is 80 per cent of the total number of regions considered. There is evidently a positive relationship between the regional public expenditures and the degree of regional employment in our example.

For the specific assessment of ERDF impacts, our method will be adjusted by taking **private investments** (Ip) as a dependent performance variable and the **ERDF Commitments** (Ic), **public investments** (Io) and **(change in) (regional) gross value added** (GVA) as explanatory variables (stimuli). The choice of private investments as dependent variables implies that they are regarded here as an (indirect) indicator for the economic growth potential in a region. We postulate that the development of the private investments does not only depend on the ERDF Commitments in a given region, but also on public investments at large and the change in gross value added in that region (implying that favourable economic performance - reflected in a relatively high value added - induces higher private investments). One may of course argue that there exists multi-collinearity between ERDF Commitments and public investments; therefore, the values of the ERDF Commitments are subtracted from the total of public investments (i.e., public investments net of ERDF expenditures, denoted by I(o-c)). Besides, it appears that the values of the ERDF Commitments are relatively very low in comparison to overall public investments (for example, in the Dutch regions supported by the ERDF, the ERDF expenditures are on average approx. 2%

of total public investments). Furthermore, the ERDF expenditures have a much higher regional fluctuation than regional public expenditures.

In Section 8.3. and 8.4. we will discuss the results of this method in the framework of empirical studies undertaken for Italy and the Netherlands.

8.3.   Assessment of ERDF Impacts on Italian Regions

The most plausible data source to be used for a frequency table analysis for EC regions is **Eurostat** (the Statistical Office of the European Communities), because of consistency in definitions of all variables needed for all regions in the European Community. Italy appears to be a relevant country for analyzing regional disparities because of the high share of ERDF expenditures, especially in the Mezzogiorno. Besides, there is a relatively good availability of the necessary regional data in the statistical data base of Eurostat compared to other European countries. The Eurostat data were available for 20 regions in Italy and for the total of Italy for the time period 1975 - 1980, including the variables Ip (private investments), Ic (ERDF Commitments) and GVA (change in Gross Value Added).

The 20 regions of Italy are depicted in the map of Figure 8.1. These are the regions of Italy at a so-called **NUTS** level **II**, the nomenclature of territorial units for statistics used by Eurostat.

Figure 8.2. Regional composition of Italy

Since there appears to be a discrepancy in definitions of the variable 'public investments' used by Eurostat and the national statistical bureau of Italy, these missing data could not entirely be completed from this latter source, so that some guesses had to be made.

The frequency tables formed by means of the available data are based on the 20 Italian regions and have been constructed for six subsequent years (see Table 8.2.). For these years all data were available in Eurostat (except for public investments), so that the results here are based on a reliable data set. The dichotomous analysis has been carried out for both ERDF expenditures and the rise in regional Gross Value Added.

Year		$Ic > Ic^*$	$Ic < Ic^*$	$GVA > GVA^*$	$GVA < GVA^*$
1975	$Ip > Ip^*$	2	5	2	5
	$Ip < Ip^*$	6	7	0	13
1976	$Ip > Ip^*$	2	7	7	2
	$Ip < Ip^*$	4	7	3	8
1977	$Ip > Ip^*$	2	6	5	3
	$Ip < Ip^*$	7	5	4	8
1978	$Ip > Ip^*$	1	8	6	3
	$Ip < Ip^*$	7	4	3	8
1979	$Ip > Ip^*$	1	8	9	0
	$Ip < Ip^*$	8	3	1	10
1980	$Ip > Ip^*$	1	9	10	0
	$Ip < Ip^*$	8	2	2	8
Total	$Ip > Ip^*$	9	43	39	13
	$Ip < Ip^*$	40	28	13	55

Table 8.2.   Frequency tables for 20 Italian regions, based on ERDF data standardized for population (without a time lag)

Legend:
Ic   = ERDF Commitments
Ip   = Private investments
GVA   = Change in Gross Value Added

These tables show the number of regions which have values below or above the regional average of the relevant variables (Ic^*, Ip^* and GVA^*) in different combinations. The variable I(o-c) is not considered here because of the absence of reliable data on Io. The pairwise combinations of variables presented in Table 8.2. are the following:

- private investments (Ip) as dependent variables and ERDF Commitments (Ic) as explanatory variable (left-hand part of Table 8.2.)
- private investments as dependent variables and the change in Gross Value Added (GVA) as explanatory variable (right-hand part of Table 8.2.).

Clearly, in most frequency tables in the years considered the largest number of regions is present in quadrant IV. Thus the situation in which both private investments and the ERDF Commitments - or the change in Gross Valued Added - are below the regional average occurs in most cases. When we add the number of regions given in the first and fourth quadrant of the frequency tables, we can easily derive Table 8.3. from Table 8.2.

Year	Left-hand column	Right-hand column
	Quadrant I + IV	Quadrant I + IV
1975	45 %	75 %
1976	45 %	75 %
1977	35 %	65 %
1978	25 %	70 %
1979	20 %	95 %
1980	15 %	90 %
Total	31 %	78 %

Table 8.3.   Number of regions in Quadrant I + IV as percentage of total number of regions.

These results support only partly the existence of a relationship between private investments as a dependent variable and ERDF Commitments (and the change in Gross Value Added) as explanatory variables.

When we first take a look at the relationship between private investments and Gross Value Added (see the right-hand column in Tables 8.2. and 8.3., respectively), we may conclude that there is in general a positive correlation between these two variables. The number of regions in the fourth quadrant is 45.8% of the total number of regions for all years. The share of the number of regions in the first quadrant compared to the total number of regions is somewhat less, but - together with the number in the fourth quadrant -, about 80% per cent of the total number of regions is contained in quadrant I and IV.

The relationship between private investments and the ERDF Commitments is somehow less clear (see the left-hand part of Table 8.3). The number of regions in the fourth quadrant is not quite high for all years (about 24% of the total number of regions). The total number of regions added up from the first and the fourth quadrant is not much higher compared to the numbers in the fourth quadrant because of the small share of regions in the first quadrant. This share is decreasing over time. Consequently, the total percentage of regions added up for the first and fourth quadrant compared to all regions together is on average just about 31%.

The above results show clearly that the Italian regions receiving financial support from the ERDF - to a level that is above the Italian regional average - do not have a share of induced private investments that exceeds the regional average. This situation suggests a **relatively small** - and sometimes even negligible - **effect** of ERDF Commitments on the private investments for those Italian regions which have a **structural** weak economic basis. However, it is still possible to offer a more positive hypothesis for the above disappointing result, viz., that as a result of the financial support of the ERDF the private investments in some regions have not reached such an extremely low level as otherwise might have taken place. This can of course only be further examined by means of an explanatory model; this will be discussed in the next chapter.

It also appeared that the position of most regions is rather stable throughout the years. Only a small number of regions appears more than twice in a different quadrant, so that changes over time are apparently not significant. Consequently, the regional development performance of Italian regions is rather stable, rigid and low.

Finally, it should be noted here that - because of the absence of a complete and reliable data set over a longer time period - we could not experiment with time lags and moving averages for the variables concerned. Such an approach might possibly lead to more satisfactory and interesting results. Such an approach could fortunately be applied to the regions in The Netherlands because of the availability of a more complete data set for this country (see Section 8.4).

8.4.   Assessment of ERDF Impacts on Dutch Regions

A similar study as described in Section 8.3 was applied to The Netherlands. The data set of the Dutch Central Bureau of Statistics and Eurostat made it possible to build a complete data set for all variables, viz., for Ip, Ic, Io and GVA for the whole period 1975 - 1987. The frequency analysis is based here on the 11 provinces of the Netherlands discussed already in Chapter 7 (see Figure 7.1.).

Compared to Italy, it was possible to extend the frequency method, by applying time lags and moving averages, because of the longer time horizon and the availability of more reliable data. Also public investment data could be considered in this case study. The combinations of variables presented in this study are the same as for Italy, but they are extended with the combination of private investments (Ip) (as dependent variables) and public investments minus the ERDF Commitments (I(o-c)) (as explanatory variables).

We examined 6 time lags varying from 0 to 5 years, so that private investments (Ip) were supposed to be dependent on the variables ERDF Commitments (Ic), public investments minus the ERDF Commitments (I(o-c)) and the change in Gross Value Added (GVA) in the same year and in the past 1 to 5 years, respectively. It appeared that there were some changes in the results when varying the time lag. Using a time lag of four years appeared to lead to satisfactory results. We refer to Blaas and Nijkamp (1991) for a comparison of all results when a series of different time lags is used. In Table 8.4. only the results for a four year lag analysis are presented.

Table 8.4 contains various interesting results. We notice that frequency tables are given here for eight years. A time lag of four years means that the private investments in 1980 are confronted respectively with the ERDF Commitments, public investments (minus the ERDF Commitments) and the change in Gross Value Added in 1976. In 1981 the private investments are then compared to the values of these three variables in 1977 etc.

It appears that regions with below average ERDF Commitments are predominantly regions with below average private investments in The Netherlands. The results are however, to some extent different from those in the Italian empirical study. If we take a look in Table 8.4. at both the private investments (supposed to be the dependent variable) and the public investments and the change in Gross Value Added, respectively (as the explanatory variables) (the central column and right-hand column of Table 8.4., respectively), it appears that there is also in this case a strong positive correlation (although somewhat less pronounced compared to the Italian case) between these two variables. In each year about 60% of the total number of regions is contained in quadrant I and IV.

Year		$Ic > Ic^*$	$Ic < Ic^*$	$I(o\text{-}c) > I(o\text{-}c)^*$	$I(o\text{-}c) > I(o\text{-}c)^*$	$GVA > GVA^*$	$GVA < GVA^*$
1980	$Ip > Ip^*$	2	3	1	4	1	4
	$Ip < Ip^*$	2	4	2	4	1	5
1981	$Ip > Ip^*$	2	2	2	2	2	2
	$Ip < Ip^*$	1	6	2	5	0	7
1982	$Ip > Ip^*$	0	3	0	3	2	1
	$Ip < Ip^*$	1	7	3	5	4	4
1983	$Ip > Ip^*$	1	2	0	3	3	0
	$Ip < Ip^*$	2	6	2	6	4	4
1984	$Ip < Ip^*$	0	4	1	3	1	3
	$Ip > Ip^*$	2	5	0	7	1	6
1985	$Ip < Ip^*$	0	4	1	3	1	3
	$Ip > Ip^*$	1	6	0	7	1	6
1986	$Ip > Ip^*$	1	4	2	3	4	1
	$Ip < Ip^*$	2	4	0	6	2	4
1987	$Ip > Ip^*$	1	4	1	4	1	4
	$Ip < Ip^*$	2	4	0	6	4	2
Total	$Ip > Ip^*$	7	26	8	25	15	18
	$Ip < Ip^*$	13	42	9	46	19	36

Table 8.4. Frequency tables for 11 Dutch regions, based on absolute data standardized for population, with a time lag of 4 years.

Legend:
Ic	= ERDF Commitments
Ip	= Private investments
I(o-c)	= Public investments -/- ERDF Commitments
GVA	= Change in Gross Value Added

Table 8.5. summarizes the results of Table 8.4. Concerning the left-hand column (Ip compared to Ic), the total number of regions in the first and the fourth quadrant is quite large in the years 1980 to 1983, but is decreasing in the following four years (although in the last years the percentage of regions does not fall below 45%). The relationship between ERDF Commitments and private investments is providing more interesting results in comparison to the Italian case (where it seemed that the size of ERDF Commitments was not sufficiently large to induce private investments to such an extent that these reach a level above average). However, for a more satisfactory statistical analysis of the influence of ERDF Commitments on private investments one should make use of an explanatory model (see Chapter 9).

Year	Left-hand column	Centre column	Right-hand column
	Quadrant I + IV	Quadrant I + IV	Quadrant I + IV
1980	55 %	45 %	55 %
1981	73 %	64 %	82 %
1982	64 %	45 %	55 %
1983	64 %	55 %	64 %
1984	45 %	73 %	64 %
1985	55 %	73 %	64 %
1986	45 %	73 %	73 %
1987	45 %	64 %	27 %
Total	56 %	61 %	58 %

Table 8.5.   Number of Dutch regions in Quadrant I + IV as percentage of total number of regions.

Besides the analysis of frequency tables based on absolute data it is also possible to construct similar tables for moving averages. It is then again possible to investigate the influence of a varying time lag. In our case study, we have compared for seven time periods the results for a time lag ranging from 0 to 2 years. Also in this case a longer time lag (i.e., two years) showed relatively the best results. These are presented in Table 8.6.

Time period		Ic > Ic*	Ic < Ic*	I(o-c) > I(o-c)*	I(o-c) < I(o-c)*	GVA > GVA*	GVA < GVA*
1	Ip > Ip*	3	2	2	3	3	2
	Ip < Ip*	1	5	1	5	2	4
2	Ip > Ip*	2	1	1	2	2	1
	Ip < Ip*	1	7	1	7	1	7
3	Ip > Ip*	1	2	1	2	2	1
	Ip < Ip*	1	7	1	7	0	8
4	Ip < Ip*	1	4	1	4	2	3
	Ip > Ip*	2	4	0	6	0	6
5	Ip < Ip*	1	3	1	3	1	3
	Ip > Ip*	3	4	0	7	1	6
6	Ip > Ip*	1	3	1	3	1	3
	Ip < Ip*	3	4	0	7	1	6
7	Ip > Ip*	1	3	1	3	1	2
	Ip < Ip*	3	4	0	7	1	6
Total	Ip > Ip*	10	18	8	20	13	15
	Ip < Ip*	14	35	3	46	6	43

Table 8.6.   Frequency tables for 11 Dutch regions, based on moving averages and standardized for population size with a time lag of 2 years; time periods 1 (1977, ..., 1981) to 7 (1983, ..., 1988)

Legend:
Ic   = ERDF Commitments
Ip   = Private investments
I(o-c)   = Public investments -/- ERDF Commitments
GVA   = Change in Gross Value Added

Finally, it is again possible to present the findings in a concise form. Table 8.7 is deduced from Table 8.6 and presents the same kind of figures as those in Tables 8.3 and 8.5. The frequency analysis based on moving averages leads evidently to better results compared to the analysis based on absolute data.

8.5.   Concluding Remarks

For the ex post assessment of ERDF Commitments in this chapter a frequency table analysis was employed. The frequency table method is mainly meant to be an

exploratory tool in the sense of generating numerical evidence on the average effect
of ERDF expenditures from the past.

Time period	Left-hand column	Centre column	Right-hand column
	Quadrant I + IV	Quadrant I + IV	Quadrant I + IV
1	72 %	64 %	64 %
2	82 %	73 %	82 %
3	73 %	73 %	91 %
4	46 %	64 %	73 %
5	46 %	73 %	64 %
6	46 %	73 %	64 %
7	46 %	73 %	73 %
Total	58 %	70 %	72 %

Table 8.7.   Number of regions in Quadrant I + IV as percentage of total number
              of regions

This type of analysis is providing a structured empirical basis for the evaluation of
these expenditures, and allows for some experimentation with impacts of time lags
between the ERDF expenditures and regional economic indicators. Applying the
frequency table analysis leads to an impact measure that gives a percentage indication
of the strength of the relationship between private investments and ERDF
Commitments (the higher the percentage the stronger the validity of the supposed
relationship).

        The results of our frequency table analysis revealed changes over time in the
correlation between private investments and ERDF Commitments. This is possibly
due to the influence of intervening factors on this correlation which fluctuate over
time. The above approach has also clearly shown the need for a simple explanatory
model, to be tested for the same regions in Italy and the Netherlands. The results of
these case studies will be discussed in the next chapter.

Chapter 9

AN EXPLANATORY IMPACT MODEL FOR ERDF EXPENDITURES
AND REGIONAL DEVELOPMENT

9.1. Introduction

In this Chapter we will present a simple explanatory model for assessing the regional impact of the ERDF (European Regional Development Fund) expenditures. This model was developed as an extension of the frequency analysis as an impact assessment tool for ERDF Commitments, described in the previous chapter. The frequency table analysis is mainly meant to be an exploratory tool. The explanatory model however, to be developed in the present chapter serves to test the existence of a causal quantitative relationship between the economic development of a region and various explanatory background variables for this development. The ERDF Commitments in this model are only one of such explanatory variables. In a way analogous to the frequency table analysis, this model is tested for two empirical studies, viz., Italy and The Netherlands.

9.2. An Explanatory Model for the Assessment of ERDF Impacts

In Section 4.3.3 we have already outlined the structure of a model based on the location factor approach focusing on the relationship between government (infrastructure) investments and economic growth indicators, notably private investments. This model will now be used as a starting point for assessing the impacts of the ERDF expenditures. The basic idea is that ERDF Commitments - together with public expenditures - will attract new entrepreneurial activities which will first manifest themselves as new private investments. Such new investments might next lead to additional employment. Furthermore, the hypothesis of **rational expectations** is used, which means that (realized or foreseen) increases in regional Gross Value Added may also lead to a rise in private investments in the region concerned.

In order to assess the impacts of the ERDF expenditures on a region's economic development, we use the following additive model (see also eq. (4.2)):

$$I_{pr} = \alpha_{op} + \alpha_1.I_{cr} + \alpha_2.I_{(o-c)r} + \alpha_3.GVA_r \tag{9.1}$$

where for each region r the following variables can be defined:

GVA_r	= change in Gross Value Added
I_{cr}	= ERDF Commitments
$I_{(o-c)r}$	= public investments -/- ERDF Commitments
I_{pr}	= private investments
α_{or}	= constant (intercept)
α_{ir}	= reaction coefficient (i = 1, 2, 3)

This basic model can be translated in terms of three complementary types of investment behaviour. This was already outlined in Section 4.3.3. Given our purpose, these equations have to make a distinction between public investments and ERDF Commitments which both can be regarded as government investments. This leads to the following three investment quotations, based respectively on an **active response** model, a **conventional** model and a **passive response** model.

The first equation, the active response model, can be written as:

$$I_{pr} = \alpha_{or} + \alpha_1.I_{cr} + \alpha_2.I_{(o-c)r} + \alpha_3.GVA_r^{(+\sigma)}, \tag{9.2}$$

where σ represents a forward looking regional entrepreneurship.

For the second equation, the conventional investment behaviour, we assume:

$$I_{pr} = \beta_{or} + \beta_1.I_{cr}^{(-\sigma)} + \beta_2.I_{(o-c)r}^{(-\sigma)}. \tag{9.3}$$

The third equation is based on a passive response behaviour and reads as follows:

$$I_{pr} = \delta_0 + \delta_1.I_{cr} + \delta_2.I_{(o-c)r} + \delta_3.GVA_r^{(-\sigma)} \tag{9.4}$$

Besides these three investment equations, a further analysis of regional employment impacts has also been undertaken by investigating the labour-investment ratio:

$$L_r = \mu_{or} + \mu_1 . I_{pr}^{(-\sigma)} \tag{9.5}$$

where L_r = employment in region r.

In this way it is possible to explore indirectly also the relationship between the ERDF Commitments and total employment in a region. However, one should carefully deal with the results of this equation because of the **intransparant nature** of forces active in **regional labour markets**.

The explanatory model can again be based on **moving averages** of the specific data and/or can be used with different **time lags**. This is dependent on the availability of   sufficiently long time series of data. This model can be applied for two types of regions, viz., those which have and those which have not received any ERDF Commitments. The model allows thus a cross-regional comparison of impacts of different explanatory variables.

To determine the existence of a causal quantitative relationship between the economic development of a region (represented by private investments and employment) and possible explanatory background variables for this development (i.e., ERDF Commitments, public investments and change in regional Gross Value Added), we will use simple **regression analyses** for the above mentioned equations. In the next two sections we will discuss the empirical results for both Italy and The Netherlands.

9.3. Results of the Model for Italy

In our Italian study a regression analysis has been applied - for the three successive investment equations and the employment equation - for five regions in Italy (viz., Abruzzi, Campania, Marche, Puglia and Sardegna; see the map of Figure 9.1), as well as for the whole of Italy. A data bank was constructed for these five regions and for the whole of Italy for the time period 1975-1990; these data included all variables on the equations mentioned in the previous section, viz., Ip, Ic, GVA (in Mio. ECU's; all variables at current prices) and L (x 1000). The public investments (Io) had to be estimated for the whole period. This was done by a cross-sectional comparison of the public investments with the private investments for two years in which the data for the public investments were available. The same ratio was then applied to those years for which data on public investments were lacking. Data for some variables were neither available in the past three to five years and also had to be estimated by assuming a continuation of the main trend of the variable at hand in the years from 1975 to 1985/1988.

The regression analyses were applied to each equation separately with a series of alternating **time lags** ranging from zero to five years (if the calculations were based on absolute data) and time lags ranging from zero to two years (if the calculations were based on moving averages). The maximum range of the time lags (five and two years, respectively) is a result of the data availability over a limited time period. In Table 9.1 the results are represented.

Figure 9.1.   The five Italian regions used in the empirical study

CALCULATIONS BASED ON ABSOLUTE DATA

Equation	Ip = a1.Ic + a2.I(o-c) + a3 .ΔGVA(+t)			Ip = b1.Ic(-t) + b2.I(o-c)(-t)		Ip = c1.Ic + c2.I(o-c) + c3. ΔGVA(-t)			L = d1.Ip(-t)
Variable	Ic	I(o-c)	ΔGVA	Ic	I(o-c)	Ic	I(o-c)	ΔGVA	Ip
Time lag	0 1 2 3 4 5	0 1 2 3 4 5	0 1 2 3 4 5	0 1 2 3 4 5	0 1 2 3 4 5	0 1 2 3 4 5	0 1 2 3 4 5	0 1 2 3 4 5	0 1 2 3 4 5

Region

CALCULATIONS BASED ON MOVING AVERAGE

Equation	Ip = a1.Ic + a2.I(o-c) + a3. ΔGVA(+t)			Ip = b1.Ic(-t) + b2.I(o-c)(-t)		Ip = c1.Ic + c2.I(o-c) + c3. ΔGVA(-t)			L = d1.Ip(-t)
Variable	Ic	I(o-c)	ΔGVA	Ic	I(o-c)	Ic	I(o-c)	ΔGVA	Ip
Time lag	0 1 2	0 1 2	0 1 2	0 1 2	0 1 2	0 1 2	0 1 2	0 1 2	0 1 2

Region

Table 9.1   Results of regression analysis for Italy; only statistically significant coefficients, based on a confidence level > 75%, are shown.

+   = 0.5 < R-squared adjusted < 1
▲   = R-squared adjusted < 0.5
Ic   = ERDF Commitments
Ip   = Private investments
I(o-c) = Public investments -/- ERDF Commitments
GVA   = Change in Gross Value Added
L   = Total employment

In Table 9.1 only the presence of positive coefficients of the relevant variables that proved to be statistically significant (at a confidence level of 75%) are presented, by means of a + sign. The number of degrees of freedom varied from six to eight. The meaning of a ▲ sign is almost the same, but here the adjusted R square may be lower than 0.5. The coefficients suggest a positive influence of all variables on the development of the private investments in a specific region. The low number of degrees of freedom is again due to the limited range of the available time series, which is reinforced by the use of moving averages and time lags cutting down the number of usable data of a given time series.

When we take a closer look at Table 9.1, we may conclude that the regression analyses based on moving averages perform relatively better than the analyses based on absolute data. From the three investments equations (9.2) - (9.4), it turns out that equations (9.2) and (9.4) show the best results. This holds true for the calculations based on both absolute data and moving averages.

When we analyse the impacts of variables separately, it appears that public investments I(o-c) have the best results in terms of the number of cases that there is a statistically significant relationship with respect to private investments. The ERDF Commitments perform also reasonably well; especially when we consider the results based on moving averages, they appear to perform to the same extent as the change in Gross Value Added. The latter variable has the worst performance when the calculations are based on absolute data.

It is also interesting that the results for the employment equations appear to be also of a high quality, at least when the calculations are based on moving averages.

The use of different time lags did not lead to unambiguous results in favour of one of the time lags used.

The use of a 75% confidence interval as a criterion for assessing the significance of the coefficients seems to be quite low. Therefore, in Table 9.2 the results are represented for coefficients which are statistically significant at a confidence level of 95%. The results do not drastically change, as it turns out that then only 20% of the coefficients that appeared to be significant with a confidence interval larger than 75% would become non-significant if we would work with a confidence interval larger than 95%. This percentage is even lower, viz., about 12%, if we would use a moving averages procedure. Thus, the conclusions drawn from the results presented in Table 9.1 appear to be also valid for the results presented in Table 9.2. Of course, in the latter case the number of statistically significant relationships is lower because of the higher confidence level.

CALCULATIONS BASED ON ABSOLUTE DATA

Equation	Ip = a1.Ic + a2 I(o-c) + a3. ▲GVA(+t)			Ip = b1.Ic(-t) + b2.I(o-c)(-t)		Ip = c1.Ic + c2 I(o-c) + c3. ▲GVA(-t)			L = d1.Ip(-t)
Variable	Ic	I(o-c)	▲GVA	Ic	I(o-c)	Ic	I(o-c)	▲GVA	Ip
Time lag	0 1 2 3 4 5	0 1 2 3 4 5	0 1 2 3 4 5	0 1 2 3 4 5	0 1 2 3 4 5	0 1 2 3 4 5	0 1 2 3 4 5	0 1 2 3 4 5	0 1 2 3 4 5
Region									
Abruzzi	+ + + + + +	+ + + + +	+	+	+ + + + + +	+ + + + +		
Campania	+ ▲	+ ▲			+ ▲	+ ▲		
Marche	+ + + + +	+ + + + + + + +	+ + +	+ + +	+ + + +	+ + + + + +	+ +	+ +
Puglia			+ + ▲ ▲	+ + ▲		+		
Sardegna	+ + + + +	+ + + + +		▲	+ + +	+ + + + + +		+ +
Italy	+ + + +		+	+		+ + + +		+ + + + + +

CALCULATIONS BASED ON MOVING AVERAGE

Equation	Ip = a1.Ic + a2.I(o-c) + a3. ▲GVA(+t)			Ip = b1.Ic(-t) + b2.I(o-c)(-t)		Ip = c1.Ic + c2.I(o-c) + c3. ▲GVA(-t)			L = d1.Ip(-t)
Variable	Ic	I(o-c)	▲GVA	Ic	I(o-c)	Ic	I(o-c)	▲GVA	Ip
Time lag	0 1 2	0 1 2	0 1 2	0 1 2	0 1 2	0 1 2	0 1 2	0 1 2	0 1 2
Region									
Abruzzi	+ + +	+ + +	+ +	+	+	+ + + +	+ + +	+	
Campania	+	+	+	+	+	+	+		+ + +
Marche	+ + +	+ + +		+ + + +	+ + +	+ +	+ + +		+ + +
Puglia	+ + +	+ + +	+ +	+ + +	+ + +	+ +	+ + +	+ +	+ + +
Sardegna		+ +			+ + +		+		
Italy	+ + +	+			+ + +	+	+	+	+ + +

Table 9.2   Results of regression analysis for Italy; only statistically significant coefficients, based on a confidence level > 95%, are shown

9.4   Results of the Model for The Netherlands

Next, the same model experiments were applied to Dutch regions. Regression analysis was applied to four major regions in The Netherlands (viz., Noord-Nederland, Oost-Nederland, West-Nederland, Zuid-Nederland; see map in Figure 9.2) and for The Netherlands as a whole.

Figure 9.2.   Map of the four Dutch regions used in the empirical study

In the Dutch case study the necessary data - except the ERDF Commitments - from the Central Bureau of Statistics were obtained. All value variables are expressed in Mio. DFL (Dutch guilders; all variables at current prices[1]). ERDF Commitments data were obtained from Eurostat and converted in Dutch guilders. Only for the last three years (1988 - 1990) estimates had to be made for some variables. The results are presented in Table 9.3. This table can be read in the same way as Table 9.1. and 9.2.

We have only presented here the results for a confidence level > 95%. Furthermore, the only important difference compared to Tables 9.1 and 9.2 is that for some regions in The Netherlands the ERDF Commitments are not considered in the regression analyses because these regions did not receive any or hardly any payments from the ERDF in the past fifteen years (West-Nederland and Oost-Nederland, respectively). From this empirical study we can also conclude that the regression

---

1

In the Dutch case study we have also undertaken a regression analysis for the simple explanatory model in terms of variables expressed in constant prices. The results were not significantly better compared to the analyses based on variables at current prices. However, this is probably due to the lack of proper specific index figures for all relevant variables used in the model.

CALCULATIONS BASED ON ABSOLUTE DATA

Equation	Ip = a1 Ic + a2 I(o-c) + a3 ΔGVA(+t)	Ip = b1 Ic(-1) + b2 I(o-c)(-t)	Ip = c1 Ic + c2 I(o-c) + c3 ΔGVA(-t)	L = d1 Ip(-t)
Variable / Time lag	Ic: 0 1 2 3 4 5 / I(o-c): 0 1 2 3 4 5 / ΔGVA: 0 1 2 3 4 5	Ic: 0 1 2 3 4 5 / I(o-c): 0 1 2 3 4 5	Ic: 0 1 2 3 4 5 / I(o-c): 0 1 2 3 4 5 / ΔGVA: 0 1 2 3 4 5	Ip: 0 1 2 3 4 5
Region				
Noord / Oost / West / Zuid	@ @ ▲	+ ▲ + ▲ + + ▲	@ @ ▲	+ + ▲ + ▲ + ▲ ▲	@ @ ▲	+ + ▲ + + ▲ ▲	+ ▲ + ▲ ▲ ▲ ▲
The Netherlands	+ +	+ ▲ + +	+ ▲

CALCULATIONS BASED ON MOVING AVERAGE

Equation	Ip = a1 Ic + a2 I(o-c) + a3 ΔGVA(+t)	Ip = b1 Ic(-1) + b2 I(o-c)(-t)	Ip = c1 Ic + c2 I(o-c) + c3 ΔGVA(-t)	L = d1 Ip(-t)
Variable / Time lag	Ic: 0 1 2 / I(o-c): 0 1 2 / ΔGVA: 0 1 2	Ic: 0 1 2 / I(o-c): 0 1 2	Ic: 0 1 2 / I(o-c): 0 1 2 / ΔGVA: 0 1 2	Ip: 0 1 2
Region				
Noord / Oost / West / Zuid	@ + + + ▲ + + + + +	@ ▲ + ▲ + + + + +	@ + + + + + + +	+ ▲ ▲ + + +
The Netherlands	+ +	+ + +	+ +	▲ ▲

Table 9.3 Results of regression analysis for The Netherlands; only statistically significant coefficients based on a confidence level > 95% are shown.
Legend:
@ = variable Ic is not considered because of absence in region concerned
Lc = ERDF Commitments
I(o-c) = Public investments -/- ERDF Commitments
GVA = Change in Gross Value Added
L = Total employment
+ = 0.5 < R-squared adjusted < 1
▲ = R-squared adjusted < 0.5

analyses based on moving averages perform much better compared to the results based on absolute data. The difference is for the Dutch case study even more clear than for the Italian case study. In contrast to the Italian case study, the investment equation based on conventional behaviour (viz., equation (9.3)) appeared to show the best results compared to the other two investment equations. This is mainly caused by the fact that the variable "change in Gross Value Added" is performing badly in these two investment equations. When we eliminate this variable in the model, the results are to a large extent similar for the three investment equations.

A look at the separate variables shows that public investments give the best results when the calculations are based on absolute data. The application of moving averages leads to very good results for the variable "ERDF Commitments". The moderate results of the public investments - compared to the Italian case study - may be understood from the less satisfactory way these data were estimated in the case of the Italian data. Furthermore, it appears that the change in Gross Value Added has hardly a positive significant relationship on private investments (this variable had also in the Italian case study the least good results, although not as poor as in the Dutch case). A possible explanation is the indirect nature of the effects of this variable on private investments. It appears that the employment equation is also performing quite well and that there is no relevant difference due to the use of different time lags when the calculations are based on moving averages. The results based on absolute data show that a shorter time lag leads to better results regarding public investments.

9.5.   **Concluding Remarks**

The simple explanatory model based on regression analysis appears to be more powerful compared to the frequency table analysis, both as a hypothesis testing device and as a mechanism for yielding estimates of the consequences of ERDF expenditures. The results of this simple explanatory model show that there are several regions which (for different time lags) have been positively influenced by ERDF Commitments. Essentially, it is possible to show the extent of influence by means of the values of the reaction coefficients of the ERDF Commitments on the private investments.

In the empirical studies for Italy and The Netherlands, it was clear that the ERDF expenditures in the past have influenced the private investments in the regions considered. According to the simple explanatory model there is some evidence that the effects differ between the regions supported by the ERDF. If we compare the regions in terms of the number of positive reaction coefficients for ERDF commitments (for different investment equations and time lags used), it appears that investments in some regions are more influenced by the ERDF Commitments than in other regions. Given the aggregate ERDF figures used, it is not entirely clear whether these differences between regions are due to a different nature of projects supported by the ERDF in specific regions. Hence, more region-specific case study research is needed.

PART D

METHODOLOGY OF EVALUATION IN TRANSPORTATION PLANNING

Chapter 10

EVALUATION AND CONFLICT ANALYSIS IN PLANNING

10.1. Conflicts in Evaluation

Modern societies demonstrate an increasing complexity. The impact patterns of decisions and actions of individuals and groups are often intricate, far-reaching and conflicting. In the recent past, this has provoked the need for many kinds of impact assessment analyses, for instance, environmental assessment, socio-economic assessment, technology assessment, etc. Impact analysis however is a necessary but not yet sufficient stage in (transportation) planning (see Chapter 3 - 5); impacts also have to be judged. Especially the field of public policy-making is often encountering difficult evaluation problems regarding the impacts of choice alternatives. In this context, various types of conflicts may be distinguished:

- **inter-actor conflicts**; examples of such conflicts are differences in priorities attached to mobility growth vis-à-vis environmental quality by **various groups** in society (e.g., the car lobby versus environmentalists) or **different decision-making bodies** (e.g., a ministry of transportation infrastructure versus a local city council);

- **inter-regional conflicts**; examples of such conflicts are the geographical transmission of negative externalities, notably, waste emission to **neighbouring regions** (for instance, the Rhine pollution) or to the **earth as a whole** (for instance, ocean pollution, ozonization, acid rain, etc.);

- **inter-temporal conflicts**; examples of such conflicts are **backward** conflicts emerging from the preservation of our cultural and natural heritage (e.g., monuments) and **forward** conflicts emerging from the present use of scarce resources which may be detrimental to the interest of future generations (e.g., depletion of scarce natural resources);

-   **intra-person conflicts**; such conflicts emanate as a result of contradictory interests **within one actor or decision-maker** (e.g., a person with an environment-conscious constituency who has at the same time a conspicuous consumption pattern). One may even argue that the latter type of conflict is essentially the source of the emergence of the other conflicts mentioned above. In any case, conflicts emerge in case of different interests regarding different choice options.

In view of the risk of biased decisions emerging from the existence of various types of conflict in public decision-making, there is a need for a more comprehensive evaluation methodology which is more tailor-made in regard to a multiplicity of considerations of policy-makers.

The emphasis on a broader judgement framework for policy decisions - based among others on financial/economic, socio-economic, environmental, energy, equity and spatial-physical criteria - is a logical consequence of the interwoven structure of advanced societies, in which interest conflicts, external effects and social interactions at different levels co-exist. Consequently, in public choice theory it has become more and more common to evaluate public plans or proposals in a more integrated and multidisciplinary welfare framework which is complementary to a single private economic or monetary approach (cf. Filippi et al., 1992).

Income **per capita** (or net economic benefit) has since long been used as the traditional measure for the economic performance of a country, a region, or a transport system. This measure has formed the major (neoclassical) criterion for judging economic developments, welfare increases, growth perspectives and the social value of public plans (including transport infrastructure plans).

In the recent past several authors have criticized this unidimensional welfare criterion for several reasons (see for a review Nijkamp, 1980, and Rietveld, 1980). This measure may to some extent be appropriate in a perfectly competitive system marked by full information and a fully operating price system, but in reality such a system hardly exists. But even under such 'ideal' conditions many essential elements of human life (e.g., residential living conditions, quality of working life, safety risk, equity and national independence) cannot be translated into a common (monetary) denominator or 'numéraire'. Especially the environmental externalities have made us aware of the severe limitations of the measuring rod of money.

Consequently, income or benefit cannot plausibly be considered as the only reliable and meaningful indicator for measuring welfare increases. Especially in the past decade the insight has grown that welfare is essentially a multidimensional variable which comprises **inter alia** (average) income, growth potential, environmental quality, distributional equity, supply of public facilities, safety, accessibility and so forth. Consequently, the welfare of countries, cities or groups in society should be represented by a vector profile (encompassing various relevant welfare constituents) instead of by an undimensional scalar monetary indicator.

Especially in transportation planning we are often facing a situation with controversial issues. For instance, the savings in time caused by new infrastructure investments can in principle be assessed by means of monetary (cost-benefit) methods (see e.g., Nijkamp and Perrels, 1987), but the rise in safety (or the higher probability of survival) can hardly be expressed in meaningful monetary units (mainly due to the limitations inherent in human capital theory; see Blauwens, 1984). A social cost-benefit analysis in transportation planning can therefore at best be a partial approach. More complete and satisfactory evaluation tools which are able to incorporate also a great variety of potential conflicts are needed.

10.2. Methods of Conflict Analysis in Evaluation

The literature on methods for conflict analysis in evaluation is rich. Various methods have been devised in the past in order to evaluate the pros and cons of different choice options. A simple method is **a checklist** approach in which the impacts of various options (e.g., transportation plans) are systematically listed according to relevant judgement criteria. This method is a survey table approach rather than a real evaluation tool.

A more interesting endeavour is provided by a **strength-weakness** analysis in which the strong and weak scores of choice alternatives are systematically recorded and compared, so that a first attempt can be made to eliminate less relevant choice options.

This elimination procedure may be extended by means of a **sieve analysis** in which - by means of critical threshold values or minimum achievement/performance values - inferior choice options can be eliminated.

Of course, in this framework also **cost-benefit analysis** has to be mentioned, or complementary methods such as cost-effectiveness analysis.

The problems inherent in assessing net social benefits on the basis of a common monetary denominator have led to the popularity of **multiple criteria analysis** in public planning, as this method does not require the use of money value in evaluating conflicting options and is more flexible in practical choice situations. This class of evaluation tools will be discussed more extensively later on in Chapter 11.

Finally, also various intermediate methods between multiple criteria analysis and cost-benefit analysis have to be mentioned here, viz., the **planning balance sheet method** (see Lichfield et al., 1975) and the **goals-achievement method** (see Hill, 1973). Clearly, **monitoring** may also be mentioned as a systematic, regular and deliberate action of collecting and analyzing relevant information on the performance of a given choice option (or set of options).

In all evaluation tools for conflicting choice options the choice of **evaluation indicators** - to be included in an **effect score matrix** - is of crucial importance, as this determines to a large extent the (estimated) performance of the alternatives at hand. Special attention has to be given here to the use of so-called achievement **norms** or **standards**, i.e., indicators on the desired performance of a plan or policy.

All above mentioned methods and approaches may form meaningful elements of a decision support approach to (transportation) planning.

The ambitions of an evaluation procedure for conflicting plans or alternatives may show a considerable range. Examples are:
-       a clarification and structuring of necessary information on choice options in view of policy decisions to be taken;
-       a reduction in the number of feasible alternatives to be judged;
-       a partial or complete ranking of all desirable choice options.

Evaluation analysis serves to provide rules for a systematic and consistent treatment of information in view of the above mentioned aims. In other words, the meaning of evaluation for public decision making regarding investment planning is **not** primarily the identification of **the optimal** and **unambiguous** solution, but rather the **rationalization** of the decision problem at hand, either in substantive terms or in procedural terms (see Simon, 1976). This means that an evaluation should focus on:

-       the provision of all relevant **information** on the judgement criteria (including opportunity costs, uncertainties, employment effects, energy use, safety or pollution effects);

-       the generation of all relevant **alternatives** (e.g., various routes of a new motorway),

-       the consideration of **interest conflicts** (e.g., environmentalists versus supporters of mobility growth);

-       the treatment of different **priorities** for various impacts (e.g., employment versus budget equilibrium);

-       the development of **procedures** and **techniques** which guarantee the **best use** of the available information, given the institutional and policy framework (e.g., process planning, multi-level planning, interactive policy-making).

Thus a series of sequential steps (including feedback loops) has to be undertaken.

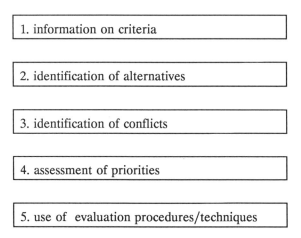

Figure 10.1.   Structure of evaluation procedure

The results of this comprehensive evaluation procedure are dependent on the available information and on the aims set by the responsible (public) decision-maker(s). Sometimes only an assessment of all impacts (short-term and long-term) of an investment plan is already sufficient, but in other cases much more emphasis has to be placed on differences in priorities, on tradeoff analysis, or on procedural questions. Thus an evaluation framework should be sufficiently flexible to cover all these different demands. In addition, an evaluation framework should make the choice conflicts and the consequences of choices more transparant. Finally, an evaluation problem should have a learning character, so that an evaluation framework may be used as a tool in process planning. This implies that - in general - an evaluation technique for alternative investment projects should be comprehensible for the decision maker(s) concerned, so that applicability and simplicity have to be strived for in any evaluation analysis (in addition to the requirements specified for impact analysis in Chapters 3 - 5). These conditions hold for both the provision of information on impacts or interest conflicts and the discrimination (i.e., ranking and/or selection) between alternative plans or projects. In Section 10.3, the various stages of the above mentioned evaluation framework will successively be discussed. It should be noticed that this framework is especially relevant for non-routine decision problems, like the construction of a new railway system, granting a permission for building a new shopping centre, etc.

10.3. Elements of Evaluation

In the present section the five elements of Figure 10.1 will be discussed in greater detail.

10.3.1. Information on criteria

As explained before, a multidimensional evaluation of public plans has to be based on a broad and representative set of criteria. These criteria may be different in nature, for instance, private economic (investment costs, rate of return, scale economies, etc.), socio-economic (employment, income distribution, access to facilities), environmental (pollution, deterioration of natural areas, noise, etc.), energy (use of energy, technological innovation, risk, etc.), spatial-physical planning (congestion, population density, accessibility, etc.), and so forth. They may include both monetary criteria and intangible criteria, quantitative and qualitative criteria, etc. In addition to gathering the necessary data, one has to process these data in a meaningful way. Thus, an impact table (or effect score matrix) for such plans may be rather detailed.

In general, the human mind has a fairly limited ability to digest a large amount of information which is at the same different in nature. Psychological experiments have demonstrated that - on average - the reliability and consistency of human decisions decreases significantly when more than approximately **seven** items are to be judged simultaneously (the 'magical number seven'; see Miller, 1978). Therefore, it seems to be reasonable to select first a set of major important criteria (no more than seven), and next to make a subdivision into subcriteria (no more than seven), etc., so that a logical hierarchical framework emerges which provides a surveyable picture of all impact criteria (see Figure 10.2).

Main criteria	**Subcriteria**
I	=
II	=
.	
.	
.	
.	
VII	=

Figure 10.2. A logical ordering of a multidimensional evaluation problem.

Examples of main classes of criteria are: macro-economic effects, labour market effects, social effects, micro-economic and financial effects, environmental effects, energy effects, safety effects, etc. It is clear that the list of main criteria and subcriteria will differ for each specific evaluation problem at hand. Sometimes, however, the policy framework and decision problem are not sharply demarcated, so that informal groups may also influence the set of relevant decision criteria. The **ultimate selection of relevant judgement criteria is a political responsibility,** supported by necessary information from the side of experts or analysts. It should be noted that the evaluation of plans or projects in a process planning framework often gives rise to the introduction of new (or adjusted) criteria which were neglected during the initial stages of the evaluation procedure. Therefore, the procedure should be sufficiently flexible to include new evaluation criteria during a later stage; this also requires feedbacks in Figure 10.1.

The selection of judgement criteria should not primarly be based on the availability of reliable information, but rather on the relevance of these criteria in the policy/evaluation framework. It will be shown later that also soft and qualitative information can be taken into account, so that there is no need to exclude imprecise or fuzzy information.

It should also be mentioned that the information on the criteria may either refer to either a static (or comparative static) framework (in which the time dimension does not play an important role) or a dynamic framework (in which long-term impacts and sequential multi-temporal impacts play a dominant role). It is evident that the use of dynamic evaluation models requires much more information; furthermore, it may also be necessary to employ a social rate of discount to translate - in an initial period - all future impacts into present values.

Finally, in this context it is also appropriate to make a distinction between the construction phase and the operating phase of new plans or projects, as the time horizon of impacts may be completely different for both phases.

10.3.2. Identification of alternatives

The evaluation of public plans or projects requires a judgement of all relevant alternatives. The number of alternatives may vary between 2 (should a certain project be undertaken or not?), any discrete number (for example, 10 alternative routes of a highway) and infinity (for example, the quantity of gasoline to be imported). It should be noted that this subdivision of evaluation projects rests only on a technical criterion concerning the number of alternatives.

The problem of only two alternatives is essentially a 0-1 selection problem in which a choice has to be made between the **status quo** and a new situation. Sometimes an intermediate stage has to be inserted, especially when the information is not yet sufficient to take a decision. In the latter case, one faces essentially a situation with three alternative choices: 'yes', 'no', 'delay in order to get more information' (the so-called principle of trichotomic segmentation).

The **discrete** evaluation problem (i.e., a distinct number of alternatives) is very common in normal plan and project evaluation problems, in which a choice out of a finite number of alternatives has to be made. Both cost-benefit analysis and multiple criteria analysis are addressing themselves to these kinds of discrete judgement analyses. Normally, most discrete evaluation methods are characterized by multiple judgement criteria, so that **multiple criteria** methods seem to be plausible evaluation methods (cf. Boyce et al., 1970; Giuliano, 1985; Miller, 1985; Shefer and Voogd, 1989).

It is clear that the number of alternatives may sometimes be very high. In such cases it is useful to first identify a subset of alternatives which are clearly discriminating. After a first selection of the most relevant projects, one may next choose the most desirable project from the set of reasonably relevant projects.

Finally, the **continuous** evaluation problem is concerned with a large number of alternatives. An example is the number of barrels of oil to be imported in a certain year. This import may depend on the production and consumption in the country concerned, the technological efficiency, the search for substitutes, climatological conditions, etc. The ultimate oil import policy may be based on several criteria: costs of oil, international political uncertainties, desired degree of self-sufficiency, etc. Such continuous policy problems based on multiple criteria (or objectives) are usually called **multiple objective programming** models. This leads to the following classification:

Number of alternatives	Type
2	zero-one
discrete	multicriteria methods
infinite	multiobjective programming models

It should also be mentioned that the total set of alternatives to be judged in an evaluation process is essentially also a matter of political responsibility. On the other hand, the expert or analyst should also take into account certain rules for designing and defining the alternative choice options to be judged:

-       the plans or projects should be feasible from a **technical** or **economic** viewpoint;

-       the plans or projects should meet at least certain **a priori** specified **standards** (for instance, employment levels, safety, pollution levels, risk, energy use);

-       the set of relevant plans or projects should fall within the 'envelope' of the various desires and options of groups in society and of the responsible decision-maker(s);

-       the various plans or projects should be defined in such a way that they are of **comparable size** (for example, it is less useful to evaluate a new big steel plant vis-à-vis a small bookstore);

-       the level of **information** (e.g., the impacts of the criteria) should be **comparable** for all plans or projects (for example, it is less meaningful to analyze in detail all employment impacts of investment project 1, if the impacts of a competing project 2 are only studied in a lucid way).

The ultimate combination of criteria and alternatives gives rise to the following impact matrix (or effect score matrix), which has to be measured in appropriate - but not necessarily in monetary - units (cf. also Dello, 1985) (see Figure 10.3).

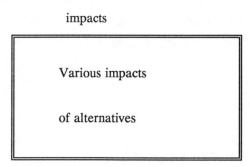

Figure 10.3.   An impact matrix

This impact matrix may contain cardinal (metric) information (e.g., number of jobs, length of a motorway), ordinal rankings (1,2,3 ...) or qualitative information (e.g., good, better, best).

The impact matrix can - without any further information about priorities - be used in several ways. In the first place, one may carry out a **dominance analysis** by examining whether a certain project (or a set of projects) is better or worse than the remaining ones. In this way the set of relevant projects to be evaluated can sometimes be truncated to a more tractable subset. It is essentially a particular kind of checklist method.

Secondly, one may carry out a **strength - weakness analysis** by identifying for each project $i(i = 1, ..., I)$ whether these outcomes of the criteria give a high or a low contribution to the policy criteria at hand (see Figure 10.4).

	Favourable outcome	Unfavourable outcome
Criterion 1	plan 1, 5	plan 2, 8
.	.	.
.	.	.
.	.	.
.	.	.
.	.	.
Criterion J	.	.

Figure 10.4. A representation of a strength-weakness analysis.

In this way one may easily identify which plans or projects are in agreement with a certain policy criterion (or set of criteria).

Thirdly, one may also **rank** all projects for each separate criterion according to the degree they contribute to that criterion (Figure 10.5). This approach implies only to a restructuring of the initially available information, but gives nevertheless meaningful insights.

Criteria	Rank order of plans (or projects)
Criterion 1 . . . . . Criterion J	Plan 1 > plan 3 > plan 7 ....

Figure 10.5. Ordinal rankings in an adjusted impact table

10.3.3. **Identification of conflicts**

The selection of a public plan or project out of a set of competing alternatives is usually characterized by conflicting views. In general, a decision-maker wants to implement a plan or project which has a maximum positive impact on income or employment, while at the same time it does no harm to environmental quality or safety or to the stock of energy resources. Such a utopian situation, however, is not likely to exist, so that in general a decision-maker has to make a certain tradeoff among conflicting criteria. The analyst may help to explain the nature of such conflicts. A useful way is to construct for each alternative project a so-called **conflict matrix** or order J x J which gives a pairwise indication of conflicts between successive criteria based on qualitative information (see **Figure 10.6**).

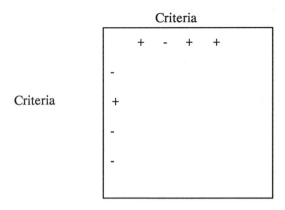

Figure 10.6. A qualitative conflict matrix for outcomes of evaluation criteria

Such a matrix can be filled with qualitative symbols having the following meaning: + + + (strongly complementary), + + (moderately complementary), + (weakly complementary), 0 (neutral), - (weakly conflicting), -- (moderately conflicting), --- (strongly conflicting).

It may sometimes be useful to disaggregate the conflict matrix for certain groups which are affected by the implementation of a certain plan or project, because the welfare impacts of a given project may have different impacts on different socio-economic groups. Analogously, one may also carry out a spatial disaggregation in order to cover the problem of different project impacts through space (for example, the impacts of a reconstruction of the inner city upon all urban districts).

One should also be aware of the fact that conflicting interests among groups may lead to a criticism regarding the set of alternatives or the set of criteria to be considered: every group wants to have its interest also reflected in the choice of the set of alternative projects or the decision criteria to be judged. In such cases, it is plausible that the expert or analyst tries to examine all combinations of alternatives and criteria which are judged to be relevant by all successive groups. This choice, of course, depends also on institutional structures in the decision-making process.

Finally, conflicts may also emerge due to lack of coordination in the decision procedure itself. Especially in the case of a multilevel policy structure or of a multiple committee structure frictions and conflicts are very likely to arise. For example, two cities may regard the construction of a new motorway connecting the two cities as necessary, whereas the state government may regard such a decision as an unpermissible destruction of the scarce open space in the area concerned.

In conclusion, the expert's task is not to solve all policy conflicts, but to contribute to a rationalization of the decision process by means of a systematic presentation of all impacts and all frictions.

10.3.4. Assessment of priorities

In as far as non-monetary values (e.g., intangibles) are included in the evaluation method, any choice among alternatives is (implicitly or explicitly) based on priorities regarding the successive policy criteria for judging the plan or project concerned.

If the decision-maker is unable to specify in advance his priorities or weights, the analyst's taks is rather modest. In that case he has the following tasks:

- to construct in a surveyable manner the whole impact matrix,
- to identify all kinds of conflicts inherent in the evaluation problem at hand, and
- to examine whether certain alternatives in the impact matrix are dominant (so that these plans or projects may be subject to further analysis) or whether certain alternatives are dominated (so that they may be excluded from a further evaluation).

Especially such a dominance analysis is very often extremely important, as it allows the researcher to restrict the set of projects to be judged and even sometimes to rank the successive projects (or subsets thereof).

If however, the evaluation of alternatives has to be based on political priorities (weights) regarding the decision criteria, the analyst's task becomes more ambitious, as he has to estimate these priorities. Several methods can be employed to assess political priorities:

- derivation of priorities on the basis of an **ex post** analysis of decisions taken in the past for similar problems. Clearly, this **revealed preference** approach is not useful for unique (i.e., non-repetitive) decision problems.
- derivation of priorities on the basis of **official documents and statements** from the side of the responsible decision-maker. This approach is sometimes useful for gathering information regarding general issues and policy objectives, but normally it is less helpful in assessing precisely preferences for detailed policy criteria.
- direct assessment of priorities on the basis of **interviews or questionnaires** among the decision-makers. Here one may use paired comparison methods, ranking methods, scaling methods, rating methods, trade-off methods or interactive assessment methods (see Nijkamp et al., 1990). This **stated preference** technique is often a fruitful method, although it is a serious problem that in practice many policy-makers - for obvious reason - do not like to express their preferences directly and in advance.

- 'fictitious' assessment of priorities on the basis of consistent **policy scenarios** reflecting hypothetical but otherwise reasonable priorities for the policy criteria at hand. This is often a useful and practical method, because it does not commit directly the policy-maker, while on the other hand the consequences of such fictitious policy priorities can easily be traced. Such scenarios may also be derived from official documents.

It is evident that in many choice situations the information about policy preferences is fairly weak. In such cases it is always necessary to carry out a sensitivity analysis with respect to the values of the policy weights. Alternatively, in case of soft information one may also employ **(multidimensional) scaling methods** (see also Chapter 4). Multidimensional scaling methods are techniques which translate soft (ordinal or qualitative) information in a consistent way into cardinal (metric) information. In that case, standard numerical operations can again be applied (see Nijkamp, 1980). Clearly, if the impact matrix contains also inaccurate or unreliable data, a sensitivity analysis should also be applied.

Finally, it should be mentioned that different decision groups (for instance, in a multi-layer structure) may have different priorities, so that the definition of a unique set of priorities is not always possible. In that case, it is more appropriate to assess several alternative priority sets for the relevant policy criteria and to calculate successively the consequences of each separate set. The results can then be further analyzed with a view to the possibility of finding a compromise solution.

10.3.5. Classification of evaluation problems

Any evaluation technique for judging the desirability of public plans or projects should be logically and consistently connected with the nature of the decision problem concerned. Given the unique nature of many decision problems, there is no unambiguous method with a universal validity, and hence each type of decision problem may require its own specific evaluation method.

Depending on the problems at hand and on the precision of the data used, several subdivisions of evaluation methods can be made:

- **discrete** versus **continuous** evaluation problems (discussed above);

- **soft** versus **hard** evaluation problems; soft problems include qualitative or ordinal information on impacts of alternatives or on priorities/weights, whereas hard problems are based on quantitative (i.e., mainly cardinal) information;

- **static** versus **dynamic** evaluation problems (discussed above);

- **multi-person** (or **multi-committee**) versus **single-person** (or **single-committee**) evaluation problems; in the case of multi-person or multi-committee problems one has to take into account the variation in preferences, while one may also consider the possibility of a multi-level decision structure;

- evaluation problems based on the **generation of efficient alternative solutions** versus those based on the **selection of one ultimate alternative**; in the first case the procedure aims at identifying only non-dominated solutions, i.e., solutions for which the value of one policy objective cannot be improved without reducing the value of a competing objective; in the second case the procedure aims at finding one alternative which is considered as satisfactory after the articulation of preferences. An intermediate approach may be based on the identification of a set of dominating alternatives;

- **single-step** versus **process** evaluation problems; the first category aims at finding the most satisfactory solution as an unambiguous result at a certain point in time; the second category considers policy making as a process during which one may add successively more information, so that the ultimate solution is identified in a series of successive steps.

10.4.   Interactive Evaluation Procedures

The notion of process planning refers to the use of interactive evaluation procedures. Interactive evaluation procedures are important vehicles in decision support systems; they are based on an information exchange between analyst and decision-maker, especially for situations in which the decision-maker has not specified his preferences or weights. The basic feature of such procedures is that the analyst suggests a certain provisional feasible compromise solution to the decision-maker, while next the decision-maker may respond to this suggestion by indicating which policy objectives in this provisional solution are unsufficiently fulfilled. This provisional solution may be determined by means of a standard compromise algorithm.

Thus, instead of presenting directly a final solution, the analyst has to develop a learning procedure in order to reach in a limited number of steps a satisfactory final compromise solution. Consequently, the first compromise solution is only a trial solution which has to be presented to the decision-maker(s) as a frame of reference for judging alternative efficient solutions. The easiest way to carry out such an interactive procedure is to ask the decision-maker(s) which values of the policy objectives are satisfactory and which are unsatisfactory (and hence have to be improved).

This can easily be done by using a checklist which includes all values of the first compromise solutions of the policy objectives (see also Figure 10.7).

Values of provisional	Satisfactory ?	
compromise solutions	yes	no
criterion 1 criterion 2 . . . . criterion J		

Figure 10.7. Checklist in interactive evaluation procedure

Let us suppose that there are K criteria (K < J) which are judged as unsatisfactory by the decision maker(s). This implies that a new solution has to be identified which is such that these K criteria lead to a better performance. Consequently, all solutions which have a worse performance may be eliminated. After such a truncation of the set of feasible solutions a new provisional compromise solution may be calculated which can be dealt with in the same way, until finally a convergent satisfactory solution will be reached. The steps of such an interactive procedure are presented in Figure 10.8.

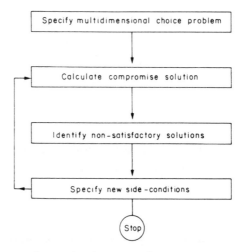

Figure 10.8. Steps of interactive evaluation procedure

The advantages of such an interactive procedure are:
-        they provide information to the decision maker(s) in a stepwise way;
-        they can easily be included in a process planning;
-        they lead to an active role of the decision-maker(s);
-        they avoid the prior specification of preferences or weights (though they can be inferred **ex post**).

10.5.   **Evaluation: Retrospect and Prospect**

Evaluation aims at rationalizing multi-faceted decision problems, either **ex ante** or **ex post**. Given the multidimensional nature of most decision problems, evaluation is usually confronted with conflicting options. This holds true for decision-making at both the individual and the collective level.

Until the beginning of the seventies, the conventional wisdom in (socio)economic choice theory taught that rational decision-making could be formally described and achieved by means of the maximization of a single objective function subject to a set of constraints. Traditional utility theory, social welfare theory, cost-benefit theory, linear and non-linear programming theory, dynamic and dual control theory were all based on the assumption of a rational decision-maker whose preferences could be encaptured adequately by an unambiguous and well defined objective function. Furthermore, the decision problem was assumed to be well specified, without any fuzzy or qualitative features (i.e., a cardinal measurement level).

However, from the beginning of the seventies the above mentioned standard approaches have increasingly been challenged and criticized for both **theoretical** and **practical** reasons.

Theoretically, the 'optimizer' concepts have been questioned since long and - instead of this abstract notion - the 'satisficer' concept has been introduced (cf. Simon, 1981). Furthermore, the assumption of an unidimensional choice criterion has been criticized, as this concept is mainly based on commensurable and cardinally measurable elements, while neglecting non-metric choice arguments (cf. Nijkamp, 1979, 1980; Rietveld, 1980; Voogd, 1983). Finally, the restrictive assumption of the non-conflicting nature of decision-making has provoked new approaches in the area of conflict and choice analysis (see Keeney and Raiffa, 1976; Spronk, 1981).

From a **practical** point of view, traditional choice analysis demonstrated also many severe shortcomings: intangible effects could not be taken into consideration; the importance of present decisions for future generations could hardly be assessed; the political priorities or value judgements of decision-makers were usually unknown and conflicts between decision-makers at inididifferent policy levels were hard to integrate in an operational choice analysis (cf. Cohon, 1978; Sinden and Worrell, 1979; Zeleny, 1982).

According to Nijkamp and Spronk (1981) the lack of relevance of choice theory for practical decision-making is due to the following factors:

- the premises of the methods are not valid;

- the abstraction level of the methods is too high;

- the methods do not fit into the decision maker's mind due to lack of training in employing such methods;

- the data necessary for applying the methods are not available;

-       the results of the methods are not translated as concrete or applicable solutions.

The above mentioned limitations became more apparent in the seventies, when many negative externalities (environmental pollution, traffic congestion, lack of safety, exhaustion of raw materials and of energy resources) emerged which could not be reconciled with traditional unidimensional evaluation criteria. In addition, social and political conflicts came to the fore, in which decision agencies were confronted with diverse interest groups and heterogeneous aspirations. Consequently, in public policy making and planning the assumption of 'the decision maker' has become a fiction, and the assumption of a single (unidimensional) evaluation criterion has become increasingly unrealistic in policy evaluation.

Admittedly, several attempts have been made to bridge these gaps by designing adjusted evaluation methods (such as social cost-benefit analysis, cost-effectiveness analysis, compensation methods, etc.), but these methods are in general only appropriate in a fully operating price and market system based on full information. In general, the presence of (positive or negative) externalities, risks, long-term effects, spatial spillovers, unreconcilable interests and qualitative information precludes a meaningful use and application of such unidimensional evaluation techniques. These factors have led to two new developments, viz.,:

-       the rise of multiple criteria and multiple objective decision methods in planning;

-       the use of disaggregate models of choice in individual choice analysis (see also Chapter 5).

All these methods aim at taking into account the heterogeneous, conflictual and qualitative aspects of complex choice problems. They all have one element in common, viz., the existence of a multiplicity of decision criteria or choice attributes. In this regard, multidimensional choice theory has become an important mode of thinking, especially as it is able to take account of a wide variety of diverging aspects inherent in any decision problem and to offer an operational framework for a multidisciplinary approach to practical choice situations. In this way, these modern methods may fulfil the specific and heterogeneous requirements imposed by decision-makers, choice processes and the practice of decision-making at both the individual and the collective level.

Instead of a narrow monetary view on impacts, modern multidimensional evaluation methods provide much broader information on - and insights into - the nature of real-world choice problems. It should be added however, that these new methods are not necessarily in contrast with traditional evaluation techniques such as cost-benefit and utility theory. They can in principle be integrated with a cost-benefit and utility framework; they are to a certain extent a natural follow-up of cost-benefit and utility analysis, especially because interest conflicts and intangible effects can be taken into account. These modern evaluation methods are also more acceptable for the practice of decision-making by including decision-makers and experts already from the beginning in an evaluation process. This may also lead to a more structured decision process, since the inventory, classification, valuation and judgement of different plan or project impacts are built up in a systematic way, based on well defined policy criteria and presented in a comprehensible way.

The previous observations have a particular relevance for transportation planning which is characterized by a blend of unpriced and priced values. At both the demand and the supply side there is a rich potential for applying various types of multiple criteria evaluation tools. Such methods will be discussed in greater detail in the next chapter.

Chapter 11

A SURVEY OF MULTIPLE CRITERIA EVALUATION METHODS

11.1. Introduction

After the discussion of multiple criteria evaluation as a tool in planning (see Chapter 10), we will now present a concise overview of some technical and substantive aspects of multiple criteria analysis. Multiple criteria analysis has essentially its roots in the history of economics. A first major contribution to the development of multiple criteria decision analysis was given by Pareto in 1896 in his trade-off analysis which generated the concept of Pareto-optimality. Pareto was looking for a criterion to judge a certain distribution of goods among people. In his opinion, interpersonal utility comparisons were hardly possible, so that an unambiguous social welfare function approach was not very meaningful (see Tarascio, 1986). Thus, he ended up with the much weaker concept of Pareto-optimality: a distribution of goods among people is Pareto-optimal, when it is impossible to improve a given person's utility performance without making other people worse off. Clearly, the Pareto-optimality concept is closely related to the efficiency concept which plays a major role in multiple criteria decision analysis.

Approximately half a century later, Koopmans (1951) introduced a similar concept in activity analysis. The problem addressed was, whether it is possible to make an optimal selection in a production process without any information about the prices of inputs and outputs. The conclusion was that indeed a distinction can be made between efficient and inefficient processes. The latter will never be chosen, whatever the prices of inputs and outputs may be. In the same year, Kuhn and Tucker(1951) introduced the concept of vector maximization, which is also related to the efficiency concept.

After the formulation of these basic concepts, multiple criteria decision analysis did not immediately take off, however. Almost all efforts in decision analysis in the 1950s were devoted to the development of methods for single criterion decision-making,

169

especially linear programming. The fact that in the practice of decision-making usually more than one objective plays a role was not really recognized in the mainstream of research. Additional constraints served mainly to count for the existence of multiple objectives. This situation continued until the late 1960s, when suddenly an expansion of multiple objective-oriented decision analysis started.

This new interest in adjusted decision techniques was accompanied by substantial changes that took place in the field of planning and policy making. Planners and politicians became increasingly aware of the need for more integrated - or at least coherent - planning (see, e.g. McLoughlin, 1969). Especially the negative effects of post-war economic development on environmental quality made it clear that economic policies no longer could be pursued without paying explicit attention to external effects (e.g., on the environment). Thus, in many countries a tendency arose towards integration of economics, environmental, energy and physical planning. This integration did not only call for the development of models that were capable of indicating the mutual impacts among the various planning fields, but also for methods generating and/or selecting alternatives which had to be judged from multiple viewpoints. The latter is exactly the aim of multiple criteria decision methods. A related factor is that post-war welfare society reached a new stage in this period. Instead of one or a limited set of unambiguous policy objectives (such as the maximization of growth), a wide variety of interest groups called for more attention to neglected aspects of the economy (e.g. distributional problems, new scarcity). This led to a multi-actor conflict situation in society, which could not be covered by means of conventional decision analysis and which called for a multidimensional policy analysis.

An influential book in this period was a study by Johnson (1968), in which a strong plea is made for decision analysis in terms of multiple criteria. The development of multiple criteria decision analysis gained momentum in the 1970s. From 1972 onwards several conferences were held on multi-criteria decision making at one or two years' intervals (see Gal, 1983). The proceedings of these conferences strongly stimulated the development of this field. This holds especially true for the first one, edited by Cochrane and Zeleny (1973). In the 1970s an explosive growth of literature on multi-criteria decision analysis took place, and the bibliographies on this topic became longer and longer. Surveys on the subject can be found among others in Changkong and Haimes

(1983), Hwang and Yoon (1981), Nijkamp (1979, 1980), Nijkamp et al. (1990), Rietveld (1980), Sinden and Worrell (1979), Voogd (1983) and Zeleny (1982). Furthermore, a very interesting sketch of almost 100 multiple objective analyses can be found in Despontin et al. (1983).

In addition to contributions from economics and operations research, in other disciplines too (psychology, e.g.) various interesting contributions to multiple criteria decision analysis have been made. For instance, analyses of search behaviour in case of conflicting options and multiple alternatives have been made among others by Skull et al. (1970), Dawes (1980), Hansen (1972), Hollnagel (1977), Kornai (1971), May (1954), Meehl (1954), Pitz (1977), Reitman (1964), Shepard (1964) and Tversky (1972).

As mentioned in Chapter 10, multiple criteria evaluation aims at providing a systematic and policy-oriented contribution to the appraisal of alternatives. Usually, the plan effect (impact score) matrix plays a central role in an evaluation procedure. An illustrative example related to the construction of a new road is given in Table 11.1.

Criteria	Alternatives		
	A1	A2	A3
C1: costs	40	60	80
C2: travel time saving	25	30	20
C3: loss of natural area	2	1.5	1.75
C4: reduction in traffic accidents	4	5	10

Table 11.1.   An effect matrix for 3 alternative trajectories of a new road.

There is - as pointed out before - a wide variety of evaluation methods for judging alternative choice options. A usual distinction is that between **monetary** and **non-monetary** evaluation methods. First, the class of monetary methods will be discussed briefly (section 11.2.), while the remaining part of this chapter is devoted to non-monetary evaluation methods.

11.2. Monetary Evaluation Methods

The class of monetary evaluation methods mainly consists of **cost-benefit** analysis (and related methods like cost-effectiveness analysis and shadow project analysis).

Cost-benefit analysis (which was already briefly discussed in Chapter 10) may be interpreted as an evaluation method which provides - to the maximum possible extent - a quantified survey of all monetary advantages and disadvantages of alternative choice options by means of a systematic cost-benefit balance (including both the construction and the operational stage of a plan or project) (see e.g. Mishan, 1982).

A distinction has to be made between private cost and benefits **and** social costs and benefits. A private cost-benefit analysis only takes into consideration the pros and cons of a plan or project accruing directly and only to the actor concerned, while a social cost-benefit analysis adopts a broader scope by considering also all relevant positive and negative effects for those who are not directly involved (as a consumer or producer) in the plan or project under consideration. In other words, social cost-benefit analysis aims at assessing the socio-economic efficiency of a plan or project at large, mainly by assessing the social cost-benefit ratio.

Cost-effectiveness analysis has a more limited scope, as it aims to identify a choice alternative which - given the level of the intended effects - can be realized as efficient as possible (i.e., at minimum costs). Alternatively, one may also aim at maximizing the policy effects, given the level of available financial resources (see e.g. the Roskill Report, 1971).

In the case of both cost-benefit analysis and cost-effectiveness analysis various limitations hamper a comprehensive use of these methods, some major shortcoming being the neglect of **intangible** effects (related inter alia to safety, environmental quality, etc.), the choice of an unambiguous **social rate of discount,** and the **opportunity costs** of distribution changes as a result of transport planning. This may lead to a biased judgement of choice alternatives. Therefore, in the past various other directions have been explored. One example is the so-called **shadow project** approach, which is essentially based on a neo-classical compensation criterion: if a certain plan or project causes intangible effects (e.g., the destruction of an ecologically valuable landscape), then the costs of restoring this landscape in its original state have to be included as items in the social cost-benefit analysis (see e.g. Klaassen et al, 1974). However, this interesting approach can normally only be applied in case of substitutable or replenishable goods.

An alternative way is to refrain from any monetary judgement and to present only a **survey table** which includes in a detailed way all relevant effects (including distributional impacts and externalities). In the latter case an unambiguous choice (or a ranking of alternatives) cannot be made, although such a table provides no doubt useful insight for policy-makers. A good example of such a survey table method is the well-known **planning-balance sheet method** (see Lichfield et al, 1975).

In various situations, however, the ambitions and demands of policy-makers are higher than just a presentation of results of empirical investigation. Often a broader social evaluation of pros and cons of alternative choice possibilities is expected. As a complement to social cost-benefit analysis one may then use a multi-criteria analysis. This will be further discussed in subsequent sections.

11.3. Multi-criteria Evaluation Methods

Multi-criteria methods are appropriate to find a (complete or partial) ranking of choice alternatives that have to be judged on the basis of a broad (i.e. not exclusively monetary) set of decision or choice criteria. In various cases weighting procedures are used to arrive at an unambiguous solution, although the use of weights is not strictly necessary.

Like in all evaluation methods the use of a plan effect (or impact score) matrix (or table) is a central step in multi-criteria evaluation. This matrix contains for all choice alternatives the numerical estimates of outcomes of all relevant criteria, measured in their own appropriate dimensions (e.g., financial costs, reduction in traffic accidents, levels of air pollution, etc.).

Next, by confronting the **a priori** specified weights set for the judgement criteria with the plan-effect matrix, a ranking of alternatives may be obtained. There are, however, various procedures for confronting these two sets (depending amongst others on the level of precision of measurement of effects) and hence a wide variety of multi-criteria evaluation methods has been designed in the recent past, ranging from extremely simple to fairly complicated ones.

Various classifications of multi-criteria choice models may be made. In Chapter 10, the following typology for these models has inter alia been proposed: **discrete** multiple criteria models versus **continuous** multiple objective models, **hard information** models versus **soft information** models.

Discrete choice models display only a finite number of distinct feasible choice possibilities (courses of action, strategies, solutions, alternative plans or projects, etc.), while **continuous** models may encompass an infinite number of choice possibilities (as is usually the case in programming models).

Hard information means information measured on a cardinal scale, while **soft** information means information based on a qualitative (ordinal or nominal) scale. Clearly, one may also distinguish mixed information, in which the information is partly cardinal, partly qualitative. Consequently, the following typology may be used (see Table 11.2):

	cardinal information	qualitative information	mixed information
discrete multiple criteria evaluation models	I	III	V
continuous multiple objective programming models	II	IV	VI

Table 11.2.   A typology of multi-criteria choice models

For each of these classes various methods can be distinguished. In sections 11.4. and 11.5. a selected set of discrete multiple criteria evaluation models and continuous multiple objective programming models will successively be discussed (see also Nijkamp and Rietveld, 1987).

11.4.   **Discrete Multiple Criteria Evaluation Models**

11.4.1. **Introduction**

The main aim of discrete multiple criteria methods is to provide a rational basis for classifying a number of distinct choice possibilities (for instance, alternative policies, plans, neighbourhoods, regions, etc.), on the basis of multiple criteria. There are many different discrete multiple objective evaluation methods currently in use (see among others Kmietowicz and Pearman, 1981, Nijkamp, 1979, 1980, Nijkamp et al., 1990, Rietveld, 1980, Voogd, 1983). A major component in all these methods is the construction of a plan impact (or score) matrix representing all relevant effects of alternatives on relevant decision criteria. Next, in order to aggregate the information of the plan impact matrix in a manageable way, usually a weighting scheme is necessary which expresses the relative importance of the various criterion scores.

The impact matrix (see also Figure 10.3) will be denoted by the symbol P:

$$
P = \begin{matrix} p_{11} & \cdots\cdots & p_{1J} \\ \cdot & & \cdot \\ p_{I1} & & p_{IJ} \end{matrix}
$$
(11.1)

This matrix has elements P_{ij}, which represent the impact of alternative i (i = 1, ..., I) on the value of criterion j (j = 1, ..., J). In the case of a qualitative evaluation problem, p_{ij} may be measured on an ordinal, binary or nominal scale. However, it is not unusual that a part of the p_{ij} elements are quantitative in nature, i.e. some of the criterion effects are determined on a cardinal scale, whereas other effects are represented in a qualitative way. This is called a mixed data problem.

The set of weights provides information on the relative importance attached to the outcomes of the successive J criteria; they will be denoted by a vector λ:

$$
\lambda = (\lambda_1, ..., \lambda_J)^T
$$
(11.2.)

Clearly, usually the vector λ does not contain purely cardinal tradeoffs, but ordinal or binary weights. Most recently developed multiple criteria methods take explicit account of the 'soft' nature of such weights.

Now, the next step is the joint treatment of preference statements (weights) and impact matrices. As mentioned before, one may subdivide multicriteria methods into 'hard' and 'soft' evaluation problems. Hard problems deal with information measured at a cardinal (quantitative) level, whereas soft problems are based on information measured at an ordinal or binary (qualitative) level. Both types will successively be discussed.

11.4.2. Quantitative information

In this subsection some examples of 'hard' multiple criteria methods will be given, viz. the **weighted summation method** (Schimpeler and Grecco, 1986, Schlager, 1968, and

Kahne, 1975), the **discrepancy analysis technique** (Nijkamp, 1979) the **goals-achievement method** (Hill, 1973) and the **concordance approach** (Guigou, 1974, Roy, 1968, and Van Delft and Nijkamp, 1977).

The **weighted summation method** assigns quantitative weights to all judgement criteria and treats these weights as 'quasi-probabilities' which should add up to 1. Thus the expected value of the outcomes of each alternative plan can be calculated by multiplying the value obtained for each criterion by its appropriate weight and by summing the weighted values of all criteria. Thus the weighted score for a specific alternative i can be written as:

$$s_i = \sum_j \lambda_j p_{ij} \tag{11.3}$$

Essentially, the weighted summation method calculates the weighted average of all (standardized) criterion scores in the evaluation matrix. This method implies a rather rigid approach since it assumes a perfect linear substitution of the values of the various criteria, which is seldom true in practical applications.

Another method for 'hard' evaluation problems is **discrepancy analysis**. This approach attempts to rank the alternatives according to their discrepancy from a (hypothetical) optimum alternative. This optimum alternative corresponds to a set of predefined goals. Statistical correlation coefficients can then be used to identify the alternative that is most similar to the reference alternative. Although this method can be very attractive in combination with computer graphics, it should be used with care because the various discrepancies in the outcomes of an alternative plan or project cannot always be made sufficiently explicit.

A method which is related to discrepancy analysis and which is often applied in planning practice, is the **goals-achievement method**. This method links each criterion to a quantitative achievement level or target value. Evaluation essentially involves taking the achievement score for each alternative plan. The values are aggregated using a weighted summation procedure similar to that described above for the weighted summation method. Hence, a similar criticism holds for this approach. However, this approach can be quite attractive for evaluation problems which need to be treated with simple, standardized and straightforward methods, e.g. in approval procedures for governmental premiums.

The **concordance approach** is also widely used. This method is based on a pairwise comparison of alternatives, thus using only the metric interval characteristics of the various scores in the evaluation of the impact matrix. The basic idea is to measure the degree to which the scores and their associated weights confirm or contradict the dominant pairwise relationships among alternatives. The differences in weights and the differences in evaluation scores are usually analyzed separately.

The central concept in a concordance analysis is the so-called concordance index $c_{ii'}$. This index represents the extent to which alternative i is better than alternative i'. This index may be defined as the sum of weights attached to the criteria included in the so-called concordance set $c_{ii'}$; this is the set of all evaluation criteria for which alternative i in the impact matrix P is at least equally attractive as alternative i'. Clearly, this set can be determined irrespective of the level of information in the impact matrix. Hence, the concordance index can be defined as follows:

$$c_{ii'} \tag{11.4}$$

A dominating alternative can now be found by employing threshold values, relative dominance indicators, or other concepts from graph theory.

In an analogous way, one may define a discordance index. This index reflects the extent to which alternative i is worse than i'. Instead of using weights in this index, the corresponding relative pairwise differences from the impact matrix are then taken into consideration. By combining the results from the concordance and disconcordance approach, final inferences on the ranking of alternatives may be made. It should be noted that the concordance method is sometimes also used for qualitative evaluation problems.

11.4.3. Qualitative information

In recent years, much attention has been paid to the development of evaluation techniques which are capable to deal, in a consistent way, with 'qualitative' or 'soft' evaluation problems. Many operational 'soft' discrete multicriteria methods are now available (cf. Hinloopen et al., 1983). The following approaches will be discussed here: the **extreme value method** (Kmietowicz and Pearman, 1981), the **qualitative sign method** (Van Delft and Nijkamp, 1977), the **eigenvalue approach** (Saaty, 1977), the **regime method** (Hinloopen et al., 1983) and the **geometric scaling approach** (Voogd, 1983). The latter two approaches are also designed to deal with 'mixed' qualitative-quantitative evaluation problems.

The **extreme value method** can be regarded as an extension of the weighted summation method discussed above. It is still assumed that the scores achieved by each plan with respect to each criterion have quantitative properties, but in addition it is postulated that the probabilities (weights) are only known in a qualitative sense, i.e. only their ordinal properties are given. In essence, the aim of this approach is to determine the alternative with the maximum or minimum expected value. This is done by transforming the discrete problem into a linear programming problem, with the ordinal probabilities as constraints. Some elementary operations lead to maximum and minimum expected values for the alternatives under consideration, which may be used to arrive at a final assessment. However, as shown by Rietveld (1982), this assessment should not be made solely on the basis of the extreme values, but should also take into account certain expected values for alternatives generated for intermediate values of the probabilities.

A relatively simple method for qualitative multiple criteria evaluation is the so-called **qualitative sign analysis**. This approach aims at identifying alternatives that provide - in regard to 'soft' criteria - better outcomes than remaining ones. In the framework of a frequency analysis, the outcomes of the effect score matrix are subdivided into distinct effect categories, viz. **very high or very favourable** ($+++$), **reasonably high or reasonably favourable** ($++$), and **moderately high or moderately favourable** ($+$). In a similar way, the weights may be classified, for instance, into very high priority (xx) and normal priority (x). By systematically classifying all alternatives into the successive resulting combined impact-weight classes, a strength-weakness analysis may be used to identify the 'strong' and 'weak' alternatives. An illustration of the use of this method can be found in Chapter 13.

The **eigenvalue approach** involves a pairwise comparison of alternatives. This comparison is made by using a nine-point scale, where the value 1 means that the alternatives being compared are of equal importance, while on the other hand a value

9 implies that one is much more important than the other. A matrix is constructed for each criterion, in which the alternatives are compared in a pairwise way with respect to that criterion. The criteria themselves are then compared in a similar way, resulting in a separate pairwise criteria matrix. Next, the information in each matrix is aggregated using an eigenvalue procedure. This involves the calculation of quantitative evaluation scores and weights, which are then used in a weighted summation procedure to determine an aggregated appraisal score for each alternative plan. This approach therefore has the same drawbacks as the expected value method discussed earlier. However, the most fundamental criticism of this approach is that it is hardly possible for the user to relate the values of the criterion weights to the values obtained for the various alternatives. In other words, the weighting is independent of the characteristics of the plans or projects under consideration, which seems to be incorrect from a theoretical point of view.

Regime analysis bears a certain resemblance to the concordance analysis. The starting point of regime analysis is the concordance index $c_{ii'}$ defined in (11.4.). Given the definition of this index, $c_{ii'}$-$c_{i'i}$ can be interpreted as an indicator of the relative attractiveness of alternative i compared to i'. Since it is assumed that the weights λ_j are ordinal, it is impossible to find a unique numerical value for $c_{ii'}$-$c_{i'i}$. Therefore regime analysis focuses on the sign of this indicator rather than on its numerical value.

It can be shown that in certain cases, ordinal information on weights is sufficient to determine this sign, so that a final ranking of alternatives can be derived from the pairwise comparison matrix, consisting of values +1 and -1. In other cases, this sign cannot be determined unambiguously, however. It can be shown that in such cases a partitioning of the set of cardinal weights can be derived, being in agreement with the ordinal information on the weights, such that for each subset of weights again the sign of $c_{ii'}$-$c_{i'i}$ can be determined. The final result of the method is a complete and transitive ranking of all alternatives, for each of the above mentioned subsets of weights. In addition, the method procedures the relative size of each subset so that one knows the relative importance of each subset. This approach will be discussed in more detail in chapter 14.

The **geometric scaling approach** is based on the principles of non-metric multidimensional scaling. The basic idea of this approach is to transform a large amount of ordinal data into a small amount of quantitative (cardinal) data, such that the new cardinal configuration is as close as possible (i.e. has a maximum goodness-of-fit) to the ordinal data. One limitation of this elegant approach is that it requires a fairly complicated computational algorithm. In addition, evaluation problems treated by this method should have a sufficient number of degrees of freedom to allow for geometric scaling. This implies that - unless sufficient ordinal information is available - no metric data can be extracted.

It is clear that several concepts from scaling analysis may also be applicable to ordinal multiple criteria problems. Various approaches can be imagined in this case. In the first place, one may use a scaling technique in order to transform a qualitative impact matrix into a cardinal matrix with less dimensions. Then the cardinal configuration of the initial qualitative matrix provides a metric picture of the Euclidean distances both between the alternatives and between the effects. This is a normal standard operation.

Second, one may also apply a joint scaling analysis to both a qualitative impact matrix and a qualitative weight vector. In that case, both the impacts and the weights have to be transformed into a cardinal metric scale. Though this is mathematically fairly difficult, one may utimately arrive at cardinal results for both impacts and weights. The final result of this analysis is that one is able to indicate precisely which rank order of alternatives is consistent with a certain rank order of ordinal weights.

The present subsection has shown that a whole series of discrete multi-criteria methods is now available, each method having its own particular weak and strong points. It illustrates that there is no universal method for solving every type of plan or project evaluation. A procedure for selecting a proper method is presented in Chapter 12. Besides, there always remains uncertainty regarding the applicability of a method, due to its implicit and explicit assumptions. It is also clear that not all methods give the same results, although this can be overcome in practice by performing a sensitivity analysis on the methodological assumptions of the discrete evaluation methods being used (see for more details Voogd, 1983).

11.5. Continuous Methods

In the present section, we will briefly discuss the class of so-called continuous methods. Much attention has been given in the past to the development of such evaluation methods. Especially 'hard' evaluation problems have been investigated, and this resulted in a wide variety of different optimization methods. The following methods will briefly be considered here: **utility function approaches** (Fishburn, 1974), **penalty models** (Theil, 1968), **goal programming models** (Spronk, 1981), **hierarchical models** (Rietveld, 1981), **min-max approaches** (Rietveld, 1980), and **reference point approaches** (Wierzbicki, 1983).

11.5.1. Quantitative information

Utility methods start from the assumption that the entire set of relevant criteria or objectives can be translated through a weighting procedure into one 'utility function'. Such a utility reflects all tradeoff and priorities (weights) attached to the successive criteria. Then this utility function has to be optimized given the constraints of the evaluation problem concerned. The utility approach is a theoretical instrument which has often been used in many neoclassical optimization problems. It is an elegant approach, but it has also obvious drawbacks. For instance, it presupposes complete prior quantitative information about all weights and trade-offs among the whole range of feasible values of all criteria.

Penalty models assume the existence of a set of desired achievement levels ('ideal values') for the criteria under consideration. Any discrepancy between an actual criterion value and an ideal value incurs a penalty calculated through some kind of penalty function. Evidently, the main difficulty in applying this kind of model is lack of information about appropriate penalty functions. For algorithmic reasons (ease of differentiation) often a quadratic function is used; however, this implies the introduction of an additional 'weight' to the deviations, which may be debatable. A special case of penalty models is the **goal programming model** dealing with penalties on under- and overachievements of fixed goal variables (see Spronk, 1981).

Next, **hierarchical models** are based on the assumption that all criteria or objectives can be ranked according to their degree of importance. Optimization is then carried out in a stepwise fashion, so that higher-ranking functions are optimized before those of lower ranks. A tolerance factor (or relaxation factor) can be specified for each function (except the most important), indicating the maximum deviation from the optimum considered acceptable by the decision-maker.

Min-max approaches are based on the use of a matrix representing the payoffs between conflicting objectives as well as their feasible ranges. In a similar way as in game theory, one may next calculate the equilibrium solution from the payoff matrix. This equilibrium solution reflects the best compromise choice for the evaluation problem. A drawback is again that there are several ways to arrive at an equilibrium solution, so that there is no guarantee that the compromise solution is unique. Here again an interactive procedure may be helpful. This approach is especially appropriate when it is necessary to take into account different views of a problem in some explicit way. Each view is represented by a criterion function (or objective function) and the information given in the payoff matrix may then be used to help the decision committee to arrive at a compromise solution.

Reference point approaches are based on the concept of an ideal point (or utopian point). This ideal point is defined as a vector whose elements are the maximum values of the individual criterion functions. The closer the criterion values of an alternative are to the values of the ideal point, the better the alternative. The compromise solution is defined as the alternative in the set of efficient solutions for which the distance to the ideal solution is minimal. An efficient solution (or Pareto solution) is a solution for which the value of one criterion (or objective) cannot be improved without reducing the value of a competing criterion (or objective). It should be noted that there are also reference point approaches which are formulated in a goal programming framework, where the reference point represents a set of aspiration levels. This approach is only appropriate if the reference points can be modified during the course of the analysis. It should therefore also be used in an interactive way.

11.5.2. Qualitative information

The continuous methods described above deal with 'hard' evaluation problems. 'Soft' continuous approaches, however, did not receive much attention in the past. Apart from some work in the field of fuzzy sets hardly any elaborative work can be reported on qualitative continuous evaluation methods. An interesting contribution, however, can be found in Leung (1983). Some recent applications can be found in Munda et al. (1992).

For global and macro decision problems, hard continuous evaluation methods have reached a stage of sufficient maturity, and hence they can be and - actually are - applied in a wide variety of policy analysis. They are especially appropriate in planning processes in which feasible solutions within certain constraints are to be found, e.g. the capacity of networks. Continuous methods may also be used to scan problems and to identify the main alternative lines of action. However, in empirical research practice one often faces also non-quantitative information. Further research in this area is therefore warranted, also in view of the qualitative nature of many decision problems in practice.

11.6. Inductive versus Deductive Evaluation Approaches

After the previous exposition on evaluation methods, in particular multiple criteria methods, we will in the present section pay attention to inductive versus deductive approaches to such methods. Some illustrations of current practice in (Dutch) transportation planning will be given in Section 11.7.

Transportation (infrastructure) planning is a proper example of a research field which badly needs an adequate decision support methodology due to the wide variety of different (mutually conflicting) judgement criteria to be taken into account in a series of sequential adaptive planning processes (see Himanen et al., 1990). Clearly, the definition of relevant appraisal criteria is far from easy due to uncertainties regarding impacts, measurement levels and spatial differentiation. In principle, two different approaches may be distinguished, viz. a **deductive** and an **inductive** approach.

The **deductive** approach starts from a listing of fairly general and main objectives and/or characteristics of the evaluation problem concerned (in terms of latent variables). In the next stage these general items are specified more precisely in terms of observable variables (see, for instance, Hutchinson, 1974; Lemer and Belloma, 1974; and Voogd, 1985). An example of this approach may be the following general listing of transportation planning issues:

a) impact on services

b) impact on safety

c) impact on historico-cultural values

d) impact on community as a whole

Next, each of these main characteristics may then be specified and measured more precisely in terms of observable variables. For instance, we may define the following more operational criteria for each of these four main apraisal criteria:

a1) educational facilities

a2) cultural facilities

a3) employment

a4) commercial facilities

a5) recreational facilities

a6) accessibility

b1) road safety and design

b2) traffic lights planning

b3) speed limits

b4) separate lanes

c1) historic buildings

c2) landscape and 'cityscape'

c3) visual aspects

d1) crowding

d2) functional separation

d3) access to centre

d4) urban homogeneity

Of course, all above mentioned factors receive only a full meaning in relation to well-defined policy strategies.

Secondly, the **inductive** approach starts in a different way, viz. by enumerating all features of all relevant policy options or alternatives. Next, these features are systematically grouped and eventually aggregated in main categories, so that a set of meaningful evaluation criteria or objectives arises.

Both methods take for granted that some hierarchy of criteria or objectives can be distinguished. In constructing such a hierarchy the concepts of specification and means-ends are useful (see also Manheim and Hall, 1968). Specification means a subdivision of one important aspect into one or more lower-level aspects. Clearly, such a subdivision implies also a close resemblance to a 'means-ends' classification.

The above mentioned discussion on transportation infrastructure planning was rather general and abstract. A more concrete illustration of this approach would have to be based on a practical planning problem, in which public choices regarding the phasing and trajectories of new infrastructure facilities are to be based on a broad set of diverse planning criteria. In the next section an empirical illustration of such an approach will be provided on the basis of a broader discussion of the planning of national highway projects in the Netherlands. It will also be shown how multiple criteria choice analysis is actually used in this context.

11.7. Highway Planning in the Netherlands

11.7.1 Introduction

The Netherlands is one of the most densely populated countries in Europe (approx. 420 inhabitants per square km) and hence road infrastructure is a crucial factor for accessibility and communication. Dutch road infrastructure planning is the responsibility of various road and highway authorities; the national highway network is under the authority of the national government. In view of congestion and lack of safety, it is foreseen that all national highways will be converted into motorways. It is evident, however, that for financial and technical reasons this expansion cannot be implemented at the same time for all highway sectors, so that a phasing of activities is necessary. In this context, a strategic network planning system has been designed, the so-called Structure Scheme for Traffic and Transport. Also the complementary Multi-Year Plan for Passenger Transport plays an important role in this framework. In the latter document, priorities for the implementation and research planning of new road projects are established. Such priorities are necessary, as the annual government budget for highway expansion is limited. This implies that an evaluation has to be made of both the urgency of adjustments and expansions of current roads (implementation planning) and new expansion plans to be investigated in greater detail (research planning) (see for an overview of Dutch infrastructure planning also Cortenraad et al., 1986).

Thus, theoretically, for each year within the planning horizon an assessment has to be made of the expected growth in demand and of the necessary implementation of new infrastructure needed to remove unacceptable bottlenecks.

Once in a certain year a bottleneck has been removed, a new priority for other infrastructure investments has to be established, and so forth. This sequential multi-period analysis of demand and supply leads to a need for a specific application of sequential evaluation techniques.

The priorities for allocating public funds to national highway projects are determined by means of a multiple criteria evaluation procedure. The following four steps can be distinguished here:

- project enumeration and classification;
- identification of judgement criteria;
- determination of an effect score table; and
- project ranking and project priority determination.

Each of these steps will briefly be described here.

11.7.2. Project enumeration and classification

The priority analysis of Dutch highway expansion covers all road infrastructure projects being part of the national highway network. After the initial listing of all projects, they are classified into three categories, the first two referring to implementation planning:

- projects which are already under construction or which have not yet been implemented, but are closely connected with projects previously completed (or still under way);
- projects for which a definite positive decision has already been taken, but for which the actual implementation has not yet started;
- projects which are still under consideration and which have to be analyzed in more detail.

It is evident that projects of types (1) and (2) have usually priority over those still on the drawing board (i.e., type (3)) on the grounds that current projects should be completed as soon as possible for the sake of efficiency and continuity in transportation policy. Clearly, type (1) projects have also a priority over type (2) projects. Consequently, the priority analysis is mainly relevant for projects of type (2) and (3), and only for type (1) if the budget limitations are severe.

11.7.3. Identification of judgement criteria

The identification of major relevant evaluation criteria is an essential step in any evaluation method. The main aim of infrastructure planning is to meet the demand for transport of people and goods, while taking into account various other aspects. The following general (latent) appraisal criteria are usually taken into consideration:

- **Accessibility**: the extent to which the project under consideration contributes to a more efficient throughflow of non-commercial traffic (e.g., recreation, commuting).

- **Economic activity**: the extent to which the project has an economic effect on the overall level of economic activity, especially in the framework of business traffic.

- **Road safety**: the extent to which the project leads to a reduction in traffic accidents and/or other forms of discomfort for road users.

- **Quality of life**: the extent to which the project has an impact on living conditions in the built environment, with special reference to environmental factors like noise and air pollution.

- **Physical planning**: the extent to which the project is in agreement with land use conditions (e.g., environmental conditions, town and country planning etc.).

The above mentioned list of latent variables indicates that a deductive approach is used in the Netherlands, so that in a later stage the various effects have to be operationalized in more concrete terms.

11.7.4. Measurement of effects

For each project under consideration all relevant effects have to be measured. The first step is thus to specify a measurable indicator (or set of indicators) for each of the five above mentioned latent judgement criteria. The effect of a project is defined as a change with respect to a zero situation. In Subsection 11.7.6. this measurement procedure will be outlined in greater detail.

In the Dutch case various assumptions have been made on the measurement procedure, viz.:

- as far as infrastructure effects during the implementation phase are negative, they are eliminated wherever possible by compensatory measures, so that such negative implementation effects can normally be left out of consideration. Accompanying

compensatory measures need to be incorporated in the cost items included under the economic activity criterion;
- any completed project will be maintained until at least the year 2020;
- the projects do not influence one another and hence can be analyzed separately, unless the list of projects indicates that they are specifically linked.

An operational listing of such relevant effects can be found in Section 11.7.6.

11.7.5. Ranking of projects

The ranking of successive infrastructure projects in the Netherlands is often based on the use of a well-known multiple criteria method, viz. concordance analysis. By means of this method road infrastructure projects are ranked in terms of decreasing social value on the basis of their comparative effects in terms of the selected criteria. In this way projects can be categorized as very urgent, urgent, less urgent, etc., taking into account a set of prevailing external conditions (e.g., the available budget). Thus the final result of this step is a classification of road projects into a number of priority groups.

Having discussed now the main elements of the evaluation procedure for Dutch highway planning, we will present in Subsections 11.7.6. and 11.7.7. some further details.

11.7.6. Assessment of the effect score table.

In order to deal with the above mentioned issues, a large-scale concordance analysis is used in the Dutch transportation planning context. The assessment of impacts is normally based on available expert knowledge and fieldwork, while the assessment of weights is based on a broad consultation of experts, policy-makers and planners. The application of the concordance method leads - for each year within the planning horizon and for the available budget in each year - to a priority ranking of new transportation plans, given the growth in transport demand (in terms of quantity, modal choice, route choice, etc.). In the present Subsection we will discuss this assessment of project effects.

For each of the above mentioned five main criteria, a set of measurable indicators is defined.
- **Accessibility.** This criterion is operationalized by taking into account the traffic intensity on a certain road section of a given length during a relevant time period,

corrected for the average speed on the section concerned. Most of these data are available in the Netherlands. The impacts of a new project take into account the special road features (e.g., length, category, number of lanes, etc.) of this new investment. A complicated factor to be taken into account is the fact that the supply of new road infrastructure will always attract additional traffic (the 'law of Say' in transportation).

- **Economic activity.** This criterion refers to the net social benefits (i.e., benefits minus costs) accuring from the implementation of a new road investment project. the benefits refer to travel time saved and to remaining reductions in relevant costs. The costs refer to construction costs, maintenance costs and operational costs.

- **Road safety.** Road safety is a latent variable which can be operationalized by means of the following indicators: number of fatalities, number of injuries and number of accidents resulting in material damage only.

- **Quality of life.** This criterion comprises mainly the effects of noise and air pollution caused by traffic. Impact assessments of noise annoyance take into consideration the road level, the car speed, the various categories of cars, the distribution of traffic over time, etc. Air pollution takes into consideration wind direction and velocity, atmosphere stability at a particular place, and the population density.

- **Physical planning.** Physical planning is related to nationally formulated objectives with respect to suburbanization/commuting, structure of large urban districts, the location of new towns etc. Clearly, some overlap with previous indicators (e.g., accessibility) is inevitable.

All effects mentioned above are measured in cardinal units, except the last one, physical planning, which is measured on a (+, 0 -) scale. In Cortenraad et al. (1986) a detailed description of all relevant effects is given.

11.7.7. The use of multiple criteria methods in Dutch transportation planning

As mentioned before, three types of transport infrastructure projects are distinguished (viz., those which are under construction, those which have been approved and those which are under consideration). For all projects in each of these three categories, the relevant impacts measured according to the above mentioned five main criteria are assessed. Hence, at the end we find an effect score matrix encompassing a characterizationn of all relevant road infrastructure projects. This is one basic input for the use of a multiple criteria method.

Next, also a set of policy weights for each of the five main criteria is established, based on a rating method. Information on weights is often obtained from the responsible Minister of Transport, regional policy authorities etc. In the Dutch case, normally a set of varying weights is used in order to test also the robustness of the results.

The data used in the multiple criteria evaluation method are mainly cardinal in nature, but also some qualitative aspects are taken into consideration. Furthermore, for the sake of simplicity and for the ease of communication with top-level decision-makers, usually a simple paired comparison method, viz. the concordance analysis, is applied. This method is easy to use despite some inherent limitations.

An interesting element is that this method is used in a sequential way, so that for each successive year a new set of relevant projects can be taken into consideration, given the decisions made in a previous period and given the available budget. This whole sequential (multi-period) system has become a fairly advanced decision support system in the Netherlands, which has had a great impact on a rational structuring of transportation plans which can usually not be implemented simultaneously in one year.

11.8. Outlook

Multiple criteria analysis may be seen as an important decision support method for planning under uncertainty. Especially in case of goal conflicts it may serve to rationalize complex decision problems, by providing both a tool for communication between all actors involved and a rigorous analytical technique for examining (implicitly or explicitly) the implications of policy trade-offs. Flexibility in the design and use of such methods is necessary to ensure a tailor-made research tool. The enormous variety in applications of such methods illustrates its great potential.

Clearly, in all empirical applications difficult analytical problems will be faced, e.g., regarding the precision of measurement, the identification of priorities, the demarcation of the impacts etc. Communication with all actors is then a sine qua non for an acceptance of results of such techniques. Recursive or cyclical planning procedures are hence necessary for a structural and generally accepted evaluation method.

It has to be added that various elements are still to be improved in the use of multiple criteria analysis for planning, e.g. the long-term effects of a decision (especially important in case of infrastructure decisions).

In any case, multiple criteria analysis offers the possibility to link analytical evaluation methods much closer to political decision processes and has, in principle, the potential to enhance the quality of decision-making. The previous expositions indicate that the use of such modern decision support methods may be of great importance for a structured transportation planning. In the final parts of this book we will provide a set of illustrative applications of the use of various multi-criteria methods in the evaluation of transportation plans, but in the next chapter we will first discuss the issue of choosing a proper evaluation method.

Chapter 12

A METHODOLOGY FOR SELECTING A TAILOR-MADE
MULTIPLE CRITERIA METHOD IN TRANSPORTATION PLANNING

12.1. A Meta-Multicriteria Choice Problem

In the previous chapter it has been shown that in the past decade a wide variety of multiple criteria evaluation methods has been designed, which aimed at structuring, systematizing and judging complex decision problems marked by multiple appraisal criteria. In this period, the general principle for rationalizing such complex choice and trade off problems was based on a straightforward approach: given (i) a certain well-defined evaluation problem and (ii) a certain specific evaluation technique, the aim is to identify the most plausible outcome for the decision problem concerned.

An overview of the field of application of evaluation methods demonstrates however, a great diversity of these methods, ranging from cost-benefit analysis and multiple criteria analysis to participation and interactive policy methods (see Chapter 11). In many practical planning situations, decision problems were in a forced manner reformulated or transformed in order to let them meet the specific requirements imposed by the evaluation technique at hand (the 'Procrustes bed' approach). This 'torturing of problems' may indeed lead to a 'tailor-made' specification of an evaluation problem, but it neglects to a large extent the specific characteristics of practical decision problems.

Surprisingly, only a few attempts have been made to regard the choice of a specific evaluation method for a practical decision problem as a multiple criteria choice problem itself (see Rietveld, 1980). This problem is essentially a **meta-multicriteria choice problem**. The solution to this problem will require a closer analysis of all relevant aspects of policy anlysis regarding a certain practical decision problem in order to develop an operational reserach methodology of choosing an appropriate appraisal technique. The field which will be examined in greater detail here is transport planning (including environmental aspects).

The approach advocated here is however also applicable to other fields of planning. In the present chapter we will focus our attention on the following problem-oriented question: which are the specific multidimensional features of various transportation planning problems and what do these features imply for the choice of an appropriate evaluation method? This question boils essentially down to a demand-supply analysis: given a certain profile of a prespecified actual evaluation problem (the 'demand side'), which evaluation method (or class of evaluation methods) from the available set of methods (i.e., the 'supply side') has a maximum correspondence to the requirements imposed by the specific evaluation problem concerned?

A further analysis of this question requires a systematic inventory and typology of transportation planning problems, based on a set of relevant classification principles. In this chapter, the following steps will be undertaken:

-       **inventory** and **classification** of various types of transportation planning problems (road construction, traffic regulations, fare policies for buses, etc.);
-       **typology** of policy-relevant attributes of transportation planning problems (information need, trade-off analysis, conflict analysis, etc.);
-       **identification** of sets of criteria to be fulfilled by the evaluation method(s) selected for the treatment of a specific transportation problem;
-       **confrontation** of these criteria with various available evaluation methods in order to identify classes of evaluation methods that are appropriate for predefined sets of transportation planning problems.

12.2.   **Characterisation of a Multidimensional Evaluation Problem**

12.2.1. **Methodology**

Transportation - and in general physical - planning is a good example of a complex planning field marked by a wide spectrum of choice problems (infrastructure construction, road traffic control, international commodity transport regulations, subsidy policy on public transport etc.). These classes of choice problems will be called **'activities'** here.

Furthermore, the number of policy considerations (criteria) to be taken into account is extremely large, for instance, costs and benefits, safety, public expenditures, deficits in public transport, efficiency in commodity transport, convenience for passengers, accessibility, environmental repercussions, energy consumption, etc. Consequently, it is clear that not all multiple criteria methods are suitable for being used in all transportation and physical planning problems. In our approach we will follow two complementary research lines to deal with this complicated choice problem: (i) the identification of a set of activities (traffic policy, infrastructure construction, etc.) which are representative for transportation problems and/or policies (the **activity profile**); and (ii) the identification of a **requirements profile** in order to select the most appropriate evaluation method for each class of activities. By combining next the activity vector with the requirements profile, one may examine whether or not for a certain class of activities one or more appropriate evaluation methods are available.

Evaluation problems in transportation planning can be distinguished **inter alia** on the basis of the following features (see Figure 12.1):

- the **type of activities** to be evaluated (for instance, highway construction, safety measures, etc.);

- the **characteristics of the effects** caused by the activities (for instance, travel time saving, reduction in accidents, etc.);

- the **nature of the decision structure** related to the activity (for instance, a hierarchical institutionalized policy structure, participatory decisions, etc.).

These three dimensions will now successively be discussed in Subsection 12.2.2. (activity profile), Subsection 12.2.3. (effects) and Subsection 12.2.4 (decision structure).

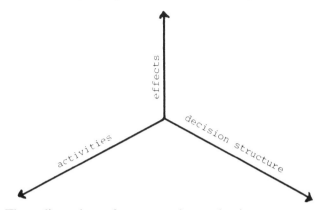

Figure 12.1   Three dimensions of transportation evaluation

12.2.2. The activity profile

The identification of classes of activities in transportation planning is not easy, as it is almost impossible to construct an exhaustive list of activities. Therefore, we will only give - by way of illustration - a limited and indicative set of activities. The following **classes of activities** may amongst others be distinguished:

1. highway construction
2. integrated traffic plan
3. reconstruction of waterways
4. construction of power lines
5. expansion of air transport
6. transport of dangerous goods
7. changing speed limits
8. LPG storage.

A further subdivision of these activities can be made on the basis of the **scope** of these activities and of their **spatial** scale.

The **scope** of these activities is determined by both the range of effects and the level and extent of policy intervention. Three categories of policy intervention may be mentioned here:

- **project**: the activity can be clearly identified and demarcated in space and time (for instance, the construction of a new street). Projects may be further subdivided into:

    •   direct governmental influence (for instance, railway construction)

    •   indirect governmental influence (for instance, subsidies on public transport);

- **plan**: the activity is composed of a coherent set of relatively less precisely defined sub-activities with a joint aim (for instance, a structure plan for physical planning including a transportation plan);

- **regulation**: the activity comprises all measures that may have an indirect impact (mainly via related activities) on transport behaviour (for instance, environmental standards, speed limits).

The **spatial scale** of activities may relate to:

- **international** activities (e.g.,cross-boundary commodity transport)
- **national** activities (e.g., railway policy)
- **regional** activities (e.g., design of a rapid transit system)
- **local activities** (e.g., urban traffic rules,).

By combining now the attributes characterizing the **scope** of activities with the spatial scale, one may construct an **activity profile** (see Table 12.1). Table 12.1 contains an illustrative - and by no means exhaustive - set of activities which are judged to be illustrative examples in the framework of a typological approach.

Class of activities	scope						spatial scale			
	project		plan		regulation					
	direct governmental influence	indirect governmental influence	facet policy	sector policy	facet policy	sector policy	international	national	regional	local
1. highway construction	x							x		
2. integrated traffic plan				x						x
3. reconstruction of waterways	x								x	
4. construction of power lines	x		x		x				x	
5. expansion of air transport		x					x			
6. transport of dangerous goods		x	x		x			x		
7. changing speed limits					x	x		x		
8. LPG storage		x			x			x		

Table 12.1   The activity profile

12.2.3. **The effects**

Effect analysis aims at assessing the foreseeable consequences of various activities. The following illustrative **appraisal criteria** in the framework of transportation planning may amongst others be distinguished:

i.   costs and benefits

ii.   changes in travel time

iii.   speed

iv.   safety

v.   accessibility

vi.   environmental effects

vii.   noise annoyance

viii. energy consumption.

These effects can next be classified according to their indigenous **features**:

- **temporal:**   (1) unique
                  (2) repetitive

                  (3) continuous short-term
                  (4) continuous long-term

- **spatial:**   (5) stationary
                  (6) mobile

                  (7) international
                  (8) national
                  (9) regional
                  (10) local

- **remaining:** (11) formal regulations applicable
                  (12) formal regulations not applicable

                  (13) marginal impact of effects
                  (14) non-marginal impact of effects.

It is clear that - as a next step of the typological approach - a survey table can be constructed which comprises all activities and their expected consequences (see Table 12.2).

a c t i v i t i e s	classes of effects								features													
	i	ii	iii	iv	v	vi	vii	viii	(1)	(2)	(3)	(4)	(5)	(6)	(7)	(8)	(9)	(10)	(11)	(12)	(13)	(14)
1	x	x	x	x	x	x	x	x	x				x	x	x	x	x	x	x	x	x	
2	x	x	x	x	x	x	x	x						x	x				x	x	x	x	
3	x				x	x			x				x	x	x		x				x	x
4	x			x		x			x				x	x			x			x		x	x
5	x	x	x	x	x	x	x	x						x	x		x		x	x	x	x	x
6	x		x	x		x				x					x			x	x	x	x	x
7	x	x	x	x	x	x	x	x					x	x		x			x		x		x
8	x					x			x					x					x	x	x		x

Table 12.2. Survey table of features of activities

12.2.4. **The decision structure**

The decision structure refers to both the **solution space** and the **decision space**. A decision problem in the framework of transportation planning may have the following solution space in terms of **alternatives** and **information content**:

(A) **alternatives:**
> discrete number
> continuous
>
> point alternatives
> sequential alternatives
>
> mutually exclusive alternatives
> mutually non-exclusive alternatives

(B) **information content:**
> quantitative
> qualitative
>
> certain
> uncertain
>
> extensive
> limited
>
> complete
> incomplete

The **decision space** of transportation planning problems can be characterized by:

(A) **institutional structure:**
        international
        national
        regional
        local

        single objective
        multiple objectives

        hierarchical
        negotiation
        informal

        routine
        non-routine

        analytical
        heuristic

(B) **aim of evaluation:**
        ex ante evaluation
        ex post evaluation

        internal communication
        external communication

        identification of one alternative
        identification of feasible alternatives
        ranking of all alternatives

Clearly, the above mentioned features can also be included in a matrix that combines activities and characteristics of the decision problem at hand, but for the sake of brevity this matrix will not be presented here (see Janssen, 1984). The next section will now be devoted to the choice of a suitable (i.e., customized) evaluation method.

12.3. Selection of an Evaluation Method

In this section the features of transportation planning problems listed above are translated into explicit criteria for selecting evaluation methods (see also Lichfield et al., 1975; Rietveld, 1980; McAllister, 1980; Voogd, 1983; Janssen, 1984). By comparing these criteria with distinct features of available methods, one obtains easily insight into the relative usefulness of different methods for different problems.

The relevant selection criteria for evaluation methods can be subdivided into **first- and second- order criteria** (cf. Duckstein et al., 1981):

-     First-order criteria are **mandatory (binary) criteria** for the selection of an evaluation method; if a method does not comply with all first-order criteria which are relevant to a certain problem, this method cannot be applied to this problem.

-     Second-order criteria are referring to **desirable** features, but are not a priori mandatory criteria for the selection of an evaluation method. Here the aim is to find a method which complies with as many second-order criteria as possible.

Next, one may also make a distinction into **generic** and **specific** criteria. Only part of the selection criteria is relevant to **all** evalutation problems. Some examples of such **generic** criteria are listed in Table 12.3. Most selection criteria are related to certain well defined transportation evaluation problems which means that appraisal methods can only be judged in relation to the problem they are intended to solve. This means that the selection criteria related to certain well defined transportation evaluation problems have to be compared with the features of a number of available and relevant evaluation methods. If a method in its basic form complies with a selection criterion, this is indicated by a symbol x. If it is possible to modify a method in such a way that - after some amendments - it may comply with a given selection criterion - even though this is not implied by its rudimentary form -, this is indicated with a symbol 0 (see Table 12.4).

G1.	The evaluation method (EM) should be able to make a consistent trade-off between different policy goals
G2.	The EM should produce results that are comprehensible to the decision-makers involved
G3.	The EM should be able to process information measured in different dimensions in a comparable way
G4.	The principles and assumptions of the EM must be explicable to decision-makers involved

Table 12.3 Generic selection criteria

Class of activities	activity profile		activity effects		decision structure		type of selection criteria	
	scope	spatial scale	criteria	features	solution space	decision space	mandatory	generic
1.	x	x	o	o	x	o	x	x
2.	x	x	x		x	x	x	o
3.			o		x		x	o
. . . .								

Evaluation methods	scope	spatial scale	criteria	features	solution space	decision space	mandatory	generic
I	x	o	x	x	x	x	x	o
II	x	x	x	o	x			x
III	x	o					x	x
. . . .								

Table 12.4.   Judgement of evaluation methods in light of the specific properties of a given decision problem

By confronting the specific row corresponding to a given evaluation problem of an activity (upper part of Table 12.4) with the class of all evaluation methods (lower part of Table 12.4), it is possible to identify the most satisfactory method by inspecting the number of 'x' symbols ensuring a maximum similarity.

12.4. Conclusion

Evaluation is a way of rationalizing and justifying complex decisions. Usually, however, a friction does exist between the nature of a specific practical evaluation **problem** and the nature of the available evaluation **technique**. This chapter has made an attempt at bridging this gap by means of a systematic typological approach.

In regard to the characteristics of transportation planning problems, the following concluding observations on a tailor-made choice of methods can be made:

- each activity causes a diversity of effects;
- the majority of evaluation problems is marked by a discrete set of alternative choice options;
- the majority of evaluation problems is marked by both quantitative and qualitative information
- lack of certainty and predictability is an important feature of many effects;
- the majority of evaluation problems is marked by conflicting objectives;
- external interest groups play an important role in many evaluation problems;
- evaluation is a matter of both an analytical and a heuristic policy style.

Given all activities, their features and effects, it appears to be possible to identify a set of appropriate customized multicriteria techniques for a specific type of evaluation problem by means of the typological analysis based on the successive matrices discussed above.

Having discussed the methodology of plan evaluation, we will in Part E present various illustrative cases which serve to demonstrate the wide range of applications of evaluation methods in transportation planning.

PART E

APPLICATIONS OF MULTICRITERIA ANALYSIS
IN TRANSPORTATION PLANNING

Chapter 13

URBAN INFRASTRUCTURE PLANNING AND HISTORICO-CULTURAL
HERITAGE: AN APPLICATION OF A QUALITATIVE SIGN ANALYSIS

13.1. Introduction

Cities are a source of economic activity, and house at the same time a wealth of historico-cultural heritage which needs to be protected. In many cities a conflict has arisen between the aim of reorienting the urban structure towards a more modern and efficient spatial lay-out and the need to preserve the historico-cultural heritage (see e.g. Nijkamp, 1988). Various aspects of the historico-cultural heritage are hardly measurable in cardinal units, so that 'soft' evaluation tools have to be used. In the present chapter a numerical illustration of conflict analysis in this area will be given, based on a qualitative sign analysis (see also Nijkamp, 1980). The aim is to present a simple method in case of qualitative information on impacts of new urban infrastructure plans.

13.2. A Brief Description of Qualitative Sign Analysis

In this section an introduction to qualitative sign analysis will be given. This method is essentially based on the assumption that qualitative data cannot be added up, but that the frequency of occurrence of a certain type of qualitative data can be numerically treated.

Consider a choice problem with I alternatives and J evaluation criteria. Next, one may distinguish (without loss of generality) three performance indices:

+ + +   very favourable impact;
 + +   fairly favourable impact;
  +   small favourable impact.

The assumption is made that all criteria are measured as benefit criteria ('the higher, the better'). Consequently, all cost criteria have to be redefined as benefit criteria.

It is evident that such 'soft' information is not very accurate, but this is a usual circumstance in many evaluation problems (for example, in monument preservation), especially in an exploratory phase of evaluation analysis. The 'soft' performance indices presuppose a certain frame of reference in order to assign the plan impact to these performance classes.

In a similar way, qualitative importance choice priorities (weights) can be incorporated in qualitative importance classes. Suppose (again without loss of generality) the following two importance classes:

XX   very high priority;

X   normal priority.

Clearly, again the assignment of these importance indices has to be based on a frame of reference regarding all plan impacts.

Next, one may construct a frequency table (Table 13.1). Each element of this table represents the frequency that a certain plan (or project) outcome (+ + +, + + or +) occurs with a certain preference score (XX or X). In other words, the left upper entry of this matrix indicates the number of times that plan 1 has a very favourable outcome (+ + +) which is considered to be very important (XX).

	XX			X		
	+ + +	+ +	+	+ + +	+ +	+
plan 1 . . . plan I						

Table 13.1.   Frequency table of combined importance-performance indices

Next, one may first attempt to eliminate **dominated** plans. All plans which have lower frequencies than any given competing plan may be eliminated. This step is essentially equal to the elimination of inferior (non Pareto-optimal) points in multiple objective programming.

The following step is the **selection** of the optimal plan. This selection may be based on certain reasonable hypotheses concerning the relative dominance of plan impacts. In light of missing information, the following hypotheses regarding the combined performance-importance indices seem to be plausible:

$$(+++,XX) > (++,XX) \sim (+++,X) > (+,XX) \sim (++ > (+,X) \qquad (13.1)$$

where the symbols > and ~ mean 'preferred to' and 'approximately equivalent to', respectively. On the basis of these rules one may usually select the optimal plan (or at least identify the most favourable plans) by comparing pairwise the rows of Table 13.1.

13.3. An Illustration of Frequency Analysis

The frequency method will now be illustrated for cultural preservation policy in the context of urban infrastructure planning. Suppose, a local government is confronted with the need for restructing urban infrastructure in a city which has a wealth of historical monuments. Several solutions (i.e., alternative plans or scenarios) may be distinguished in order to cope with the clear conflict between economic development and structural decline or loss of monuments. Clearly, each solution has certain advantages and disadvantages, given the available limited budget. After a thorough investigation of all plans it appears to be possible to represent the performances (effectiveness scores) of all plans by means of a qualitative impact table.

The following six feasible plans or alternatives (i.e., $I = 6$) may be distinguished for the urban development policy at hand:

1)   a very modest change in the urban infrastructure, accompanied by a marginal improvement of all monuments;

2)   a partial rehabilitation of most monuments and a partial demolition of others, followed by constructing new residential buildings without substantial changes in the urban infrastructure;

3)   a better preservation of approximately one half of all monuments and a demolition of all others, followed by the construction of new dwellings;

4)   a complete restoration of a limited number of all monuments and a demolition of all others, followed by a construction of new residential buildings, on the basis of lower densities, but with a maintainance of the original urban layout;

5)   a complete demolition of all monuments and a construction of new residential

buildings and of a modern urban infrastructure;

6)   an increase of tourist taxes so as to increase the budget for conservation of monuments and a partial demolition of less important ones.

Next, the assumption may be made that the local government wants to judge these alternative plans on the basis of the following seven evaluation criteria (i.e., $J = 7$):

1)   improvement of the urban and residential quality of life

2)   socio-economic distribution of the impacts of the new plans;

3)   costs of the alternative plans;

4)   impact on the urban employment;

5)   consequences for urban population density;

6)   accessibility of the city centre;

7)   supply of urban amenities.

It is clear that the cost criteria 3) and 5) have to be translated into benefit criteria, so that a low amount of costs will be represented by an effectiveness score $+ + +$.

For the above mentioned urban development plans we now assume the qualitative impact table shown in Table 13.2. The local government has to decide on these above plans on the basis of this 'soft' impact table, given its own priorities regarding the evaluation criteria.

criteria	plans					
	1	2	3	4	5	6
1	+	+ +	+ +	+ + +	+ + +	+ +
2	+ +	+ + +	+ + +	+ +	+ +	+
3	+ + +	+ +	+	+	+	+ +
4	+	+ +	+ +	+ +	+	+ + +
5	+	+ +	+ +	+ + +	+ + +	+ +
6	+	+	+ +	+ +	+ + +	+ + +
7	+	+ +	+ +	+ +	+ +	+ + +

Table 13.2.   Qualitative impact table of monument conservation and infrastructure plans.

Next, the priority scores shown in Table 13.3 will be assumed for the seven policy criteria indicated above. Thus, the assumption is made that there is one priority score for each criterion (i.e., a linear qualitative weighting system). In the case of a non-linear weighting system an entire matrix of preference scores has to be constructed.

criterion	1	2	3	4	5	6	7
weight	XX	X	XX	XX	X	X	X

Table 13.3. A vector of priority scores for monument conservation and infrastructure

On the basis of Tables 13.2 and 13.3, the frequency table of combined performance-priority scores can be constructed (see Table 13.4). Table 13.4 gives rise to fairly straightforward conclusions. First, several plans may be eliminated, because it is easily seen that plan 6 dominates absolutely plan 1, 3, 4 and 5. After the elimination of plans 1, 3, 4 and 5, the only choice remains between plan 2 and plan 6. But it can also easily be checked that - given our hypothesis (13.1) - plan 6 may be selected as the best policy decision.

Thus it appears that qualitative sign analysis is an easily applicable multiple criteria evaluation method. A disadvantage is, however, that in various cases it does not necessarily lead to an unambiguous solution. As a tool for scoping of alternatives it is however a useful method.

plans	XX			X		
	+ + +	+ +	+	+ + +	+ +	+
1	1	0	2	0	1	3
2	0	3	0	1	2	1
3	0	2	1	1	3	0
4	1	1	1	1	3	0
5	1	0	2	2	2	0
6	1	2	0	2	1	1

Table 13.4. Frequency table of combined performance-priority scores

Chapter 14

RAIL INFRASTRUCTURE PLANNING AND QUALITATIVE INFORMATION: AN APPLICATION OF REGIME ANALYSIS

14.1. Introduction

In the practice of transportation planning, cardinal information (measured on a ratio scale) is often not available, so that then conventional evaluation methods - either monetary-based methods (such as cost-benefit analysis, cost-effectiveness analysis or shadow project methods) or cardinal multiple criteria methods (such as goals-achievement analysis or weighted summation analysis) - cannot be applied as methodologically sound tools for decision analysis. In the past years a wide variety of qualitative multiple criteria choice methods has been developed (see also Chapter 11). Examples of classes of adjusted methods are: survey table methods (for instance, score card methods and computer-graphic methods); interactive computer methods (for instance, based on an interplay between expert and decision-maker); weighted methods (based on a set of weights reflecting the relative importance attached to the successive value criteria).

Unfortunately, various of these qualitative multiple criteria methods treat qualitative information as pseudo-cardinal information, so that their methodological basis is questionable. Despite the less correct treatment of categorical or ordinal information in several of these methods, they have become fairly popular analytical tools thanks to their simplicity. On the other hand, some more complicated analytical techniques (such as geometric scaling methods) are scientifically more justified, but less accessible to decision-makers because of their complicated statistical-mathematical contents. Consequently, there is apparently a conflict between simple but wrong methods on the one hand and complex but good methods on the other. In the search of a compromise between the requirements emanating from methodological soundness, accessibility and

213

mathematical-statistical simplicity recently a new method has emerged, the so-called
regime method (see Hinloopen et al., 1990). The next section will present some basic
principles of this method, while next the usefulness of this method will be illustrated by
means of an application to rail infrastructure plans in Belfast.

14.2. Principles of the Regime Method

The regime method for qualitative multiple criteria analysis is based on the
following considerations;

-       the technique should not use methodologically unpermitted operations (for
        instance, summation or multiplication of ordinal numbers)

-       the technique should be as much accessible as possible to a decision-maker

-       the technique should be easily applicable on a computer

-       the application of the regime method should in principle lead to an unambiguous
        solution, so that always a dominant choice option is identified.

In the sequel of this section, the essence and structure of the regime will be further
described.

Suppose we have a discrete choice problem with I choice options or alternatives
i (i = 1, ..., I), characterized by J judgement criteria j (j = 1, ..., J). The basic information
we have is composed of qualitative data regarding the ordinal value of all J judgement
criteria for all I options. In particular we assume a partial ranking of all I alternatives
for each criterion j, so that the following effect matrix can be constructed.

$$
E = \begin{matrix}
e_{11} \cdots \cdots e_{1J} \\
\cdot \qquad\qquad \cdot \\
\cdot \qquad\qquad \cdot \\
\cdot \qquad\qquad \cdot \\
e_{I1} \cdots \cdots e_{IJ}
\end{matrix}
\qquad\qquad (14.1)
$$

The entry e_{ij} (i = 1, ..., I; j = 1, ..., J) represents thus the rank order of alternative i
according to judgement criterion j. Without loss of generality, we may assume a rank
order characterized by the condition 'the higher, the better'; in other words: if $e_{ij} > e_{i'j}$,
then choice option i is preferable i' for judgement criterion j.

As there is usually not a single dominating alternative, we need additional information on the relative importance of (some of) the judgement criteria. In case of weighting methods this information is given by means of preference weights attached to the successive criteria. If we deal with ordinal information, the weights are represented by means of rank orders w_j ($j = 1, ..., J$) in a weight vector w:

$$w = (w_1, ..., w_J)^T \qquad (14.2)$$

Clearly, it is again assumed that $w_j > w_{j'}$, implies that criterion j is regarded as more important than j'.

Next, the regime method uses a pairwise comparison of all alternatives, so that the **mutual** comparison of two choice options is not influenced by the presence and effects of other alternatives. Of course, the eventual rank order of any two alternatives is co-determined by remaining alternatives (cf. the independence of irrelevant alternatives (IIA-problem)).

In order to explain the mechanism of the regime method, we will first define the concept of a **regime**. Consider two alternative choice options i and i'. If for criterion j a certain choice option i is better than i' (i.e. $s_{ii'j} = e_{ij} - e_{i'j} > 0$), it should be noted that in case of ordinal information, the order of magnitude of $s_{ii'j}$ is not relevant, but only its sign. Consequently, if $\sigma_{ii'j} = \text{sign } s_{ii'j} = +1$, then alternative i is better than i' for criterion j. Otherwise, $\sigma_{ii'j} = -1$, or (in case of ties) $\sigma_{ii'j} = 0$. By making such a pairwise comparison for any two alternatives i and i' for all criteria $j(j = 1, ..., J)$, we may construct a $Jx1$ **regime vector** $r_{ii'}$,

$$r_{ii'} = (\sigma_{ii'1}, ..., \sigma_{ii'J})^T, \quad \forall \, i, i'; \, i' \neq i \qquad (14.3)$$

Thus, the regime vector contains only $+$ and $-$ signs (or in case of ties also 0 signs), and reflects a certain degree of (pairwise) dominance of choice option i with respect to i' for the unweighted effects for all J judgement criteria. Clearly, we have altogether $I(I-1)$ pairwise comparisons, and hence also $I(I-1)$ regime vectors. These regime vectors can be included in an $JxI(I-1)$ **regime matrix** R:

$$R = r_{12}r_{13}...r_{1I.}..........r_{I1}...r_{I(I-1)} \qquad (14.4)$$

I-1   I-1

It is evident that, if a certain regime vector $r_{ii'}$ would only contain + signs, alternative i would absolutely dominate i'. Usually however, a regime vector contains both + and - signs, so that then additional information in the form of the weight vector (14.2) is required.

In order to treat ordinal information on weights, the assumption is now made that the ordinal weights w_j (j=1, ..., J) are a rank order representation of an (unknown) underlying cardinal stochastic weight vector $w^* = (w^*_1, ..., w^*_J)^T$ with max $\{w^*_j\} = 1$, $w^*_j \geq 0$, $\forall_j$. The ordinal ranking of the weights is thus supposed to be consistent with the quantitative information incorporated in an unknown cardinal vector w^*; in other words: $w_j > w_{j'} \rightarrow w_j^* > w_{j'}^*$. Next, we assume that the weighted dominance of choice option i with regard to i' can be represented by means of the following stochastic expression based on a weighted summation of cardinal entities (implying essentially an additive linear utility structure):

$$v_{ii'} = \sum_{j=1}^{J} \sigma_{ii'j} \, w^*_j \qquad (14.5)$$

If $v_{ii'}$ is positive, choice option i is dominant with respect to i'. However, in our case we do not have information on the cardinal value of w_j^*, but only on the ordinal value of w_j (which is assumed to be consistent with w_j^*). Therefore, we introduce a certain probability $p_{ii'}$ for the dominance of i with respect to i':

$$p_{ii'} = \text{prob} \, (v_{ii'} > 0) \qquad (14.6)$$

and define as an aggregate probability measure:

$$p_i = \frac{1}{I-1} \sum_{i' \neq i} p_{ii'} \qquad (14.7)$$

Then it is easily seen that p_i is the average probability that alternative i is higher valued than any other alternative. Consequently, the eventual rank order of choice options is then determined by the rank order (or the order of magnitude) of the p_i's.

However, the crucial problem here is to assess $p_{ii'}$ and p_i. This implies that we have to make an assumption about the probability distribution function of both the w_j^*'s and of the $s_{ii'j}$'s. In view of the ordinal nature of the w_j's, it is plausible to assume for the whole relevant area a uniform density function for the w_j^*'s. The motive is that, if the ordinal weight vector **w** is interpreted as originating from a stochastic weight vector **w***, there is without any prior information no reason to assume that a certain numerical value of **w*** has a higher probability than any other value. In other words, the weight vector **w*** can adopt with equal probability each value that is in agreement with the ordinal information implied by **w**. This argument is essentially based on the 'principle of insufficient reason', which also constitutes the foundation stone for the so-called Laplace criterion in case of decision-making under uncertainty (see Taha, 1976). However, if due to prior information in a specific case there is reason to assume a different probability distribution function (a normal distribution, e.g.), there is no reason to exclude this new information. Of course, this may influence the values of $p_{ii'}$ and hence the ranking of alternatives. The precise way in which in general rank order results will be derived from a probability distribution in case of qualitative information will now only be sketchily treated here (see for details Hinloopen and Nijkamp, 1990, and Hinloopen and Smyth, 1985). But it may suffice to mention here that in principle the use of stochastic analysis, which is consistent with an originally ordinal data set, may help to overcome the methodological problem emanating from impermissible numerical operations on qualitative data.

The regime method then identifies the feasible area within which values of the stochastic variables w_j^* have to fall in order to be compatible with the conditions imposed by equations (14.1) - (14.6). By means of a random generator numerous values of w_j^* (and of the quantitative effects e_{ij}^*) can be generated. This allows us at the end to calculate the probability score (or success score) p_i for each alternative i (see equation (14.7)). In this respect an unambiguous solution can always be found.

A final remark concerns the meaning embodied in $\sigma_{ii'j}$. Our approach implies that in case of a pairwise comparison of two non-numerically different alternatives the differences in effects are assumed to be negligible, i.e., $\sigma_{ii'j} = 0$. This assumption corresponds essentially to that implied by Kendall's rank correlation coefficient. Thus, only if two distinct choice options can be distinguished in measurable terms (either cardinal or ordinal), we have a possibility to represent these differences somehow in numerical form. If these differences are measured in an ordinal sense, then these differences may again be interpreted as stochastic variables which stem from an underlying cardinal uniform probability distribution. This approach is then again based on the principle of insufficient reason and hence similar to that described above for the weights.

14.3. Appraisal of Urban Rail Investment Plans

In this section the evaluation of rail investments in the city of Belfast will be dealt with as an illustration of the use of the regime method (see Hinloopen and Smyth, 1985).

Until 1976, the three rail routes entering Belfast's city centre were unconnected, with the exception of abandoned freight lines. In that year a cross city rail link was introduced incorporating a new Central Station and through-running between the southern and eastern commuter routes. This left the railway line to Larne Harbour, the province's principal ferry and roll-on roll-off port, largely isolated. In 1978 the government accepted in principle a recommendation - made as a result of a public inquiry - to construct a rail link between the Central Station and the city's other principal station at York Road.

Against the background of diverging interests of various parties involved, an investigation of a wider range of costs and benefits accruing from the proposed railway scheme was undertaken. The intention of this study was to inform various interested parties of the effects of constructing the link in a clear way with the aim of stimulating at a later stage a detailed investigation of the various costs and benefits identified. Furthermore, it was argued that the case for the alternative route option - the Riverside alternative - had not yet been adequately investigated.

In the evaluation study, based on the regime method, four different alternatives have been distinguished, viz., Do-Nothing (Al), Riverside (Elevated) (A2), Cross-River (A3), and Riverside (Depressed) (A4). The related impact matrix is presented below, for both the effects on the successive interest groups and the set of socio-economic criteria (see Tables 14.1 and 14.2).

alter-natives	impacts on interest groups			
	operators	employment growth	users	non-users
A1	4	1	1	2
A2	3	3	3	1
A3	2	2	2	3
A4	1	3	3	4

Table 14.1.   Impact matrix of effects on interest groups

alter-natives	evaluation criteria			
	economic	environment	traffic safety	accessibility
A1	3	1	3	3
A2	2	3	2	2
A3	1	4	3	3
A4	1	2	1	1

Table 14.2.   Impact matrix for relevant evaluation criteria

By assuming that the weights attached to the successive impacts on interest groups in Table 14.1 are horizontally ranked in decreasing order of importance, the standard regime method could easily be applied. The following results of the regime analysis for Table 14.2 were obtained:

$p_1 = 0.83$

$p_2 = 2.5$

$p_3 = -1.00$

$p_4 = 1.66$

Thus A2 appeared to be the most favourable alternative plan.

If one assumes also a decreasing rank order of the weights for the criteria in Table 14.2, we find again that A2 is the most favourable outcome. Thus, altogether plan 2 appears to be a dominating plan.

14.4. Concluding Remarks

The above analysis has demonstrated that for discrete choice problems which are marked by complete (or partial) uncertainty reflected by ordinal (or mixed) information, the regime method may be an operational tool. It leads to a probability statement regarding the choice of alternatives, and in so doing it leads to a unique solution (which is a major advantage compared to other 'soft' multiple criteria methods - like the concordance method -, which often do not lead to an unambiguous solution). Also its ability to deal with both qualitative information (including ties) and mixed information, makes it a powerful vehicle for evaluation analysis. Various empirical applications (e.g., housing market, transportation and physical planning) have demonstrated its usefulness for practical evaluation problems.

The regime method has a rich field of potential applications in transportation and infrastructure planning. Examples are:

-       optimal route scheduling problems in goods transport, in which besides efficiency criteria also intangible safety criteria play a role.

-       modal choice problems for different socio-economic groups in society, in which besides financial aspects also speed and convenience play a role.

-       planning of alternative trajectories for new motorways, in which besides public expenditures also accessibility and time saving play a role.

-       evaluation of different deregulation regimes, in which besides efficiency also convenience of passengers plays a role.

It should be added that according to the methodology for evaluation method selection proposed in Chapter 12 alternative evaluation methods may also have a relevance in actual applications, so that the choice in favour of regime analysis is certainly not unambiguous but depends on the specific features of the problem at hand. This means that some creativity and flexibility is needed in applying multi-criteria evaluation techniques to transportation planning issues.

As a further illustration of the broad spectrum of evaluation methods, we will present in the next chapter an example of airport planning using a vested evaluation method.

Chapter 15

AIRPORT PLANNING AND FUNCTIONAL SPECIALIZATION:
AN APPLICATION OF A NESTED REGIME METHOD

15.1. Changes in Airline Patterns

In recent years, airline policies have become a focal point of transportation research, mainly because in this field deregulation principles have been experimented and applied in many countries. The liberalization of airline policy has had tremendous impacts on air fares, competitive positions, level of services and/or capacity of carriers between different airports (cf. Banister and Button, 1991; Banister et al., 1992; Barrett, 1990).

An obvious result in many countries - at least in the first deregulation stage - has been the emergence of various small-scale carriers focussing mainly on commuter services from smaller airports to larger hubs. This situation has provoked questions regarding the centrality and the development potential of various airport locations, mainly because concentrating and deconcentrating tendencies seem to emanate simultaneously. In various countries we face a situation with on or more large central airports (mainports or hubs) and a larger set of regional airports. From the viewpoint of both airport investment planning and airline policy of carriers, it is extremely important to have more insight into desirable planning directions in view of the functional specialization between various types of airports.

In the present chapter this evaluation problem will be dealt with, based on a case study from the Netherlands. The methodology applied here will be based on the regime method discussed in Chapter 14.

15.2. Brief Description of the Dutch Airport Network

The Netherlands has one large international airport (Schiphol near Amsterdam) and five regional airports, viz., one in the Randstad area (near Rotterdam) and four in the periphery (Groningen, Twente, Eindhoven and Maastricht). Schiphol airport is facing the problem of a rapid increase of airline activities, so that the problem emerges whether in the future this airport should be expanded or whether the regional airports could also be included in the national and international airline network of the Netherlands. At the moment all of them have already international connections. However, their share in the total Dutch airline activities is still fairly modest (approximately 6 percent), of which Rotterdam takes approximately one half.

In addition to a complementary task of the regional airports, they also fulfil a feeder function for the main airport of Schiphol. This 'hub and spokes' system amounts to approximately 20 percent of all activities from the regional airports to Schiphol.

It is noteworthy however, that the regional airports are not only regarded as complementary to the central national airport of Schiphol, but also have their indigenous value, viz., as an incubator for new development potential in the regions concerned, based e.g., on business services, freight logistics etc. Although the catchment area of a regional airport may be fairly small, the ensuing external economies may still be significant for the region under consideration, so that a regional airport may indeed act as a growth pole.

Since the adoption of deregulation principles in airline policies, the importance of regional airports tends to grow, as many new (and often small-scale) airlines are based at these regional airports. This also implies that various regional airports are facing nowadays capacity problems, apart from noise annoyance for the built environment.

All these questions have led to a reconsideration of the tasks of all Dutch airports. And it is clear that especially the issue of concentration versus deconcentration plays a crucial role in the discussion. A main question here is whether a functional specialization of various airports has to be strived for or whether the national airport network should be dominated by the central airport of Schiphol.

In order to structure the discussion on various options three different models for the national airport network will be considered (see also Van Hasselt, 1986).

(1) **Airport network model 1: maximum use of Schiphol airport supported by efficient complementary infrastructure**

This is a typical concentration model, in which regional airports only play a modest role. In order to ensure this central position of Schiphol, new complementary motorways and rapid railways (TGV, e.g.,) have to be constructed in order to expand its catchment area. This model would also imply facilities for international companies, new industrial areas for complementary activities (like high tech and commercial services, etc.).

(2) **Airport network model 2: Schiphol airport as a part of a nation-wide network of airports**

This model is more integrative in nature and would be more in agreement with current deregulation and liberalization tendencies. This would imply a less rapid growth of the central airport and a more important role of regional airports (especially for international connections). This model would require an improvement of infrastructure at all regional airports.

(3) **Airport network model 3: Schiphol airport as a central airport in combination with two functionally specialized airports**

This is a model based on modest deregulation, as it takes for granted that only two regional airports will play a significantly more important role, viz., Maastricht and Rotterdam. Maastricht would have a direct access to Germany, Belgium and France, while the newly planned airport of Rotterdam might also be used to solve peak capacity problems of Schiphol airport. This intermediate model would discriminate negatively with respect to the remaining three regional airports.

It is clear that all above mentioned network models have advantages and disadvantages, and therefore it is necessary to evaluate these options on the basic of relevant judgement criteria. This will be done in the next section.

15.3. Judgement Criteria for Dutch Airport Network Models

The development of Dutch airports has to be judged against the background of official policy documents, such as the Structure Scheme on Civil Aviation published in 1979 and its later revisions. From such documents a set of relevant judgement criteria can be derived.

A. Economic aspects

These aspects refer to the contribution of airport activities to economic development (at a national and/or regional scale). The economic criterion however, is still a latent variable and needs to be operationalized by means of the following indicators:

A1: efficiency of airport network in terms of public spending;

A2: contribution to international trade;

A3: savings in costs of new infrastructure/facilities;

A4: reduction of leakage effect to foreign airports;

A5: contribution to employment.

B. Infrastructure aspects

The infrastructure effects concern the access to and from the airports for ground transport and related consequences. Here the following indicators are used:

B1: suitability of current (road and railway) infrastructure for the airport network at hand;

B2: accessibility of airports for passengers from all over the country;

B3: incubator potential for new regional economic activities.

C. Physical planning aspects

These aspects include:

C1: efficiency in land use for residential purposes for employees directly or indirectly associated with a new airport configuration;

C2: efficiency in direct land use for a new airport configuration;

C3: efficiency in indirect land use (e.g., for business services) related to a new airport configuration;

C4: efficiency in infrastructure land use (roads, railways, etc.) for a new airport configuration.

D. Environmental aspects

Environmental aspects mainly refer to noise annoyance and to a lesser extent to a deterioration of air, water, soil or landscape due to new infrastructure equipment. The following indicators are considered here:

D1: damage to physical environment and landscape;

D2: noise annoyance for surrounding areas.

E. Aviation aspects

Aviation aspects are related to the level and quality of services provided by a given airport network configuration. The following indicators are relevant here:

E1: flexible adjustment to a new airport configuration;

E2: efficiency of handling passengers and cargo;

E3: safety and flexibility for air traffic;

E4: efficiency in safeguarding airports.

F. Socio-cultural aspects

Socio-cultural aspects refer to the general contribution to human well-being and are reflected here by the following two indicators:

F1: flexible adjustment to tourist demand from catchment area;

F2: fulfilment of demand for recreational airline acitivities.

It goes without saying that most of the above mentioned indicators can only be measured at an ordinal level. In Van Hasselt (1986) a presentation of the impact score matrix ('the higher the better') for the three relevant models of airport configurations in the Netherlands is given (see Table 15.1). The way in which this information will be handled by means of a nested regime analysis will be discussed in Section 15.4.

	economic					infra-structural			physical planning				environ-mental		aviation				socio-cultural	
airport networkA1 A2 A3 A4 A5 model	A1	A2	A3	A4	A5	B1	B2	B3	C1	C2	C3	C4	D1	D2	E1	E2	E3	E4	F1	F2
(1)	3	3	1	1	1	1	1	1	3	3	3	1	2	3	3	3	3	3	1	3
(2)	1	1	2	3	3	2	3	3	1	1	1	2	1	2	1	1	1	1	3	1
(3)	2	2	3	2	2	3	2	2	2	2	2	3	3	1	2	2	2	2	2	2

Table 15.1.   Impact score matrix of 3 airport network configurations in the Netherlands

15.4. An Application of a Nested Regime Method

The information contained in Table 15.1 lends itself for a two-stage evaluation. First, the results can be analyzed at the distinct level of the main criteria, and next at the overall level (in the way suggested in Chapter 11). First, we will analyze the impact score matrix 15.1 more intuitively for each judgement criterion.

The first category of criteria, the economic aspects, does not lead to an immediate conclusion at first glance; the second class of infrastructure criteria shows that model (1) is no doubt inferior; the third class of physical planning aspects suggests that model (2) is not a plausible option; the environmental aspects in the fourth category show that model (2) is inferior; the aviation aspects in class E lead to a clear selection of model (1) as the dominant alternative, while socio-cultural aspects do not clearly discriminate among the three competing options. Thus an ambiguous solution cannot be identified beforehand, so that a more rigorous methodology may be used here. Therefore, an appropriate evaluation technique has to be used here. In view of the large number of soft criteria, the regime method may be used here as an appropriate analytical tool.

The regime method will be applied here in a stepwise and nested way, viz., (1) at the individual level of each of the main criteria A ... F, and (2) next at the level of an overall judgement of all criteria together. The latter step incorporates thus essentially the first step; hence the name **'nested regime method'**.

If we assume that there are no reasons to discriminate between the weights attached to each of the subcriteria A1 ... A5, the regime method - with equal weights - can be applied in a straightforward way. The results can be found in Table 15.2. If we adopt the same procedure also for all other main criteria, a set of results for each main criterion may be obtained (see Table 15.2).

airport network model	probability (success score) for each of the main criteria					
	A	B	C	D	E	F
(1)	0.207	0.000	0.956	0.761	1.000	0.500
(2)	0.517	0.926	0.022	0.261	0.000	0.500
(3)	0.775	0.574	0.522	0.478	0.500	0.500

Table 15.2.   Result of regime analysis for each main judgement criterion

These results indicate that model (2) is only competitive for criterion B; for all other criteria it is inferior. Thus, unless criterion B would be given excessively high weights, model (2) does not seem to be a plausible option. Consequently, the major choice to be made concerns model (1) or (3). The latter question can be dealt with by applying again the regime analysis to the new rank order of options presented in Table 15.2. If we assume equal weights for A ... F, we find the results presented in Table 15.3. Model (1) seems to emerge as the best option. However, it is interesting to observe that, in case of a high priority for criteria A and B and a low priority for the remaining criteria, model (3) emerges as an interesting option. In general however, various sensitivity analyses suggest that in most cases model (1) is to be regarded as the most plausible option, followed by model (3), whereas model (2) is definitely inferior.

airport network model	equal weights for all criteria	high weights for criteria A and B
(1)	0.929	0.499
(2)	0.037	0.251
(3)	0.535	0.750

Table 15.3   Results of regime analysis for an overall judgement of airport network configurations in the Netherlands

In conclusion, the nested regime method presented above is able to capture both broad evaluation criteria (rather imprecisely defined first-order decision criteria) and specific evaluation criteria (rather detailed and focused second-order decision criteria).

Chapter 16

LOCATION OF PARKING FACILITIES IN A HISTORICAL TOWN:
AN EX POST MULTIPLE CRITERIA EVALUATION

16.1. **Introduction**

Transportation planning is not only concerned with moving vehicles and network infrastructure (such as roads or railways), but also with point infrastructure (such as parking lots). In the present section an empirical application will be dealt with, which addresses the issue of an optimal location of an urban parking lot. The case study concerns the city of Enkhuizen (in the province of North-Holland in the Netherlands). The city houses an interesting museum on the history of the interior lake of the Netherlands (currently named the IJsselmeer, but in former times the Zuiderzee). The construction and opening of a new exterior part of this Zuiderzee-museum - located near the border of the IJsselmeer - required sufficient parking facilities for private cars. The city itself is an extremely interesting old place characterized by an impressive architectural and historico-cultural heritage which deserves strict protection, so that parking policy in this city does not only have a transport aspect but also a conservation aspect. The city is also a centre of tourism, with a strong orientation towards water sports (e.g., sailing).

In view of many conflicting issues, the city has made an exploration of all possible relevant locations for a sufficiently large parking lot which would favour visits to the exterior Zuiderzee-museum (and the old city) without being in conflict with the historical value of the place itself. From the set of alternative choice possibilities the city has ultimately selected the best compromise solution, viz., an extra-urban parking lot (annex visitor's centre) which was connected with the exterior part of the Zuiderzee-museum (and the old city) by means of small ferry boats. In this chapter we will ex post evaluate whether this choice has been the most appropriate one (see also Reins, 1985).

231

16.2. Description of Alternative Locations and Evaluation Criteria

A total of seven alternative locations will be taken into consideration in our posterior analysis:

(1)   A location near a former cement factory in the city

(2)   A location on a camping site next to the museum

(3)   A location on a camping site in a recreation area

(4)   A more distant location next to a cemetry

(5)   An extra-urban location

(6)   A semi-extra-urban location

(7)   A location near the sluices of a new dike (annex provincial road) in the IJsselmeer.

A major problem is not only formed by the land use and the location of the parking lot, but also by various routes that can be chosen by tourists to reach a particular parking lot. This may vary for each distinct alternative, so that a given location can be subdivided into some variants (denoted by a, b, ...). The total number of meaningful choice options appears to be 15 in this case.

Next, a set of eight decision criteria may be assumed, each of them focusing on a particular policy aspect of the location of a new parking lot in Enkhuizen. These criteria are:

1.   A maximum number of visitors - arriving by car and buses - to the museum should use the parking lot

2.   The parking lot should be as close as possible to the museum

3.   The parking lot should have a good accessibility

4.   The construction costs of the parking facilities should be as low as possible

5.   There should be a minimal disturbance of the quality of life

6.   The architecture and the historical character of the city should be strictly protected

7.   Recreational functions should not be disturbed by the parking facilities

8.   The loss of remaining functions of the area to be used for parking should be minimized.

A closer investigation of the outcomes of all choice alternatives with respect to all relevant judgement criteria has next led to the assessment of a complete (8 x 16) impact matrix. This matrix can be found in Table 16.1.

Location criterion	Variants															
	1a	1b	2a	2b	3a	3b	3c	3d	4a	4b	4c	4d	5	6	7
1	6.5	6.5	15	15	10	10	10	10	3.5	3.5	3.5	3.5	15	13	1
2	12.5	12.5	14.5	14.5	9	9	9	9	4.5	4.5	4.5	4.5	1.5	1.5	16
3	4	5	2.5	6	11.5	2.5	11.5	7	9.5	8	13.5	1	13.5	15	16
4	14.5	14.5	10.5	10.5	5.5	13	3	4	2	10.5	5.5	10.5	7.5	7.5	16
5	1	10	3	10	10	3	10	10	10	10	10	3	10	10	16
6	7.5	13.5	7.5	13.5	2.5	2.5	7.5	7.5	13.5	13.5	7.5	7.5	7.5	1	16
7	14.5	7.5	4	1	10	9	6	2.5	11	7.5	12	2.5	13	14.5	16
8	14.5	14.5	1.5	1.5	5	5	5	5	10.5	10.5	10.5	10.5	10.5	10.5	16

Table 16.1.   An impact matrix of alternative locations of an urban parking lot

The numbers in this matrix are measured in rank orders (including ties). A first inspection of this table teaches us already at the outset that alternative 7 scores in most cases as the best choice. Thus based on a visual inspection (i.e., a dominance analysis; see Chapter 11) we find immediately a conclusion. The dominance of the extra-urban parking lot near the new dike is only less strong, if criterion 1 would be assigned an extremely high value. These findings ar confirmed by applying a multi-criteria method. A concordance analysis applied with varying weights (including the above mentioned extreme cases) led to the conclusion that - also in extreme cases - alternative 7 has to be regarded as the best compromise choice. It is interesting to note that this alternative was also the choice option actually selected and implemented by the city.

16.3. Retrospect

The previous analysis has brought to light that evaluation methods of a multi-criteria type can also be extremely useful in judging **ex post** the relative merits of an actually taken decision.

Next, it is also noteworthy that after the construction of an impact matrix it is very important to judge by means of a simple strenght-weakness analysis the relative performance of each possibility. It is noteworthy that in our case there was hardly any need to apply a multi-criteria method, as the effects themselves were already self-evident.

Furthermore, a further analysis of the impact matrix may also lead to an immediate elimination of inferior alternatives (for instance, (4d) is dominated by (1b) or (4b), (3d) is (almost entirely) dominated by (3c)). Thus, evaluation may require the use of multiple criteria methods, but it should first of all follow the natural rules of common sense.

REFERENCES

Anas, A., and R.R. Cho, Existence and Uniquenes of Price Equilibria, **Regional Science and Urban Economics**, vol. 16, 1986, pp. 211-239.

Andrioli, F.D., F. Rensen, and G. Slob, Accessibility as a Locational Factor for Business Establishments, **Tijdschrift voor Economische en Sociale Geografie**, vol. 70, 1979, pp. 17-26.

Armstrong, H., and J. Taylor, **Regional Economics and Policy**, Philip Allan, Deddington, 1985.

Aschauer, D.A., Highway Capacity and Economic Growth, **Economic Perspective**, vol. 14, no. 5, 1990, pp. 14-24.

Bahrenberg, G., M.M. Fischer, and P. Nijkamp (eds.), **Recent Developments in Spatial Data Analysis**, Gower, Aldershot, 1984.

Banister, D., and K. Button (eds.), **Transport in a Free Market Economy**, MacMillan, London, 1991.

Banister, D., J. Berechman, B. Andersen, S. Barrett, and G. de Rus Mendoza, Regulatory Regimes in European Transport and Market Contestability, **Europe on the Move** (P. Nijkamp, ed.), Avebury, Aldershot, 1993, (pp. 213-230).

Barentsen, W., and P. Nijkamp, Nonlinear Dynamic Modelling of Spatial Interaction, **Environment & Planning B**, vol. 15, 1989, pp. 433-446.

Barra, T. de la, **Integrated Land Use and Transportation Modelling**, Cambridge University Press, Cambridge, 1990.

Barrett, S., Deregulating European Aviation, **Transportation**, vol. 16, no. 4, 1990, pp. 311-327.

Bartels, C.P.A., and J.J. van Duijn, **Regionaal-Economisch Beleid in Nederland**, Van Gorcum, Assen, 1981.

Bartels, C., W.R. Nicols, and J.J. van Duyn, Estimating the Impacts of Regional Policies, **Regional Science and Urban Economics**, vol. 12, 1982, pp. 4-41.

Batey, P.W.J., and M.J. Beheny, Methods in Strategic Planning, **Town Planning Review**, vol. 49, 1978, pp. 502-518.

Batten, D.F., J. Casti, and B. Johansson (eds.), **Economic Evolution and Structural Adjustments**, Springer Verlag, Berlin, 1987.

Batty, M., Plan Generation: Design Methods Based on Sieve Maps, Potential Surfaces, Lattices and Markov Chains, Geographical Papers no. 25, Department of Geography, University of Reading, 1974.

Beckmann, M., and T. Puu, **Spatial Economics: Density Potential and Flow**, North-Holland Publishing Co., Amsterdam, 1985.

Benayoun, R., J. de Montgolfier, J. Tergny and O. Larichev, Linear Programming with Multiple Objective Functions: Step Method (STEM), **Mathematical Programming**, vol. 1, 1971, pp. 366-375.

Bennett, R.J., and R.J. Chorley, **Environmental Systems: Philosophy, Analysis and Control**, Methuen, London, 1979.

Bennett, J.L., **Building Decision Support Systems**, Addison Wesley, Reading, Massachusetts, 1983.

Berndsen, R., **Qualitative Reasoning and Knowledge Representation in Economic Models**, Ph.D. Dissertation, Faculty of Economics, Catholic University Brabant, Tilburg, 1992.

Berry, B.J.L., **The Geography of Economic Systems**, Prentice-Hall, Englewood Cliffs, 1976.

Bertuglia, C.S., and G.A. Rabino, The Use of Mathematical Models in the Evaluation of Actions in Urban Planning, **Sistemi Urbani**, no. 2, 1990, pp. 121-132.

Biehl, D., Determinants of Regional Disparities and the Role of Public Finance, **Public Finance**, vol. 35, no. 1, 1980, pp. 44-71.

Biehl, D., **The Contribution of Infrastructure to Regional Development**, DG XVI, European Community, Brussels, 1986.

Blaas, E., and P. Nijkamp, **The Paradise - Model**, DG XVI, European Community, Brussels, 1991.

Blair, P.D., **Multiobjective Regional Energy Planning**, Martinus Nijhoff, Boston, 1979.

Blauwens, A.J., De Tijd, De Dood en het Comfort, Inaugural Address, Department of Economics, Erasmus University, Rotterdam, 1984 (mimeographed).

Blommestein, H.J., **Eliminative Econometrics**, Ph. D. Dissertation, Department of Economics, Free University, Amsterdam, 1987.

Blommestein, H.J., and P. Nijkamp, Causality Analysis in Soft Spatial Econometric Models, **Papers of the Regional Science Association**, vol. 51, 1983, pp. 65-78.

Bovy, P., J. P. Orfeuil, and I. Salomon, A Billion Trips a Day, **Europe on the Move** (P. Nijkamp, ed.), Avebury, Aldershot, 1993 (pp. 67-94).

Boyce, D., N.D. Day and C. McDonald, **Metropolitan Plan Making; An Analysis of Experience with Preparation and Evaluation of Alternative Land Use and Transport Plans**, Monograph 4, Regional Science Research Institute, Philadelphia, 1970.

Bracken, I., **Urban Planning Methods: Research and Policy Analysis**, Methuen, London, 1981.

Broersma, J., Doelstellingen, Instrumenten en Effectiviteit van Sectorpolitiek in de Lid-Staten van de E.E.G., Master's Thesis, Economic Faculty, Free University, Amsterdam, 1977.

Brotchie, J., P. Newton, and P. Hall (eds.) **The Spatial Impact of Technological Change**, Croom Helm, London, 1988.

Brouwer, F.M., **Integrated Environmental Modelling**, Kluwer, Dordrecht, 1989.

Brouwer, F., J. Maybee, P. Nijkamp, and H. Voogd, Sign-Solvability in Economic Models through Plausible Districtions, **Atlantic Economic Journal**, vol. 17, no. 2, 1989, pp. 21-26.

Brouwer, F.M., and P. Nijkamp, Qualitative Structure Analysis of Complex Systems, **Measuring the Unmeasurable** (P. Nijkamp, H. Leitner and N. Wrigley, eds.), Martinus Nijhoff, Dordrecht, 1985, pp. 509-532.

Bruinsma, F., Infrastructuur, Investeringen en Werkgelegenheid, **Tijdschrift voor Vervoerswetenschap**, vol. 26, no. 1, 1990, pp. 74-90.

Bruinsma, F., P. Nijkamp, and P. Rietveld, Infrastructure and Metropolitan Development in an International Perspective, **Infrastructure and Regional Development** (R.W. Vickerman, ed.), Pion, London, 1991, pp. 189-205.

Burrough, P., **Principles of Geographic Information Systems for Land Resources Assessment**, Pergamon Press, Oxford, 1982.

Button, K., and Ph. Barde (eds.), **Transport Policy and the Environment**, Earthscan, London, 1991.

Button, K., and D. Pitfield (eds.), **Transport Deregulation**, MacMillan, London, 1991.

Camagni, R., From City Hierarchy to City Network, **Structure and Evolution of Spatial Systems** (T.R. Lakshmanan and P. Nijkamp, eds.), Springer Verlag, Berlin, 1993, (pp. 66-89).

Campbell, T.D., and J.C. Standley, **Experimental and Quasi-Experimental Designs for Research**, Rand McNally, Chicago, 1966.

Chadwick, G.F., **A Systems View of Planning**, Pergamon Press, Oxford, 1976.

Changkong, V., and Y.Y. Haimes, **Multi-objective Decision Making, Theory and Methodology**, North-Holland Publishing Co., Amsterdam, 1983.

Cochrane, J.L., and M. Zeleny (eds.), **Multiple Criteria Decision Making**, University of South Carolina Press, Columbia, 1973.

Cohon, J.L., **Multiobjective Programming and Planning**, Academic Press, New York, 1987.

Cortenraad, W.M.H., K.J. Moning, and J.H. Jonk, Allocation of Priorities for National Highway Projects in the Netherlands, **Rijkswaterstaat Communications**, no. 45, The Hague, 1986, pp. 3-8.

Cumberland, J.H., **Regional Development**, Mouton, Den Haag, 1981.

Davidson, R.R., and P.M. Farquahar, A Bibliography on the Method of Paired Comparison, **Biometrics,** vol 32, 1976, pp. 241-252.

Dawes, R.M., The Robust Beauty of Improper Linear Models in Decision Making, **American Psychologist**, vol. 15, 1980, pp. 132-148.

Delft, A. van, and P. Nijkamp, **Multicriteria Analysis and Regional Decision-Making**, Martinus Nijhoff, Dordrecht, 1977.

Dello, P., Strategic Choice and Evaluation: Some Methodological Considerations, **Evaluation of Complex Policy Problems** (A. Faludi and H. Voogd, eds.), Delftsche Uitgevers Maatschappij, Delft, 1985, pp. 109-123.

Deno, K.T., and R. Eberts, Public Infrastructure and Regional Economic Development, **Journal of Urban Economics**, vol. 30, 1991, pp. 329-343.

Despontin, M., J. Moscarola, and J. Spronk, A User-oriented Listing of Multiple Decision Methods, **Revue Belge de Statistique, d'Informatique et de Recherche Opérationelle**, vol. 23, no. 4 (special issue), 1983, pp. 51-88.

Diamond, D., and N. Spence, **Regional Policy Evaluation**, Gower, Aldershot, 1983.

Diamond, D., and N. Spence, **Infrastructure and Industrial Costs in British Industry**, HMSO, London, 1988.

Dieperink, J.P.H., and P. Nijkamp, A Multiple Criteria Location Model for Innovative Firms in a Communication Network, **Economic Geography**, vol.63, no. 1, 1987, pp. 66-73.

Doorn, J. van, and F. van Vught, **Nederland op Zoek naar zijn Toekomst**, Spectrum, Utrecht, 1981.

Douglas, M., and A. Wildavsky, **Risk and Culture**, University of California Press, Berkeley, 1982.

Duckstein, L., I. Bogardi, and M.E. Gershon, Multi-objective Decision Making: Model Choice, Working Paper, IIASA, Laxenburg, 1981.

Duda, R.O., and J.G. Gashnig, Knowledge Based Expert System Come of Age, **Byte**, vol. 6, no. 9, 1981, pp. 238-281.

Dunn, R., Parameter Instability in Models of Local Unemployment Responses, **Environment and Planning A**, vol. 14, 1982, pp. 75-94.

Eckenrode, R.T., Weighting Multiple Criteria, **Management Science**, vol. 12, 1965, pp. 180-192.

European Roundtable of Industrialists, **Missing Networks; A European Challenge**, Brussels, 1991.

Evers-Koelman, I., H.A. van Gent, and P. Nijkamp, Effecten van de Aanleg of Verbetering van Verkeersinfrastructuur op de Regionaal-economische Ontwikkeling, **Tijdschrift voor Vervoerswetenschap**, vol. 23, no. 1, 1987, pp. 32-60.

Fandel, G., **Optimale Entscheidung bei Mehrfacher Zielsetzung**, Berlin, Springer, 1972.

Farquhar, P.H., Research Directions in Multiattribute Utility Analysis, **Essays and Surveys on Multiple Criteria Decision Making** (P. Hansen, ed.), Springer, Berlin, 1983. pp. 268-283.

Filippi, F., A. La Bella, and M. Silvestrelli, Il Metodo Degli Autovelori per la Valutazione delle Alternative di Sviluppo dei Sistemi di Trasporto, **Strumenti Quantitativi per l'Analisi dei Sistemi di Trasporto** (L. Bianco and A. La Bella, eds.), Franco Angeli, Milano, 1992, pp. 191-218.

Fischer, M.M., and P. Nijkamp, Categorical Data and Choice Analysis in a Spatial Context, **Optimization and Discrete Choice in Urban Systems** (B. Hutchinson, P. Nijkamp, and M. Batty, eds.), Springer Verlag, Berlin, 1981, pp. 1-30.

Fischer, M.M., and P. Nijkamp, From Static towards Dynamic Discrete Choice Modelling: A State of the Art Review, **Regional Science and Urban Economics**, vol. 17, no. 1, 1987, pp. 3-23.

Fischer, M.M., and P. Nijkamp (eds.), **Regional Labour Markets**, North-Holland Publishing Co., Amsterdam, 1987.

Fischer, M., and P. Nijkamp (eds.), **Geographic Information Systems, Spatial Modelling and Policy Evaluation**, Springer Verlag, Berlin, 1993.

Fischer, M., P. Nijkamp, and Y. Papageorgiou (eds.), **Spatial Choices and Processes**, North-Holland Publishing Co., Amsterdam, 1990.

Fishburn, P.C., **Utility Theory for Decision-Making**, Wiley, New York, 1970.

Fishburn, P.C., Lexicographic Orders, Utilities and Decision Rules, a Survey, **Management Science**, vol. 20, 1974, pp. 1442-1471.

Folmer, H., **Regional Economic Policy**, Martinus Nijhoff, Dordrecht, 1985.

Folmer, H., and P. Nijkamp, Methodological Aspects of Impact Analysis of Regional Economic Policy, **Papers of Regional Science Association**, vol. 57, 1986, pp. 165-181.

Fontaine, P., M. Garbely, and M. Gilli, Qualitative Solvability in Economic Models, **Computer Science in Economics and Management**, vol. 4, no. 3, 1991, pp. 285-301.

Forkenbrock, D.J., T.F. Pogue, N.S.J. Foster, and D.J. Finnegan, Road Investment to Foster Local Economic Development, Report Midwest Transportation Center, University of Iowa, 1990.

Fotheringham, A.A., and M.E. O'Kelley, **Spatial Interaction Models: Formulations and Applications**, Kluwer Publishers, Dordrecht, 1989.

Friedmann, J., **Retracking America**, Anchor Press, Garden City, 1973.

Friend, J.K., and W.N. Jessop, **Local Government and Strategic Choice**, Pergamon Press, Oxford, 1976.

Frisch, R., Co-operation Between Politicians and Econometricians on the Formalization of Political Preferences, **Economic Planning Studies**, Dordrecht, Reidel, 1976, pp. 41-86.

Gal, T., On Efficient Sets in Vector Maximum Problems - a Brief Survey, **Essays and Surveys on Multiple Criteria Decision Making**, (P. Hansen, ed.), Berlin, Springer, 1983, pp. 94-114.

Garbely, M., and M. Gilli, Evaluating the Number of Zero Eigenvalues in a Dynamic Model, **Econometric Decision Models** (J. Gruber, ed.), Springer Verlag, Berlin, 1990, pp. 496-501.

Garcia-Mila, T., and T.J. McGuire, The Contribution of Publicly Provided Inputs to State Economics, **Regional Science and Urban Economics**, vol. 22, no. 2, 1992, pp. 229-241.

Geenhuizen, M. van, P. Nijkamp, and P. Townroe, A Company Life History Approach to Economic Dynamics and Innovation, Research Memorandum, Department of Economics, Free University, Amsterdam, 1989.

Gent, H.A. van, and P. Nijkamp, Mobility, Transportation and Development, **IATTS Research**, vol. 11, no. 1, 1987, pp. 62-68.

Giaoutzi, M., and P. Nijkamp (eds.), **Informatics and Regional Development**, Avebury, Aldershot, U.K., 1987.

Giaoutzi, M., P. Nijkamp, and D. Storey (eds.), **Small and Medium Size Firms and Regional Development**, Croom Helm, London, 1988.

Gilli, M., and Causor, A Program for the Analysis of Recursive and Interdependent Causal Structures, Ciser's Manual, Department of Econometrics, University of Geneva, 1980.

Giuliano, G., A Multicriteria Method for Transportation Investment Planning, **Transportation Research A**, vol. 18, 1985, pp. 29-42.

Glickman, N.J., **The Urban Impacts of Federal Policies**, The John Hopkins Press, Baltimore, 1980.

Golledge, R.G., and H. Timmerman (eds.), **Behavioural Modelling in Geography and Planning**, Croom Helm, London, 1988.

Golob, Th., B. Ruhl, H. Meurs, and L. van Wissen, An Ordinal Multivariate Analysis of Accident Counts as Functions of Traffic Approach Volumes at Intersections, **Accident Analysis and Prevention**, vol. 20, no. 5, 1989, pp. 335-355.

Graaff, H. de, and P. Nijkamp, Data on Infrastructure and Regional Development in the Netherlands, Economic and Social Institute, Free University, Amsterdam, 1986 (mimeographed).

Green, P.E., and V.R. Rao, Rating Scales and Information Recovery - How many Scales and Response Categories to Use?, **Journal of Marketing**, vol. 34, 1970, pp. 33-39.

Guigou, J.L., **Analyse des Données et Choix à Critères Multiples**, Dunod, Paris, 1974.

Haag, G., and W. Weidlich (eds.), **Interregional Migration**, Springer, Berlin, 1986.

Hägerstrand, T., What about People in Regional Science, **Papers of the Regional Science Association**, vol. 24, 1970, pp. 7-21.

Hakimi, S.L., Optimum Locations of Switching Centers and Medians of a Graph, **Operations Research**, vol. 12, 1964, pp. 406-409.

Halpern, J., Duality in the Cent-dian of a Graph, **Operations Research**, vol. 28, 1980, pp. 722-735.

Halpern, J., Finding Minimal Center-median Convex Combination (cent-dian) of a Graph, **Management Science**, vol. 24, 1978, pp. 535-544.

Handler, G.Y., and P.B. Mirchandini, **Locations on Networks**, M.I.T. Press, Cambridge, Mass., 1979.

Harris, B., The Comprehensive Planning of Location, **Planning Theory in the 1980's** (R.W. Burchell and G. Sternlieb, eds.), Centre for Urban Policy Research, Rutgers University, New Brunswick, N.J., 1978, pp. 88-103.

Harvey, D., **Explanation in Geography**, Edward Arnold, London, 1969.

Hasselt, B. van, De Regionale Luchthavens in Nederland: Betekenis en Perspectief, Master's Thesis, Department of Economics, Free University, Amsterdam, 1986.

Heckman, J., Statistical Models for Discrete Panel Data, **Structural Analysis of Discrete Data with Econometric Applications** (C.F. Manski and D. McFadden, eds.), MIT Press, Cambridge, Mass., 1981, pp. 114-178.

Hewings, G.J.D., P. Nijkamp, and I. Orishimo (eds.), **Information Technology and Urban and Regional Systems**, Springer Verlag, Berlin, 1988.

Hickling, A., Evaluation is a Five-Finger Exercise, **Evaluation of Complex Policy Problems** (A. Faludi and H. Voogd, eds.), Delftsche Uitgeversmaatschappij, Delft, 1985, pp. 16-32.

Higgins, B., and D.J. Savoie (eds.), **Regional Economic Development**, Unwin Heyman, London, 1988.

Hill, M., **Planning for Multiple Objectives**, Regional Science Research Institute, Monograph no. 5, Philadelphia, 1973.

Himanen, V., P. Nijkamp, and J. Padjen, Environmental Quality and Transport Policy in Europe, **Transportation Research A**, vol. 26, no. 2, 1992, pp. 147-157.

Hinloopen, E., De Regime Methode, Master's Thesis, Interfaculty Actuariat and Econometrics, Free University, Amsterdam, 1985 (mimeographed).

Hinloopen, E., and P. Nijkamp, Information Systems in an Uncertain Planning Environment - Some Methods, **International Journal of Development Planning Literature**, vol. 1, no. 1, 1986, pp. 105-129.

Hinloopen, E., and P. Nijkamp, Qualitative Multiple Criteria Choice Analysis; The Dominant Regime Method, **Quality and Quantity**, vol. 24, no. 1, 1990, pp. 37-56.

Hinloopen, E., P. Nijkamp and P. Rietveld, Qualitative Discrete Multiple Criteria Choice Models in Regional Planning, **Regional Science and Urban Economics**, vol. 13, 1983, pp. 77-102.

Hinloopen, E., and A.W. Smyth, A Description of the Principles of a New Multicriteria Evaluation Technique, The Regime Method, **Proceedings Colloquium Vervoersplanologisch Speurwerk 1985**, Delft, 1985, pp. 430-441.

Hitchens, D.M.W.N., and P.N. O'Farrell, The Competitiveness and Performance of Small Manufacturing Firms, **Environment and Planning A,** vol. 21, 1989, pp. 1241-1263.

Hollnagel, E., Cognitive Functions in Decision Making (H. Jungermann and G. de Zeeuw, eds.), **Decision Making and Change in Human Affairs,** Reidel, Dordrecht, 1977, pp. 431-444.

Hutchinson, B.G., **Principles of Urban Transport Systems Planning,** McGraw-Hill, New York, 1974.

Hutchinson, B., P. Nijkamp, and M. Batty (eds.), **Optimization and Discrete Choice in Urban Systems,** Springer Verlag, Berlin, 1985.

Hwang, C.L., and K. Yoon, **Multiple Attribute Decision Making - Methods and Application,** Springer, Berlin, 1981.

Hwang, C.L., and A. Masud (eds.), **Multiple Objective Decision Making,** Springer, Berlin, 1979.

Isard, W., and L. Anselin, Integration of Multiregional Models for Policy Analysis, **Environment and Planning A,** vol. 14, 1982, pp. 359-376.

Issaev, B., P. Nijkamp, P. Rietveld, and F. Snickars (eds.), **Multiregional Economic Modelling,** North-Holland Publishing Co., Amsterdam, 1982.

Isserman, A.M., Research Designs for Quasi-experimental Control Group Analysis in Regional Science, Research Paper, Regional Research Institute, West Virginia University, Morgantown, 1990.

Janis, I.L., and L. Mann, **Decision-Making,** Free Press, New York, 1977.

Janssen, R., Evaluatiemethoden ten behoeve van het Milieubeleid en -beheer, Economic and Social Institute, Free University, Amsterdam, 1984.

Janssen, R., **Multiobjective Decision Support for Environmental Problems,** Ph.D. Dissertation, Department of Economics, Free University, Amsterdam, 1991.

Johnsen, E., **Studies in Multi-objective Decision Models,** Monograph No. 1, Economic Research Center in Lund, Lund, Sweden, 1968.

Johnson, C.R., Constructive Critique of a Hierarchical Prioritization Scheme Employing Paired Comparisons, **Proceedings IEEE Conference on Cybernetics and Society,** Cambridge, 1980, pp. 373-378.

Kahn, H., and A.J. Wiener, **The Year 2000,** MacMillan, New York, 1967.

Kahne, S., A Contribution to Decision Making in Environmental Design, **Proceedings of the IEEE,** 1975, pp. 518-528.

Kahneman, D., P. Slovic, and A. Tversky, **Judgment under Uncertainty**, Cambridge, 1982.

Kamann, D.J., **Spatial Differentiation in the Impact of Technology on Society**, Avebury, Aldershot, 1988.

Keen, P.G.W., and M. Scott Morton, **Decision Support Systems**, Addison Wesley, Reading, Massachusetts, 1978.

Keeney, R.L., and H. Raiffa, **Decision Analysis with Multiple Conflicting Objectives**, Wiley, New York, 1976.

Kendall, M.G., **Rank Correlation Methods**, New York, Hafner Publishing Company, 1955.

Kessel, N., Effectanalyse in de Ruimtelijke Ordening, Planologisch Memorandum 1983-8, Faculty of Civil Engineering, Delft University of Technology, 1983 (mimeographed).

Klaassen, L.H., J.A. Bourrdrez, and J. Volmuller, **Transport and Reurbanisation**, Gower, Aldershot, 1981.

Klaassen, L.H., A.C.P. Verster, and T.H. Botterweg, **Kosten-batenanalyse in Regionaal Perspectief**, Tjeenk Willink, Groningen, 1974.

Kmietowicz, Z.W., and A.D. Pearman, **Decision Theory and Imcomplete Knowledge**, Aldershot, U.K., Gower, 1981.

Koopmans, T.C., Analysis of Production as an Efficient Combination of Activities, **Activity Analysis of Production and Allocation** (T.C.Koopmans, ed.), Yale University Press, New Haven, 1951, pp. 39-97.

Krueckeberg, D.A., and A.L. Silvers, **Urban Planning Analysis: Methods and Models**, John Wiley, New York, 1974.

Kruijssen, P., and H. Voogd, Expert Systems for Urban Development Planning, **Informatics and Regional Development** (M. Giaoutzi and P. Nijkamp, eds.), Gower, Aldershot, 1988, pp. 270-298.

Kuhn, H.W., and A.W. Tucker, Non-linear Programming, **Proceedings of the Second Berkeley Symposium on Mathematical Statistics and Probability** (J. Neyman, ed.), University of California Press, Berkely, 1968, pp. 481-493.

Kutter, E., Dilemma's in Car Mobility, **Transportation Planning in a Changing World**, (P. Nijkamp and S. Reichman, eds.), Gower, Aldershot, U.K., 1987, pp. 48-60.

Lancaster, K., **Consumer Demand**, Columbia University Press, New York, 1971.

Laurini, R., Expert Systems and Image Generations for Urban Planning, **Informatics and Regional Development** (M. Giaoutzi and P. Nijkamp, eds.), Gower, Aldershot, 1988, pp. 279-291.

Leman, C.K., and R.H. Nelson, Ten Commandments for Policy Economists, **Journal of Policy Analysis and Management**, vol. 1, no. 1, 1981, pp. 97-117.

Lemer, A., and S.J. Bellomo, **H.U.D. Envoronmental Guidelines Study**, U.S. Deptartment of Housing and Urban Development, Washington D.C., 1974.

Leung, Y., Urban and Regional Planning With Fuzzy Information (L. Chatterjee and P. Nijkamp, eds.), **Urban and Regional Policy Analysis in Development Countries**, Gower, Aldershot, 1983, pp. 231-249.

Leung, Y., **Spatial Analysis and Planning under Imprecision**, North-Holland Publishers Co., Amsterdam, 1989.

Lichfield, N., P. Kettle, M. Whitbread, **Evaluation in the Planning Process**, Pergamon Press, Oxford, 1975.

Lichfield, N., Plan Evaluation Methodology: Comprehending the Conclusions, **Evaluation Methods for Urban and Regional Plans** (D. Shefer and H. Voogd, eds.), Pion, London, 1990, pp. 79-98.

Lierop, W.F.J. van, and P. Nijkamp, Disaggregate Residential Choice Models, **Scandinavian Housing and Planning Research**, vol. 8, no. 4, 1991, pp. 133-151.

Liew, C.K., and C.J. Liew, Measuring the Development Impact of a Transportation System, **Journal of Regional Science**, vol 25, 1985, pp. 241-258.

Love, R.F., and J.G. Morris, Modelling Inter-city Road Distances by Mathematical Functions, **Operations Research Quarterly**, vol. 23, 1972, pp. 61-71.

Love, R.F., and J.G. Morris, Mathematical Models of Road Travel Distances, **Management Science**, vol. 25, 1979, pp. 130-139.

Lucas, H.C. (ed.), **The Information Systems Environment**, North-Holland Publishing Co., Amsterdam, 1980.

Maggi, R., I. Masser, and P. Nijkamp, Missing Networks in European Transport and Communications, **Transport Reviews**, vol. 12, no. 4, 1992, pp. 311-321.

Malecki, E.J., Industrial Location and Corporate Organization in High Technology Industries, **Economic Geography**, vol. 61, 1981, pp. 345-369.

Manheim, M.L., and F.L. Hall, Abstract Representation of Goals, Professional Paper, Massachusetts Institute of Technology, Cambridge, Mass., 1968.

Martin, J., **Strategic Data Planning Methodologies**, Prentice Hall, New York, 1982.

Masser, I., Strategic Land Use Planning, **Systems Analysis in Urban Policy-Making and Planning** (M. Batty and B. Hutchinson, eds.), Plenum Press, New York, 1983, pp. 89-106.

May, K.O., Transivity, Utility and the Aggregation of Preference Patterns, **Econometrica**, vol. 22, 1954, pp. 1-13.

McAllister, D.M., **Evaluation in Environmental Planning**, MIT Press, Cambridge Mass., 1980.

McLaughlin, J.B., **Urban and Regional Planning, a Systems Approach**, Faber, London, 1969.

McLennon, D., and J.B. Parr (eds.), **Regional Policy: Experiences and New Directions**, Robertson, Oxford, 1979.

McNichols, C.W., and T.D. Clark, **Microcomputer Based Information and Decision Support Systems for Small Business**, Prentice Hall, New York, 1983.

Meehl, P.E., **Clinical Versus Statistical Prediction**, University of Minnesota Press, Minneapolis, 1954.

Meyer - Krahmer, T., Innovative Behaviour and Regional Industrial Potential, **Regional Studies**, vol. 19, no. 6, 1985, pp. 523-554.

Miller, D.H., Equity and Efficiency Effects of Investment Decisions: Multi-criteria Methods for Assessing Distributional Implications, **Evaluation of Complex Policy Problems** (A. Faludi and H. Voogd, eds.), Delftsche Uitgeversmaatschappij, Delft, 1985, pp. 336-350.

Miller, D.H., **Plans and Publics: Assessing Distribution Effects**, Planologisch Memorandum 81-2, Department of Urban and Regional Planning, Delft University of Technology, 1981.

Miller, G.A., The Magical Number Seven, Plus or Minus Two: Some Limits on our Capacity for Processing Information, **Psychological Review**, vol. 63, no. 2, 1978, pp. 81-97.

Mills, E. (ed.), **Handbook of Urban Economics**, North-Holland Publishing Co., Amsterdam, 1988.

Mishan, E.J., **Cost-Benefit Analysis**, Allen & Unwin, London, 1982.

Moning, K.J., and W.M.H. Cortenraad, De Prioriteitenstelling van Rijkswegenprojecten voor de Middellange Termijn (M.P.P.), **Beleidsanalyse**, vol. 1-2, 1985, pp. 28-35.

Moore, B., and J. Rhodes, Regional Economic Policy and the Movement of Manufacturing Firms to Development Areas, **Economica**, vol. 43, 1976, pp. 17-31.

Munda, G., P. Nijkamp and P. Rietveld, Multicriteria Evaluation in a Fuzzy Environment, Research Memorandum, Dept. of Economics, Free University, Amsterdam, 1992.

Nelder, J.A., and R.W.M. Wedderburn, General Linear Models, **Journal of the Royal Statistical Society A**, no. 135, 1972, pp. 370-384.

Nijkamp, P., **Multidimensional Spatial Data and Decision Analysis**, Wiley, London, 1979.

Nijkamp, P., **Environmental Policy Analysis**, Wiley/Chichester, New York, 1981.

Nijkamp, P. (ed.), **Technological Change, Employment and Spatial Dynamics**, Springer, Berlin, 1986.

Nijkamp, P. (ed.), **Handbook of Regional Economics**, North-Holland Publishing Co., Amsterdam, 1987.

Nijkamp, P., Regional Planning and Urban Impact Analysis, **Scandinavian Housing and Planning Research**, vol. 4, 1987, pp. 101-118.

Nijkamp, P, Culture and Region, **Environment & Planning B**, vol. 15, no. 1, 1988, pp. 5-14.

Nijkamp, P., H. Leitner and N. Wrigley (eds.), **Measuring the Unmeasurable**, Martinus Nijhoff, Dordrecht, 1985.

Nijkamp, P., and J. Paelinck, **Operational Theory and Method in Regional Economics**, Saxon House, Farnborough, 1976.

Nijkamp, P., and A. Perrels, Trans-National Road Infrastructure and the Development of Peripheral Areas, **Planning without a Passport** (J.J.M. Angenent and A. Bongenaar, eds.), Netherlands Geographical Studies, Amsterdam, 1987, pp. 122-134.

Nijkamp, P., and A. Reggiani, Dynamic Spatial Interaction Models: New Directions, **Environment & Planning A**, vol. 20, 1988, pp. 1449-1460.

Nijkamp, P., and A. Reggiani, **Interaction, Evolution and Chaos in Space**, Springer, Berlin, 1992.

Nijkamp, P., and S. Reichman (eds.), **Transportation Planning in a Changing World**, Gower, Aldershot, U.K., 1987.

Nijkamp, P., and P. Rietveld, Structure Analysis of Spatial Systems, **Multiregional Economic Modelling** (B. Issaev, P. Nijkamp, P. Rietveld and F. Snickars, eds.), North-Holland Publishing Co., Amsterdam, 1982, pp. 35-49.

Nijkamp, P., and P. Rietveld (eds.), **Information Systems for Integrated Regional Planning**, North-Holland, Amsterdam, 1984.

Nijkamp, P., P. Rietveld, and F. Snickars, Regional and Multiregional Models, **Handbook of Regional Economics** (P. Nijkamp, ed.), North-Holland Publishing Co., Amsterdam, 1987, pp. 257-194.

Nijkamp, P., P. Rietveld, and H. Voogd, **Multicriteria Analysis in Physical Planning**, Elsevier, Amsterdam, 1990.

Nijkamp, P., and I. Salomon, Future Spatial Impacts of Telecommunications, **Transportation Planning and Technology**, vol 13, 1989, pp. 275-287.

Nijkamp, P., and J. Spronk, **Multiple Criteria Analysis**, Gower, Aldershot, 1981.

Osgood, C.E., G.J. Suci, and P.H. Tannenbaum, **The Measurement of Meaning**, University of Illinois Press, Urbana, 1957.

Ozbekhan, H., Towards a General Theory of Planning, **Perspectives of Planning** (E. Jantsch, ed.), OECD, Paris, 1969, pp. 31-50.

Paelinck, J.H.P., Qualitative Multiple Criteria Analysis, Environmental Protection and Multiregional Development, **Papers of the Regional Science Association**, vol. 36, 1976, pp. 59-74.

Papadimitriou, C.H., and K. Steiglitz, **Combinatorial Optimization Algorithm and Complexity**, Prentice-Hall, Englewood Cliffs, 1982.

Paraskevopoulos, C.C., Patterns of Regional Economic Growth, **Regional and Urban Economics**, vol. 4, no. 1, 1974, pp. 77-105.

Pellenbarg, P.H., Bedrijfsmigratie in Nederland, Part VI, Geographic Institute, State University, Groningen, 1977.

Pelt, M.J.F. van, A. Kuyvenhoven, and P. Nijkamp, Sustainability, Efficiency and Equity: Project Appraisal in Economic Development Strategies, **Environmental Impact Assessment** (A.G. Colombo, eds.), Kluwer, Dordrecht, 1992, pp. 287-312.

Pitz, G.F., Decision Making and Cognition, **Decision Making and Change in Human Affairs** (H. Jungerman and G. de Zeeuw, eds.), Reidel, Dordrecht, 1977, pp. 403-424.

Pitz, G.F., and J. McKillip, **Decision Analysis for Program Evaluators**, Beverly Hills, Los Angeles, 1984.

Pleeter, S., **Economic Impact Analysis: Methodology and Applications**, Martinus Nijhoff, Boston, Mass., 1980.

Polya, D., **Patterns of Plausibility Inference**, Princeton University Press, Princeton, 1954.

Porter, M., **The Competitive Advantage of Nations**, MacMillan, London/New York, 1990.

Pred, A.R., **City-Systems in Advanced Economies**, Wiley, New York, 1977.

Reijns, A., Evaluatie van Parkeerlokatiekeuze Gemeente Enkhuizen, Working Paper, Dept. of Regional Economics, Free University, Amsterdam 1985 (mimeographed).

Reitman, W.R., Heuristic Decision Procedures, Open Constraints, and the Structure of Ill-defined Problems, **Human Judgments and Optimality** (M.W. Shelley and G.L. Bryan, eds.), Wiley, New York, 1964, pp. 282-315.

Rietveld, P., **Multiple Objective Decision Methods and Regional Planning**, North-Holland Publishing Co., Amsterdam, 1980.

Rietveld, P., Using Ordinal Information in Decision Making Under Uncertainty, Research memorandum 1982-12, Department of Economics, Free University Amsterdam, Amsterdam, 1982.

Rietveld, P., The Use of Qualitative Information in Macro-Economic Policy Analysis, **Macro-Economic Planning with Conflicting Goals** (M. Despontin, P. Nijkamp, and J. Spronk, eds.), Springer, Berlin, 1984, pp. 263-280.

Rietveld, P., Infrastructure and Regional Development, **The Annals of Regional Science**, vol. 23, 1989, pp. 255-274.

Rietveld, P., Employment Effects of Changes in Transport Infrastructure, **Papers of the Regional Science Association**, vol. 66, 1990, pp. 19-30.

Rima, A., and L.J.G. van Wissen, **Modelling Urban Housing Market Dyamics**, North-Holland Publishing Co, Amsterdam, 1988.

Rivers, J.E., **Computerized Information Systems for Effective Organizational Management**, Gower, Aldershot, 1984.

Roskill, **Commission on the Rural London Airport: Report**, Her Majesty's Stationary Office, London, 1971.

Rouwendal, J., **Decision and Equilibrium on the Housing Market**, Martinus Nijhoff, Dordrecht, 1989.

Roy, B., Classement et Choix en Présence de Points de Vue Multiples (la Méthode ELECTRE), **R.I.R.O.**, vol. 2, 1968, pp. 57-75.

Saaty, T.L., A Scaling Method for Priorities in Hierarchical Structures, **Journal of Mathematical Psychology**, vol. 15, 1977, pp. 234-281.

Schimpeler, C.C., and W.L. Grecco, The Expected Value Method, an Approach Based on Community Structures and Values, **Highway Research Record**, vol. 238, 1986, pp. 123-152.

Schlager, K., The Rank-based Expected Value Method of Plan Evaluation, **Highway Research Record**, vol. 238, 1968, pp. 153-158.

Scholten, H., The Role of Geographical Information Systems in Physical Planning, **Informatics and Regional Development** (M. Giaoutzi and P. Nijkamp, eds.), Gower, Aldershot, 1988, pp. 292-307.

Scholten, H.J., and J.E.M. Stillwell (eds.), **Geographical Information Systems for Urban and Regional Planning**, Kluwer, Dordrecht, 1991.

Shefer, D. and H. Voogd (eds.), **Multicriteria Methods for Urban and Regional Plans**, Pion, London, 1989.

Shepard, R.N., On Subjectively Optimum Selection Among Multi-attribute Alternatives, **Human Judgments and Optimality** (M.W. Shelley and G.L. Bryan, eds.), Wiley, New York, 1964, pp. 257-281.

Simon, H.A., **Models of Man**, Wiley, New York, 1957.

Simon, H.A., From Substantive to Procedural Rationality, **Method and Appraisal in Economics** (S. Latsis, ed.), Cambridge University Press, Cambridge, 1976, pp. 61-78.

Sinden, J.A. and A.C. Worrell, **Unpriced Values**, Wiley, New York, 1979.

Skull, F.A., A.L. Delbecq and L.L. Cunnings, **Organizational Decision Making**, McGraw-Hill, New York, 1970.

Spronk, J., **Interactive Multiple Goal Programming for Capital Budgeting and Financial Planning**, Boston, Kluwer Nijhoff, 1981.

Stefik, M., The Organisation of Expert Systems, **Artificial Intelligence**, vol. 8, March 1982, pp. 135-172.

Steuer, R.E., Linear Multiple Objective Programming With Interval Criterion Weights, **Management Science**, vol. 23, 1976, pp. 305-316.

Taha, H.A., **Operations Research**, MacMillan, New York, 1976.

Tansel, B.C., R.L. Francis, and T.J. Lowe, Location on Networks: a Survey, **Management Science**, vol. 29, 1983, pp. 482-511.

Tarascio, V.J., **Pareto's Methodological Approach to Economics**. Chapel Hill, The University of North Carolina Press, 1968.

Tervo, H., and P. Okko, A Note on Shift-Share Analysis as a Method of Estimating the Employment Effects of Regional Economic Policy, **Journal of Regional Science**, vol. 23, 1983, pp. 115-121.

Theil, H., **Optimal Decision Rules for Government and Industry**, North Holland Publishing Co., Amsterdam, 1968.

Tinbergen, J., **Economic Policy: Principles and Design**, North Holland Publishing Co., Amsterdam, 1956.

Torgerson, W.A., **Theory and Method of Scaling**, Wiley, New York, 1958.

Verdier, J.M., Advising Congressional Decision-Makers, **Journal of Policy Analysis and Management**, vol. 3, no. 3, 1984, pp. 421-438.

Voogd, H., **Multicriteria Evaluation for Urban and Regional Planning**, Pion, London, 1983.

Voogd, H., Prescriptive Analysis in Planning, Planologisch Memorandum, Department of Urban and Regional Planning, Delft University of Technology, Delft, 1984 (mimeographed).

Voogd, H., Transportation Policy Analysis, **Sistemi Urbani**, December, 1985, pp. 355-394.

White, D.J., The Foundations of Multi-objective Interactive Programming - Some Questions, **Essays and Surveys on Multiple Criteria Decision Making**, (P. Hansen, ed.), Springer, Berlin, pp. 181-203.

Wilson, A.G., **Catastrophe Theory and Bifurcation**, Croom Helm, London, 1981.

Wit, J.G., and H.A. van Gent, **Vervoers- en Verkeerseconomie**, Stenfert Kroese, Leiden, 1986.

Wold, H., Causality and Econometrics, **Econometrica**, vol. 22, 1954, pp. 162-177.

Wrigley, N., **Categorical Data Analysis**, Routledge, London, 1986.

Yu, P.L., **Multiple-Criteria Decision Making**, Plenum Press, New York, 1985.

Zeleny, M., **Multiple Criteria Decision Making**, McGraw-Hill, New York, 1982.

Zionts, S., and J. Wallenius, An Interactive Programming Method for Solving the Multiple Criteria Problem, **Management Science**, vol. 22, 1976, pp. 652-663.

Transportation Research, Economics and Policy

1. I. Salomon, P. Bovy and J-P. Orfeuil (eds.): *A Billion Trips a Day. Tradition and Transition in European Travel Patterns.* 1993
ISBN 0-7923-2297-5

2. P. Nijkamp and E. Blaas: *Impact Assessment and Evaluation in Transportation Planning.* 1994 ISBN 0-7923-2648-2

Kluwer Academic Publishers – Dordrecht / Boston / London